Asia and the
New International
Economic Order

Pergamon Titles of Related Interest

Laszlo/Kurtzman/Bhattacharya RCDC (REGIONAL COOPERATION AMONG DEVELOPING COUNTRIES)
Nicol/Echeverria/Peccei REGIONALISM AND THE NEW INTERNATIONAL ECONOMIC ORDER

UNITAR-CEESTEM Library on NIEO

Laszlo & Kurtzman Eastern Europe and the New International Economic Order

Laszlo & Kurtzman Western Europe and the New International Economic Order

Laszlo & Kurtzman Political and Institutional Issues of the New International Economic Order

Laszlo & Kurtzman The Structure of the World Economy and the New International Economic Order

Laszlo & Kurtzman The United States, Canada and the New International Economic Order

Laszlo et al. The Implementation of the New International Economic Order

Laszlo et al. World Leadership and the New International Economic Order

Laszlo et al. The Objectives of the New International Economic Order

Laszlo et al. The Obstacles to the New International Economic Order

Lozoya & Bhattacharya The Financial Issues of the New International Economic Order

Lozoya & Cuadra Africa, Middle East and the New International Economic Order

Lozoya & Bhattacharya Asia and the New International Economic Order

Lozoya & Green International Trade, Industrialization and the New International Economic Order

Lozoya & Estevez Latin America and the New International Economic Order

Lozoya & Birgin Social and Cultural Issues of the New International Economic Order

Lozoya et al. Alternative Views of the New International Economic Order

Miljan, Laszlo & Kurtzman Food and Agriculture in Global Perspective

Related Journals*

INTERNATIONAL JOURNAL OF INTERCULTURAL RELATIONS
REGIONAL PLANNING
TECHNOLOGY IN SOCIETY
WORLD DEVELOPMENT

*Free specimen copies available upon request.

 PERGAMON POLICY STUDIES ON THE NEW INTERNATIONAL ECONOMIC ORDER

Asia and the New International Economic Order

Edited by
Jorge A. Lozoya
A.K. Bhattacharya

A Volume in the New International
Economic Order (NIEO) Library
Published for UNITAR and the
Center for Economic and Social
Studies of the Third World (CEESTEM)

Pergamon Press
NEW YORK • OXFORD • TORONTO • SYDNEY • PARIS • FRANKFURT

Pergamon Press Offices:

U.S.A.	Pergamon Press Inc., Maxwell House, Fairview Park, Elmsford, New York 10523, U.S.A.
U.K.	Pergamon Press Ltd., Headington Hill Hall, Oxford OX3 0BW, England
CANADA	Pergamon Press Canada Ltd., Suite 104, 150 Consumers Road, Willowdale, Ontario M2J 1P9, Canada
AUSTRALIA	Pergamon Press (Aust.) Pty. Ltd., P.O. Box 544, Potts Point, NSW 2011, Australia
FRANCE	Pergamon Press SARL, 24 rue des Ecoles, 75240 Paris, Cedex 05, France
FEDERAL REPUBLIC OF GERMANY	Pergamon Press GmbH, Hammerweg 6, Postfach 1305, 6242 Kronberg/Taunus, Federal Republic of Germany

Library of Congress Cataloging in Publication Data

Main entry under title:

Asia and the new international economic order.

(Pergamon policy studies on the new international economic order)
"A volume in the new international economic order (NIEO) library published for UNITAR and the Center for Economic and Social Studies of the Third World (CEESTEM)."
Includes index.
1. Asia--Foreign economic relations--Addresses, essays, lectures. 2. Asia--Economic conditions--1945- --Addresses, essays, lectures. 3. Asia--Social conditions--Addresses, essays, lectures.
I. Bhattacharya, Anindya K. II. Lozoya, Jorge Alberto. III. United Nations Institute for Training and Research. IV. Centro de Estudios Economicos y Sociales del Tercer Mundo. V. Series.
HF1583.A84 1981   337.5   80-25758
ISBN 0-08-025116-1

Printed in the United States of America

Contents

Preface to the UNITAR-CEESTEM New International Economic Order Library

AN INFORMATION NOTE BY THE PROJECT DIRECTOR

The UNITAR-CEESTEM NIEO Library is the most extensive and comprehensive series of publications ever to appear on the New International Economic Order. The result of three years of intensive research by over 200 independent experts in all parts of the world, its 97 studies and associated research reports cover practically all aspects of the world economic and political scene as they relate to the issues of the New International Economic Order.

The worldwide research effort that produced the NIEO Library was born in the winter of 1976-77, when UNITAR and CEESTEM (Centro de Estudios Economicos y Sociales del Tercer Mundo, Mexico) decided to initiate a series of inquiries into the problems and the opportunities associated with the establishment of the New International Economic Order. These institutions agreed that the NIEO constitutes one of the highest priority items on the international agenda; and that independent, objective, and scholarly investigation of its objectives, obstacles, and indicated strategies will be of great value both to decision makers directly concerned with the negotiation of the issues, and to scholars and the international community at large. The NIEO Library is a result of the research that was undertaken by the central professional staffs of the institutes, and by their jointly formed international network of collaborators and consultants.

What are some of the reasons behind this assessment of the importance of the NIEO in contempoorary economic and world affairs? Although most people know that the world economy is encountering serious difficulties on both national and international levels, few people outside a small circle of experts realize the seriousness and breadth of the problems. Contrary to some current perceptions, the NIEO is neither a passing pressure of the poor countries on the rich, nor merely a demand for more aid and assistance. It is a process which has deep historical precedents, and an undisputed historical significance.

We need not go back further than the end of World War II to find an entire array of historical events which set the stage for the later emergence of the call for the NIEO. While these events arose from their own historical antecedents, they themselves produced the setting for the breakdown of the postwar economic system, and the widening gap between rich and poor nations.

The first, and perhaps most decisive, event was the liberation of the oppressed peoples of Africa and Asia, in the great wave of decolonization that swept the world in the years following World War II. The newly independent states were said to be sovereign and equal to all other states, old and new, large and small. Their admittance to the U.N. underscored this. However, the fresh political and juridicial status of the new countries was far from matched by their actual economic conditions. The majority felt that their de jure political colonization ended only to be replaced by a de facto economic colonization.

The historical process which gave the majority of the world's population the status of citizens of sovereign and equal states, but left them in a situation of economic underdevelopment and dependence, triggered the "revolution of rising expectations." Desires for rapid economic growth led Third World governments into ambitious plans and programs of national development. Most of the plans envisaged a quick repetition of the industrial growth processes of the developed world, following a path already long trodden by the countries of Latin America. When the unintended side effects of traditional patterns of industrialization became evident — uncontrolled growth of cities, relative neglect of rural areas and agriculture, threats to the environment, and the increasing stratification of people in modern and traditional sectors, often with serious damage to social structure and cohesion — many of the original development strategies underwent modification. The goal of rapid economic growth was not surrendered, however. Quantitative growth targets were formally included in the official development strategies of the First and Second U.N. Development Decades (for the 1960s and the 1970s, respectively).

However, the midterm review of the achievement of the Second Development Decade's goals showed mixed results. The greatest disappointment came in the area of agricultural production and official development aid. On the average, the U.N. official development aid targets have not even been half achieved. At the same time, service charges on past loans began to put enormous pressures on developing countries' balance of payments, and world poverty showed no signs of diminishing. There was insufficient progress in commodity trade and inadequate access to the markets of developed countries, particularly for agricultural products; tariffs have escalated, especially for semi-processed and processed products; and new tariffs and non-tariff restrictions were introduced by many developed countries on a number of items, including textiles and leather goods. The plight of the least developed, island, and landlocked developing countries gave rise to additional concern. While some progress was achieved (for example, through the introduction of a generalized system of preferences by the developed countries, and the proposals of the Tokyo Declaration concerning multilateral trade negotiations), the negative developments weighed more heavily in the balance and created widespread dissatisfaction in the developing world.

Another set of factors came into play as well. This was the sudden and unexpected rise of Third World economic and political power. The Middle East oil embargo of 1973-74, and the subsequent four-fold increase in the price of oil created a world energy crisis. It affected all oil importing nations, developed as well as developing. It also exhibited the dependence of the developed countries on the developing world for several major natural resources, and proved the ability of the Third World to wield economic and political power effectively. The consequences included rises in the price of food due to the increased cost of chemical fertilizers, and further tensions between producers and consumers of raw materials. But the OPEC-type of exercise of Third World economic and political power proved unable to improve the condition of the developing countries as a whole. Despite significantly higher gross resource flows from the oil-exporting to the oil-importing developing countries, the economic plight of the latter worsened due to the higher cost of energy. Developed countries found themselves beset by economic problems on their own, including not only higher oil prices but inflation, unemployment, and unused industrial capacity. Economic rates of growth slowed while, in most countries, balance of payment deficits grew. Even where surpluses could still be generated, concerns focused on the domestic economy and the political will to increase levels of aid and assistance to the Third World faltered.

Compounding the economic difficulties of the developed nations were signs of breakdown in the international monetary system which affected all countries, developed as well as developing. Amidst growing tensions between the United States, Japan, and the European Community over matters of trade, the Bretton Woods systems collapsed and gave rise to a system of floating exchange rates. The value of the U.S. dollar began to erode, creating serious difficulties for those countries which, like most of the Third World, held their reserves in dollars. The creation of Special Drawing Rights provided some access to foreign exchange independently of dollar holdings, but such access favored the countries already developed, and the rest remained seriously dissatisfied with the workings of the international monetary system. It became evident that some of the fundamental tenets of the postwar world economy were being called into question; indeed, that some had already collapsed.

The NIEO made its appearance as an international political issue in the context of this series of events. Encouraged by the success of OPEC but fearful of splintering Third World solidarity through the newly won wealth of a few of its countries, Presidents Boumedienne of Algeria and Echeverria of Mexico, among others, called for structural reforms in the international economic system. Their governments' initiative resulted in the adoption of such major U.N. resolutions as those of the Sixth and Seventh Special Sessions and the Charter of Economic Rights and Duties of States. These, in turn, provided the impetus for a long series of declarations, resolutions, position papers, and studies on various NIEO issues by the United Nations system and the international community at large.

The coming together of these historical factors was not purely coincidental. The wave of decolonization was the culmination of a long-term historical process of democratization, and the rise of the concept of universal rights for individuals and societies. It led, in turn, to a mounting desire for rapid industrialization by the newly independent countries. This met with major frustrations. But as economic interdependence intensified, as trade and markets expanded, and access to energy and raw materials became crucial to the developed world's giant economic machinery, the concentration of economic power itself was modified. It was no longer wielded by a few powerful governments but also fell into the hands of oil-exporting nations and transnational corporations.

The historical process which gave birth to a host of independent nation-states placed into sharp relief the inequities of the previous economic system, and provided some of the developing countries with fresh degrees of economic leverage. Since not only do they control the supply of a number of important fuels and raw materials but they also absorb about 25 percent of the developed world's exports, their demands can no longer be ignored. And they insist that a healthy growth in the world economy cannot be brought about within the framework of the existing economic system.

When the General Assembly, in December 1977, called for another Special Session in 1980 to assess progress in the establishment of the NIEO, it took a decisive step in bringing the North-South debate to the Organization, where it belongs. It created an ongoing forum for discussions and negotiation in the interim through the Committee of the Whole which, during 1978, managed to define its role and function despite earlier disagreements. Together with the work of the bodies charged with the preparation of the International Develoment strategy for the Third United Nations Development Decade, the Organization created the forums for substantive progress in the area of restructuring the economic relations of developed and developing countries. Faced with mounting pressure on national economies in all parts of the world, the international community now finds itself facing a watershed decision: to make use of these forums, or to continue to use mainly bilateral and sectoral corrective measures to mitigate tensions while entrusting the resolution of problems to the mechanisms of the free market.

This decision is intimately linked to an entire array of basic questions. Among them:

● The question of cost and benefit. Who will have to bear the burden of instituting NIEO, and will the results be worth the sacrifices? Will benefits really accrue to the poor people to help fulfill their basic needs, and will developing countries be made truly more self-reliant — or will the main beneficiaries be the already rich elites?

Will the developed countries also benefit from NIEO (a positive-sum game), or will it mainly mean the redistribution of the current stock of wealth from them to the developing countries (a zero-sum game)?

● The question of legitimacy. Is the free market the basic mechanism of world trade and the best vehicle of development, or is it merely a convenient fiction to cover up the current unjust manipulations of the major economic groups?

● The question of morality. Do the rich countries have a moral obligation to help the poor, and especially the poorest? Does this responsibility extend to those countries who had no historical part in the creation of poverty in the Third World?

● The question of political feasibility. How strongly will different organized groups in society support or oppose governmental policies aimed at the achievement of the NIEO — and how much solidarity exists in these domains internationally, among the developing and the developed countries themselves?

It is unrealistic to expect that real progress will be made on specific NIEO issues (such as official development aid, technical assistance, debt renegotiation, removal of tariff barriers, technical cooperation among developing countries, the link between SDRs and development, voting power in the World Bank and IMF, transfers of technology, regulation of transnational corporations, a system of consultations on industrialization, and restructuring the economic and social sectors of the United Nations) so long as the basic issues are not resolved and a consensus does not emerge concerning them. NIEO can be achieved if, and only if, it is perceived that its benefits are universal and can reach all segments of the world's population (especially the neediest); if it is held that its costs do not exceed its benefits; if its regulatory mechanisms are seen to be legitimate; if some real sense of moral responsibility exists among members of the human community; and if sufficient political support is available nationally as well as inter-nationally for the indicated measures.   If one or more of these preconditions are not met, the NIEO wil not be achieved; member states will continue to practice the existing, predominantly piecemeal, ad hoc, and mainly bilateral modes of adjusting to stresses and reaching compromises.

The basic purpose of the UNITAR-CEESTEM NIEO Library is to provide an independent and objective assessment of these issues, and to report its findings in time for the historic events of 1980: the Special Session of the General Assembly devoted to the assessment of progress toward the NIEO; and the immediately following regular session, during which the International Development Strategy for the 1980s and beyond (the U.N.'s Third Development Decade) is to be debated and adopted. It would be clearly an enormous waste of time and effort to enter into these negotiations without forming a clear idea of the issues that bear on their success. But reporting on them is not a simple matter of using insight and intuition; it requires painstaking and organized empirical research. The requirement is to identify the forces that operate for or against the NIEO in all parts of the world. Intuitive answers concerning its cost and benefits, legitimacy, morality, and political feasibility occur to all persons knowledgeable in these areas, but such answers tend to vary and are thus not sufficiently reliable. Expert research on the current obstacles and opportunities associated with the NIEO in the different regions of the world, and with respect to the diverse sectors of the world economy, needs to be conducted. The results of such research may shed some much needed light on the chances of success in establishing a new international economic order generally, and on the types of objectives and modes of negotiations that could lead to it specifically. For, although it is unlikely that a dominant consensus already exists in the world concerning the cost and benefit, legitimacy, morality, and political feasibility of the NIEO (if it did exist, the international community would probably not be experiencing the sense of frustration it is today), the precise estimates of costs versus benefits, legitimacy versus illegitimacy, morality versus indifference, and political feasibility versus futility by different societal groups could reveal highly differentiated potentials for achieving a dominant consensus in the future. Today's chaotic welter of opinions and pressures concerning the NIEO need not remain such, but could crystallize into a decisive mood favoring or opposing it.

To those who object to such analysis on the grounds that economic theory, rather than wide-ranging socio-political considerations, must serve to decide the fate of NIEO, we may reply that economic theory, while relevant, is in itself over-generous: it can often prove both sides of conflicting positions. Since both sides in a dispute can marshal some variety of economic theory in their defense, and no common criteria exist for assessing the relative merits of all theories, economic rationality (as conveyed by economic theories) becomes marginal in the negotiating process. We need to go one step deeper, inquiring into the reasons particular theories are summoned to defend particular points of view, as well as measuring the intensity of commitment to these viewpoints and the negotiating power of the parties subscribing to them.

Thus, the focus of the UNITAR-CEESTEM Library is not on a given economic theory, but the perceptions and opinions underlying the positions taken by diverse actors. The configuration and strength of these perceptions and opinions will ultimately determine whether negotiations in the area of the NIEO can be successful; and, if so, which strategies will have optimum chances of success.

The Library contains volumes arranged in three different series. There is, first of all, a series of overview studies. These provide background, context, and basic reference data. They include a volume defining and classifying the principal objectives of the NIEO as agreed or debated in the United Nations and other major international forums; a volume giving an overview and assessment of alternative viewpoints on the NIEO espoused by various nongovernmental groups and researchers in different parts of the world; a third defining the most critical obstacles confronting the establishment of the NIEO; and a fourth dealing with the specific problems of food and agriculture as they are debated in the framework of the United Nations. A fifth volume suggests the basic strategies which appear indicated and appropriate to accelerate progress toward the NIEO; and a final volume communicates the results of the associated UNITAR-CEESTEM International Opinion Survey of Decisionmakers and Experts on the crucial questions of the NIEO.

The second series contains geographic studies. Volumes in this series review the positions and postures of national governments and the attitudes of business, labor, the public media, and the opinions of the population at large in various nations and regions of the world. Individual volumes focus on the United States and Canada, Western Europe, Eastern Europe including the Soviet Union, Asia including Australia, Latin America, and Africa and the Middle East.

The third series of the NIEO Library is devoted to functional studies. Here, experts give their views and assessments of such issues as the possible and the desirable structure of the world economy; the patterns and problems of international trade and industrial development; international financial matters; and the associated political and institutional, as well as social and cultural, problems and opportunities.

Among them, the 17 volumes of the Library cover practically all the principal issues encountered in efforts to establish a New International Economic Order, through in-depth discussion by independent investigators, coming from different societies in different parts of the world.

The UNITAR-CEESTEM Library offers wide-ranging analyses, and sometimes divergent viewpoints, on a broad range of topics. It does not offer simplistic solutions, nor does it advocate one viewpoint indiscriminately over others. It seeks to illuminate the range and complexity of the issues, provide clarification of individual items, and to lend a sense of the vastness and significance of the NIEO as a whole.

It is the hope of all of the researchers and consultants of the UNITAR-CEESTEM project on the NIEO that our results, published as the NIEO Library, may render some service to the decision maker and negotiator who must cope with the problems of the international economic order, as well as to the student of international economic and world affairs interested in further research on these topics. It is our view that the NIEO is a historically necessary, and humanly and politically appropriate, attempt to create a world order that is sustainable for generations, equitable for all, and capable of meeting the most urgent needs and demands of the peoples and nations of the world community.

Ervin Laszlo

Introduction

The UNITAR/CEESTEM Library on the New International Economic Order (NIEO) examines obstacles and opportunities associated with current efforts to create a new and more equitable world community. This volume deals with the establishment of the NIEO in the Asian continent, defined as South, Southeast, and East Asia. The major functional themes addressed in this volume are trade, industrialization, food, raw materials, natural resources, regional integration, and socio-cultural issues.

The great diversity of cultures and levels of socio-economic development in the Asian region renders a discussion of common obstacles and strategies difficult in the context of the NIEO. The consensus that emerges in this volume is that Asia cannot as yet be treated as a single unit, but that a major common objective should be the strengthening of an Asian consciousness and identity, similar to that which exists in Europe and Latin America.

An overview of the Asian region reveals the following features. The continent is divided into three separate units – the dry farming area of South and Southwest Asia, the wet paddy land of Southeast Asia, and the plantation economy of East and Southeast Asia. The socio-economic indicators point to an equally bewildering diversity in historical development of the region, ranging from a large population base, low productivity of agriculture, and low export ratio in national income in South Asia, to relatively land-abundant, food-surplus countries with high export ratio in Southeast Asia, to food-deficit, plantation economies with high import ratio in East and Southeast Asia. The degree of government control over the economy ranges from extensive central planning in South Asia to a much greater reliance on free-market enterprise in Southeast and East Asia, to strong central control in China, Vietnam, and Kampuchea. In terms of international trade patterns, South Asia relies primarily on exports of heavy manufactured products; the food-surplus countries of Southeast Asia on rice, maize, cattlefeed, etc.; and the resource-rich countries of Southeast and East Asia on exports of natural resources such as oil, rubber, tin, iron ore, lumber, sugar, copper, plywood, as well as light manufactured products. The forms of government range from constitutional, parliamentary systems in India and Japan to military governments in many countries in the region, and to centrally planned government in the People's Republic of China and others.

Thus, the stunning diversity of Asia rules out the standard North-South compartmentalization and calls for an analysis of the NIEO issues in strictly functional terms rather than in country or regional terms. What follows is an issue-area analysis of NIEO principles impinging on Asia, as defined above.

In the area of producers' associations, it is clear that many commodities produced in the Asian region are not well suited for such associations, because, unlike oil, demand is relatively elastic due to the existence of substitutes; or they are perishable, such as bananas; or monopoly control is found in developed countries, such as is the case of manganese ore, phosphate rock, and bauxite. For commodities that cannot profitably come under international control, costs of production should be reduced, and efficiency in production, marketing, and distribution should be raised; and a major drive should be launched for the removal of tariff and nontariff barriers in industrial countries for primary products. The establishment of many producer associations is suggested, not on a commodity-by-commodity basis, but on a basket of commodities in a Common Fund in which the earnings of those commodities that go up in price are used to support those that go down. It is acknowledged, however, that oil producers would never enter into such an agreement, since they assume that oil prices would only move upward.

International buffer stocks are also impractical due to problems of standardization, specification, and storage of many products; the difficulty of agreeing on a "fair," "remunerative," or "appropriate" price; and the possibility that price stabilization would not prevent the encroachment of synthetics on the market for natural commodities. On the last point, some believe that the pricing policy of the International Tin Agreement has hampered the development of tin and, at the same time, enabled substitutes to capture a larger share of the packaging business. The lack of adequate information on market behavior, coupled with inadequate financing, limits the capacity of Asian cooperation on this front.

The competitiveness of natural products versus synthetic substitutes emerges as one of the major issues in the effort to accelerate the establishment of a NIEO in Asia. The main obstacle to the price competitiveness of natural products is the instability of market share for such products. The share of natural rubber, for example, has declined to only about 30 percent in recent times in the total production of rubber, compared to about 60 percent in 1955. A variety of reasons is offered for the higher unit labor costs in natural products — inefficient production methods, deficiencies of business management, excessive bureaucratic controls, lack of an efficient civil service, constraints on technology transfer, market restrictions by transnational corporations (TNCs), and environmental and waste considerations. It is suggested that, in order to overcome such obstacles, agreements must be reached between producing and consuming countries on long-term transactions of specific commodities. Specified minimum targets must be agreed upon and adhered to by both parties; price agreements should be concluded at least one year in advance of the delivery date and should be based on the current market price at the time of the agreements. Efficient technology and management techniques should be introduced, along the lines of what is already in operation in Malaysian or Sumatran rubber estates and in the Indonesian palm oil industry.

As far as trade in manufactures is concerned, a great deal of concern is expressed over the increasing degree of protectionist sentiments in industrial countries. It is felt that the main obstacle to an abating of protectionism is the inability or the unwillingness of industrial nations to bring about structural changes in their own economies so that, in the interest of a more rational division of labor, labor-intensive and low-technology manufacturing activities can be phased out in order to accommodate the relatively "low-wage" manufactured products from developing economies, including the Asian nations. While increasing protectionism in industrial countries affects all GATT (General Agreement on Tariffs and Trade) trading partners, it assumes a particularly serious role in curtailing manufactured exports from developing countries in the Asia-Pacific area. In the case of the Republic of Korea, for example, while tariffs on imports have been progressively reduced, developed countries have expanded nontariff barriers to trade such as import license, import quota, voluntary regulation, and so on. As far as the manufactured exports from the Asia-Pacific region are concerned, protectionism in developed countries shows a pattern of change from selective restrictions to categorical controls, from single-nation to multiple-nation restrictions, and from short-term to long-term restrictions. The solution proposed is that UNCTAD should continue to take up the challenge and press for the removal of tariff and nontariff barriers to Third World trade. It is also suggested that too much stress has been laid on Third World international trade and too little on Third World intra- and interregional trade. It is felt by some that Third World tariffs ought to be cut for all products across the board, along the lines of what has been initiated already in ASEAN (Association of Southeast Asian Nations), although such an approach might run into difficulties with GATT's principles of reciprocity and nondiscrimination in international trade.

In the field of food and natural resources, the case study of India shows that many of the current obstacles to the establishment of a NIEO can be removed by appropriate policies and programs at both the national and international levels. At the international level, such action should take the form of reducing trade barriers to imports from developing countries, providing greater financial and technological aid to improve productivity, and providing for adequate stocks of food as envisaged by the World Food Security System. At the national level, policies should be aimed at promoting growth with social justice that will generate additional income and employment opportunities for the economically weaker sections of society. The kinds of measures that need to be taken at the domestic level include: the strengthening of the agrarian structure based on peasant proprietorship supplemented by cooperative and joint farm enterprises, the application of science and technology to animal production and breeding, the appropriate marketing strategies for rural products, and greater use of animal energy.

In the area of industrialization, the Indian experience illustrates the fact that the long-run dependence of Asian countries on Western powers impedes the harnessing of appropriate strategies for social, technological, and economic well-being of these countries. This dependence syndrome is internalized in the ruling elites of Asia and pervades every facet of Asian culture, including technological choice and economic production and distribution. Despite impressive industrial gains, per capita real income in India has remained stagnant to date, labor force participation rates have continued to decline, and unemployment continues to be a serious problem. Both the government emphasis on the secondary sector of heavy industries and the role of transnationals have accentuated the employment problem. The transnationals have rarely encouraged backward linkages, and their contribution to forward linkages have actually resulted in replacing traditional, labor-intensive, local industries such as aluminum, stainless steel, and light consumer goods. The dependence on orthodox Western and Soviet models of development has prevented the introduction of approproate technology, especially in rural areas. Both existing internal income distribution and external relations with transnationals have to be significantly modified if Asia is to make any appreciable progress toward industrialization and appropriate technology. There should be internationally agreed-upon formal relationships between the TNCs and host governments to guarantee the certainty of economic benefits to the host country as well as to reduce the risks of a curtailment of their national sovereignty, implied in the global decision-making processes of the TNCs. National and regional models of development must attack the problems of the nonorganized, primary sector in ariculture and tackle the issues of the malaccumulation and maldistribution of national income. In the long run, the process of industrialization must conform to the basic needs of the Asian populace.

The issues of trade and industrialization in Asia are intimately linked to regional integration efforts. Tariff reductions would not be of much benefit to countries in the region which are not structured to take advantage of them. However, historically, trade has been a major engine of growth and regional cooperation in Asia remains a basis for hope, assuming that Asians can get along with each other. However, the divisive emphasis placed by international organizations on both self-sufficiency and trade-related specialization is a key obstacle to bringing about increased regional cooperation in Asia. Simply put, the key question is: Who would do the importing if every country is self-sufficent and geared to exporting?

In the Asian context, international trade is also tied to economic planning harmonization. In view of the active role of the governments in the region in allocating resources, and in view of the fact that stable price systems cannot be presupposed in Asia, a tariff reduction scheme alone will not get very far in Asia. What is necessary is plan harmonization and coordination of policy objectives. The problem of cooperation is particularly acute in the case of food and industrialization. In each case, the principle of comparative advantage is denied by overlapping and competing forces. While pure comparative advantage principles may be unacceptable in the heterogeneous context of Asia, marginal adjustments may be acceptable, and it is in this context that regional cooperation assumes a particularly significant role.

As far as social change is concerned, the gains from trade do not filter down to the general public. In fact, disparities in income levels have been increasing significantly both within and among regions. Therefore, any strategy aimed at bringing about a NIEO in Asia should put stress on linking external trade relations with desired domestic changes. In other words, external trade should be viewed more as a function of a centralized national authority than a function of the authority of international prices. The decision-making disorder of many nations in the Asian region is a major obstacle to the achievement of a NIEO. Overdependence on advanced-country models of development based on industrial, scientific, and technological revolutions results in an identity crisis. Domestic policy measures should attack the population explosion, especially in urban areas, and should foster the growth of managerial, entrepreneurial, and technical skills among the population – two critical factors in the achievement of a NIEO in Asia. Ways must be found to cope with increased demands for decentralization of power and elaboration of consensus systems to diffuse traditional suspicions, antagonisms, and polarizations by building participative organizations, institutions, and societies. There is more lack of contact between Asians than between any other regional groups in the world. To a large extent, this is caused by the substantial information gap in Asia. Japan, for example, is a net importer of information, i.e., the Japanese know more about the world markets than the world knows about Japan. This gap should be closed by educating the public in national self-interest (cheaper consumer prices on developing-country food imports, for example) and by establishing Asian regional institutes to bring together students, scholars, businessmen, and politicians to discuss common objectives and common problems. In the long run, Asians ought to promote collective self-reliance based on national consciousness, and individual and collective identity in the region.

A major new force in the emerging world order in Asia is the People's Republic of China. Among the developing nations of Asia, the PRC stands out as a special case in view of its political importance, its success in achieving relative equality in the distribution of national income, and its ability to sustain moderate economic development without substantial external assistance. Although, as of now, China has only a limited capacity for making concrete contributions to bringing about a NIEO in Asia, its moral support for NIEO principles is of crucial significance to the Third World. China has already given firm support to the Arusha Programme for Collective Self-reliance, the Integrated Programme of Commodities, the Common Fund, the proposed International Code of Conduct on the Transfer of Technology, and other component positions of the NIEO. In the long run, it is the autonomous and self-reliant nature of China's development, coupled with its effort to span a "modernity lag" and its political sympathies for the Third World, that will determine China's attitude to the global economic system and to the NIEO proposals.

In conclusion, although in view of the great diversity of Asian countries it is difficult to implement NIEO strategies across the board, there are selected functional areas where NIEO principles can be fruitfully applied. This volume pinpoints some of the these issue-areas and also draws attention to the policy actions that must be undertaken if there is to be real and appreciable progress in Asia toward the establishment of a New International Economic Order.

The editors wish to point out that the views expressed in this volume are those of the authors in their individual capacities and not necessarily those of the sponsoring organizations or of the governments.

The editors would like to express their appreciation for the excellent work done by Ms. Susanne Kyzivat, an intern at UNITAR.

Jorge Lozoya
A.K. Bhattacharya

1 Social and Cultural Imperatives
Romesh Thapar

Asia cannot be treated as a single cultural matrix, and certainly not in the context of a new international order. The United Nations' divisions, still based on rather mechanical North-South equations, are unreal in terms of Asian complexities and challenges. The continent embraces the incredibly advanced technology of Japan, now outpacing United States consumer goods production in many fields, and the growing giants of India and the People's Republic of China, compelled despite contrasting social systems to seek new organizational answers to the pressures of huge populations. In addition, Asia is dotted with divided (partitioned!) peoples, island nations, tribal enclaves, and cultures imbibing influence and drawing sustenance from a variety of sources in the northern and southern hemispheres.

Within the sprawling continent, a number of regional manifestations are, however, becoming visible. While the PRC and Japan, with their common collectivist ethos, build a centrist, political dynamism, the peoples further south, in India, Vietnam, and Southeast Asia, are moving toward a decentralized expression which is a response to cultural pluralities. These trends, profound in many ways, are in their early formative stage. Varying experiences within the developing continent will be watched, studied, and digested, increasingly breaking the invisible links which still hold Asia in some kind of psychological and philosophical subservience to the former centers of imperial power. This qualitative change in Asian thinking and striving holds revolutionary germs in relation to the the the New International Economic Order.

Parallel to the debate on a new division of world income between the rich and poor nations (a reform to be achieved through diplomacy and hard bargaining) there is a growing assertion that the nations of the Third World are caught in a series of illusions created by the affluent centers of economic power, illusions which hold their ruling elites in a terrible grip, and until this status quo situation is shattered there is no hope for self-reliant development which alone can be the base of a New

1

International Economic Order. In other words, a fundamental restructuring of economic power is called for. But Asia is realizing that, before this self-reliance in action becomes possible, there will have to be a major reorganization of ideas and concepts – even perspectives. Significantly, this realization is common to the advanced and backward regions of the continent.

The sharpness of the debate on the New International Economic Order has uncovered many layers of inequality, exploitation, discrimination, and dependence. The old imperial stranglehold continues in many disguised forms and has to be exposed and tackled before any healthy economic relationships can evolve. The existence of countries which have broken with the world capitalist system lends weight to this body of opinion. It is becoming clear that the existing situation calls for internal changes in class power and an alteration in social priorities.

These trends are very much a part of the spiritual ferment of the developing world of which Asia is critically important. A new power and purpose has become evident by the change in the early 1970s in the Third World's voting strength in the United Nations, and the extraordinary demonstration of economic repercussions in the hike in oil prices in 1973.

These phenomena are rooted firmly in the realities of our unequal world, and they will find wide relevance in the years ahead. Indeed, they will develop a certain depth, cutting across many divided and conditioned views on the New International Economic Order. Without a focus on such social and cultural imperatives, no full understanding is possible on the directions men and movements will take during the next decade in Asia.

The cultural mosaic of the region, based on old civilizations which live on into the present, creates a multitude of national and subnational strivings which have to be respected and nurtured, and also given the opportunity to grow and prosper within whatever framewords are envisaged for political, economic, and social development. The old domination, inherited from a long history of conquests and subjugations, have to be replaced by sensitive working relations based on equality. They cannot be replaced by a new kind of cultural domination in which ideas of what constitutes economic progress (complete with the enormous waste involved) are transferred from the northern to the southern regions, and continue to give the latter a persistent but false inferiority complex. Naturally, economic programming, with a proper balance and integration within ethnic boundaries, determines political and social stability. The problems arising from this complicated, and often little understood, situation have a direct bearing on many developmental priorities, and there is no way of understanding the thrust of regional thinking except from a local point of view.

The shared experience of colonialism which has spawned a variety of common and urgent problems (the rapid growth of elites largely isolated from the mass of the people; the continuing dependence of these economies on more powerful and developed centers, either directly or through transnational corporations; the economic, political, and social distortions, together with the feeling of individual helplessness), unite a sharply contrasted grouping of nations. But it would be an error of profound magnitude to imagine, in the context of a New International Economic Order, that regional yardsticks can provide a meaningful measure of what progress has been achieved and what has still to be done.

In other words, despite the "collective image," Asia internally contains an enormous amount of cultural tension which spills over to political and economic areas. As a result, the quantum of tension increases with every year.

The critical effort to recognize, locate, and comprehend national and sub-national strivings is of very special concern in the context of the dynamics of growth. It is this effort, when translated into regional programs and policies, that must be governed by the impulses of self-reliant expression. It is a passion which may not be immediately visible. Indeed, it may well be heavily covered over by the intense activities of rather imitative ruling elites. But it is bound to surface and impact political, economic, and social growth, because it is a deep cultural need in the communities of Asia.

Actually, at both the individual and collective levels, it battles with and confronts in various open and subtle ways the trends which seek to mold life and living into rigid mechanistic, petrified models. Efforts are being made to impose the models of advanced societies (or societies which happened to pioneer the industrial, scientific, and technological revolutions) on two-thirds of the world as an inevitable part of the process of modernization. Considerable brainwashing has been done in leading influential circles of the Third World to make easier the projection of those values which underpin these much-publicized models. As the debate on the New International Economic Order is more fully joined, this model-making, with its wide ramifications, will come under close scrutiny.

The crisis of identity in modernization, or the survival of individual cultures amid industrial and technological change, is ever present in the consciousness of Asia, and cannot but influence the contours of the NIEO. The crisis needs emphasizing because the peoples of Asia are spanning a century of change in decades while attempting to retain their variety, their integrity, and their coherence. In a sense, this is the heart of the problem of self-reliant development. A failure in this area could spark psychological upsets the like of which we have not known. In Asia, modernization, as interpreted today, will need fundamental reassessing and redesigning to buttress social and cultural self-defense. This will have to be done at feverish speed, before the foundations of the available authentic identity are destroyed beyond repair, creating new and more terrible crises of social alienation and atomization.

The destruction of individual and collective identity in this course of modernization proceeds at an unthinking pace because the inevitability of this destruction is subtly programmed into the consciousness of the Third World. It is too widely assumed that any resistance to this process is tantamount to opposing progress and favoring backward-looking revivalism. In many societies, a rigid fascination with modernization has meant accepting all its negative and unproductive features, in spite of the fact that many socially disruptive elements of imitative modernization become uncontrollable and result in demands for "instant" changes.

We have now arrived at a most interesting phase. A more searching analysis of what modernization actually signifies is beginning to gain favor at many levels of development. The repercussions of modernization are sparking a rethinking, based on the experience of the world undergoing modernization. The first faint signs of this resurgence are visible in India and the PRC. However, the devotees of the status quo and its values try to sidestep the cultural and social content of the NIEO.

The multicultural structure of Asian nations, brought about by conquests and famines, calls for specific political and economic concepts that will favor the future development of this region. In the context, for example, of preserving individual and collective identity in the process of modernization, together with national self-reliance and integrity, widespread support has come to be extended to demands for decentralizing power and elaborating consensus systems to defuse traditional suspicions, antagonisms, and polarizations. This creates a challenging scenario for political parties in the region. These trends contrast sharply with the centralization of power that is inherent in industrial, scientific, and technological advances even in federal countries like the United States and the USSR. Significantly the Asian experience cuts across the ideological commitments of the political Right and Left and places the emphasis rather heavily on the gut problems of building participating organizations, institutions, and societies.

The decentralized society, drawing its popular sanctions from fair and just consensus techniques, necessarily flourishes at various levels of autonomous functioning. From its success, the participative society takes nourishment. Despite the distortions in political experience, and the anguish and trauma which prevail over many areas of the developing world, the enormous groups demanding equal treatment and opportunity know vaguely that these hopes will be wrecked unless deep and all-pervasive changes take place in the social infrastructure which serves the people. The present infrastructure, designed originally to cater to the elites of industrial societies, is totally unsuited to the spiritual and physical needs of an Asia stirring from colonial stupor to take up the slack of centuries. New vested interests, linked to international centers of economic power and damaging to national self-reliance, have seen startling growth in certain regions. These are mobilized to defend their self-interests, but the pressure to find the path of self-reliance is growing and making their position ultimately untenable.

The transition from imitative practice to more authentic experimentation in political, economic, and social structuring is, however, still held back by the lack of preparation within the organizations dealing with these central questions. Vague commitments have to be replaced by hard-headed systems which make full use of many facets of modernization, while, at the same time, safeguarding the essential cultural and spiritual continuities reinforcing the self-reliant attitudes of a society in rapid growth. Surprisingly, no political formation has as yet been able to present a viable alternative to the imitative model. Shared emotions force the crystallization of thinking here and there, but the framework is lacking for a more thorough overhaul. This may well be due to the absence of alternative thrusts in those societies, such as Japan, which have modernized recently and, in many respects, outstripped those whom they sought to imitate. A modicum of identity remains in these modernized societies, but the key problems related to a new value system have not been tackled. No significant experience can be drawn upon.

In Asia, development is proceeding even while the question of identity in modernization is being raised. India and the PRC, large and populous, are very clearly opposed to an unthinking and unmindful submergence in what is called modernization. This powerful opposition will have to find the missing framework for the alternative model or it, too, will be in danger of being confused, diverted, and derailed. However, it is not unreasonable within Asia to see developments where the contradiction between highly centralized industrial, technical progress and decentralized autonomous progress will have to be resolved organizationally, institutionally, and structurally. And when it is resolved, it will become worthy of emulation in older industrial societies. After all, the latter societies, despite protests to the contrary, are themselves realizing that the models by which they live are not the guarantee of social stability. Advanced thinking the world over, irrespective of ideology, is stressing that the participative content of social organization and functioning will determine the health and viability of the systems upon which a New International Economic Order will be built.

The size of India and the PRC, physically and demographically, builds a framework of political, economic, and social thinking which is in many ways different from what Western textbooks preach. If India and the PRC temporarily stray back to the rigid models of the developed nation-states, the correction is not long-delayed; although the ruling elites exert great pressure to conform to the experience of the older industrialized societies, and often prevail despite warning signals, the return to reality is a constant counterpressure. This continuous struggle over the texturing of political, economic, and social growth, with its several related challenges to the value system underpinning existing societies, cannot fail to condition the Asian contribution to the NIEO.

The consumer society, based essentially on the "free play" of a much manipulated market with its frenzied excitement over an incredible range of unnecessary wants, has given birth to so much tension that it is no longer, as many believe, the sole perspective setter for societies in growth. Indeed, the variety of social crises rocking the otherwise stable economies of the developed world indicate the bankruptcy of culture and humanity which results when people are manipulated by the "free play" of the consumer goods market. The remarkable upsurge of work in the social sciences since the end of World War II, and the capacity of research to uncover the malaise which afflicts seemingly healthy societies, has sensitized the thinking world to the pollution of unplanned and perspectiveless development concerned only with deceptive rates of growth and profits. What is described as an extraordinary lack of social and cultural investment is, in fact, attributable to the emphasis of business on higher growth rates and profits. Such decadent economic thinking has to be exposed for what it is, or else it will seriously infect the NIEO.

This is no mean task. To begin with, the entire infrastructure of economic "collaboration" and "cooperation" is motivated by the urge to bargain for the best terms (a process which almost invariably is damaging to the interests of the less fortunate) and, then, to push development in directions familiar to the industrially advanced. This brings about a marriage of elites who seek to nourish one another, a marriage that is sanctioned by a communication network and an economic infrastructure that militates against the interests of developing peoples. The example of the PRC and India, reduced to the statistics of growth as seen through the eyes of Western economists, is instructive. No matter what centralizing ideological systems hold sway in these countries (population: 1500 million), if a way of life is sought comparable to the standards set in developed lands, the production figures in key areas would have to be staggering. No complex calculations are required to arrive at these conclusions. Obviously, unless there is some remarkable scientific and technical breakthrough in the field of energy production and material substitution, the social and cultural texturing will have to be completely different from that of present-day developed societies.

We need also to remember that our shrinking world cannot possibly underwrite two different levels of living. One must impact the other in the natural process of leveling. It is here that we will have to intervene actively, and on the solid foundation of tested social and cultural values, to prevent choices that would perpetuate those differences in levels of living that the NIEO seeks to dissolve. The intervention cannot be fuzzy or romantic, of the kind so often proposed. Qualitative changes in international thinking cannot be achieved without a major revolution in values and perspectives. We will have to return to this central issue over and over again if we are serious about a New International Economic Order. Everyone knows that this is the gut problem with a spillover effect on all efforts to bring the many-sided crises of our world into some kind of focus. And yet the thinking on it is by and large left to the futurists – as if it belongs to an age far far ahead. This is the myth we are living with, a myth which has the effect of paralyzing our capacity to cut a path through the frightening maze in which we find ourselves.

All over the Third World, and especially in Asia, it is possible to see how a refusal to restructure the base of developing societies in relation to the new realities is heightening the political crises through which these societies are passing. The initial democratic impulses, born in the womb of the freedom struggles against colonialism, are being snuffed out as more and more millions are persuaded that authoritarian remedies alone can cut the tangled knots of a colonial heritage. It matters little that authoritarianism has so far achieved next to nothing in transforming these societies. The stamping out of participative experiments in life and living, which alone can provide a meaningful base for a democratic order, and the mobilization sought behind charismatic, and often corrupt, individuals and groups has aborted the social and cultural revolution in these lands. The elites spawned by these authoritarian regimes are cosmopolitan, imitative in the worst sense of the term, and far removed from the imperative social concerns which should motivate them. Those trends do immense damage to the dignity, creativity, and identity of the peoples of the region. They can only be reversed by a determined effort to present a series of interrelated alternatives which gradually sketch a different framework of political, economic, and social thinking.

The alternative society is still in a very early phase of sketching. The open, multicultural Indian federation, underpinned by a varied and highly individualistic population, contrasts with the more cohesive, closed, almost single-nation, collectivist ethos of the PRC. Yet, the thrusts into the future of both these sprawling and populous lands are conditioned by the enormity of their extremely complex problems. Ideologies notwithstanding, both peoples seek social and cultural justice as the bedrock of political development. In contrast to what is happening in the smaller nations of Asia, including the extraordinary workshop that is Japan, these two giants are compelled to devise more integral perspectives on development. Their efforts, if successful, will offer many lessons for the world community, and particularly for the Third World. They will build alternative systems of growth which are bound to spark corrective thinking in the industrialized societies. The world of waste cannot forever coexist with the world of want. The struggle to resolve the problems of the rich and poor within nations is now impinging upon the relationship between nations and is directly influencing thinking on a New International Economic Order. A conflict of value systems is inevitable and will, in the long run, replace the present North-South divisions with which we are only too familiar.

If Asia's presence in the NIEO is to be conditioned by a new value system more related to both cultural continuity and economic necessity, the societies which will emerge will be qualitatively different from those glorified as models on the pages of glossy magazines. Can such a contradiction or confrontation persist for long? In the give-and-take of a shrinking world, criss-crossed by communication networks, profound mutations are likely to occur. The wisdom inherent in a social order largely devoid of waste, fundamentally egalitarian, and wedded to decentralized, participative action, skirting the obvious vulgarities of affluence, working for the simplification of life and living, and expanding the areas of creative leisure, cannot but assert itself in the long run. The processes are foreseeable, but it is necessary to caution against those who advance simplistic solutions to our ills and imagine that the transition to a new value system, even among the deprived, will be speedy or easy to attain.   Quite the contrary. The old, established ways are extremely difficult to demolish. Indeed, even the poorest of the poor, in whose name economic, political, and social revolutions are launched, are heavily programmed by the titillations of affluence and cannot easily detach themselves from such interests and desires. This is the reality of our condition and highlights the complexity of the task before us.

It is important to note that, as adjustments are sought by developing societies and dislocations persist, there will be massive migrations from the less privileged regions of the world, particularly those that are overcrowded or are unable to offer steady employment. These migrations, consisting largely of working people, will also embrace a variety of skilled personnel attracted by better emoluments and conditions of work. The so-called brain drain is too easily described. It is often a reflection of training facilities which have not been properly fused with national needs, or of specializations which do not really cater to the problems of the developing society. The lack of international balance is bound to create these movements of people; but we have to remember that migrations have always been a part of global life, even though they are culturally and ethnically more visible today because they consist of underprivileged working people moving into regions of affluence. In considering the present migrations, the North needs to recall the movement of some 100 million from Europe during the past 200 years to all corners of the planet, and to the Americas in particular. This fact of our comparatively recent history is largely slurred over, even though it could well be argued that the exit of so many from the continent of Europe defused demographic tensions and helped create the basis for economic health. An overcrowded Europe could have had a very different history of growth and accomplishment.

The migrations now started from the South will gather in momentum and continue despite the restrictions, at least until such time as the economic gaps between the two hemispheres are narrowed and the contrasting areas of waste and want become a memory of the past. At this moment, to arrange for healthier transitions to a NIEO, deeper communication is needed to neutralize the collision of communities and rash hatreds focusing on color, creed, and culture. These movements of people, and the emotional and psychological tangles they create, are very much a part of the social and cultural problematique of the NIEO.

One day, a common value system which is just and workable and which preserves cultural identities, even as modernization takes over, will unite the communities of our planet. Until then, populations will move transnationally as they do within multicultural nations. This is a natural demographic assertion and very much a part of the process which eliminates the gulfs between the rich and the poor or poverty-stricken countries – a perspective that inspires those working for a New International Economic Order.

In a strange kind of way, the debate on an <u>international</u> economic order must of necessity become concerned with <u>internal</u> economic orders. The rich, the poor, and the poverty-stricken will have to evolve commonly accepted yardsticks if they are to understand each other and extend their cooperation. In other words, as we debate international social justice, we will have to scrutinize internal social justice. This is exactly what is happening despite attempts to evade basic issues. If the debate is superficial at the moment, or skimming the surface, it is because there is a general failure to understand the new social texturing which is being sought by societies in development. The repeated stress on self-reliance based on egalitarianism, on national dignity, and on individual and collective identity within the awe-inspiring sweep of three revolutions working simultaneously – the industrial, the technical, and the scientific – is a reflection of the new texturing, and the social and cultural imperatives within that texturing. No caucus, international or internal, can hold back for long the movements of thought and action which are gathering for the confrontation with the status quo or its unchanging mechanisms.

Specifically, the effort to establish a NIEO capable of transforming the life of the overwhelming majority of mankind is nourished by the new relations between peoples and the heightened sensitivity to human deprivation and suffering. National cultures, which are increasingly asserting themselves, are now able to contribute to the general pool of enlightenment and uplift which is universal in scope. So long as warlike preparations do not interfere with the natural growth of these relationships, there can be a sustained enriching of a New International Economic Order which is not only just but carries within it the seeds of significant social transformations both in developed and developing societies. National cultures growing self-reliantly within the format of a universal civilization represent a new harmony. The culture of a small nation, despite the limitation of means, is now able to survive and live in dynamic equality with more expansive cultures. This does not mean that the processes of assimilation and rejection, which are at the heart of cultural strength and authenticity, cease or lessen. As our world grows "smaller" with the rapidity of movement and instant communication, a mutually beneficial collaboration between cultures cannot be confined, contained, or restricted – but it can be disciplined by intense selectivity and sensitivity. This is the true nature of the confrontation between industrially powerful and influential cultures and those which are not so endowed. The elaboration of a new economic order helps to defuse the unhealthy aspects of the confrontation by strengthening the self-reliance of the weak. This play between economic, political, and socio-cultural forces within nations and between nations needs fuller comprehension if we are to be the architects of our future.

The organization and implementation of a NIEO demand wide-ranging economic and social changes within the structure of all countries and in the relations among states. This is a gigantic undertaking, but it would be fraught with grave danger if the pattern of change was unvaried from culture to culture. This danger is ever present because the southern hemisphere is very much a part of the capitalist system headquartered in the North. The NIEO has, therefore, to stress self-reliant societies which alone can nourish a diversity of cultures within an evolving universalism.

Nations that perceive these momentums in the developing situation, and link themselves realistically to the hard facts of their economics, politics, and culture, are likely to survive the transition and influence the building of a new order. Those that lose their anchorages are in danger of being lost for years in paralyzing imitation and costly correctives. At this moment, the choice faces the countries of the Third World and, for that matter, every constitutent of Asia.

In this connection, it is customary to speak of two competing patterns of development — the capitalist, which now flourishes, having started some three centuries ago, and that which has taken shape in what is described as the socialist world. The lazy assumption that these patterns are universal in character is faulty, particularly in those regions where the breakaway from the capitalist system has taken place or is taking place. Apart from the serious contradictions which have crystallized in the postimperialist phase of development, the corpus of socialist throught and action is being variously interpreted as more and more countries abandon the capitalist path, or plan to extricate themselves from the international capitalist system. We are, in fact, entering a phase of extensive experimentation in the areas of economics and politics, experimentation which naturally is considerably influenced by the social and cultural infrastructures of each society. The trends we are witnessing are likely to be accentuated. The universalism we speak of may well be characterized by an experimentation influenced by both capitalist and socialist traditions, a marriage which will attempt the creation of a participative society founded firmly on the principles of justice. This dream can be frustrated, repeatedly, but not made to disappear by the sectarian partisans of the capitalist or socialist systems.

The political and social environment of the last decades of the century cannot but heavily influence the sketching of the New International Economic Order, an order which must drastically curb the waste of a minority of the human race and urgently meet the wants of the overwhelming majority. The old structure of power commanded by the rich, exploitive nations is under threat. In its place, a pluralism is beginning to flourish. This pluralism creates a healthy competition between various ideas and concepts, theoretically and in practice, destroying the rigid frameworks and models of the ideologues which invariably assist the more powerful to dominate those who are rising to claim their rights. In the creation of a new economic order, this varied experience will have to play an increasingly important cross-fertilization role. We have only just begun to understand this aspect of the new global situation.

Naturally, the richness of the exchange between cultures will be dependent on the degree to which our societies are equal, open, and accessible. This is a tall order, considering that the crisis of economic development (variously manifested) in both the northern and southern regions initially prepares the base for authoritarianism. It does not need underlining that authoritarianism, with its heightened nationalism, is the natural enemy of normal exchange between nations. Authoritarianism is highly imitative of status quo models and frameworks and is deeply suspicious of the new thinker, the passionate experimenter, and the impatient reformer. The surface improvements associated with authoritarian rule are a screen for the perpetuation of class, caste, tribal, and communal hegemonies. These dimensions of the problem are not always evident because so much of the discussion until now has been within familiar frameworks and confined to technical economic matters. If the struggle for a NIEO is to be relevant to Asia, and the developing world in general, it will have to move away from its present inhibitions and work toward a more fundamental and universal restructuring of economic, political, and socio-cultural life.

We are presently on the edge of some such development. The old models of growth are almost dead. The exponents are exhausted. The world waits for the new infrastructures which will serve the needs of freedom, justice, and equality within nations and between them. It is a moment of considerable historic importance. The actions taken today will mold our tomorrows. We seem to be aware of the significance of what we do, but we are reluctant to abandon the old props and supports. Any exercise that helps strengthen the resolve to achieve a breakthrough is of tremendous value. At least, it can be said that the nations of Asia, as well as other countries of the Third World, are poised to follow the new models of growth, and to fuse with them the vital social and cultural imperatives. This is no mean asset in the battle for a New International Economic Order.

2 Japan and the New International Economic Order
Masahiro Sakamoto

NIEO AND THE JAPANESE POSITION

In spite of manifold and contradicting contents, the NIEO seems to have been an established notion since the early 1970s. Because the economic gap between developed and developing countries has been widening and many developing nations still remain in an absolute poor stage, NIEO's advocates stress the need to change international economic mechanisms and institutional frameworks to a more favorable situation for the developing countries. The free trade principle has not reduced the imbalance between the rich and the poor countries. NIEO's proposals emcompass a wide range of contents: enlargement of development aid, improvement of terms of trade of LDCs (including indexation schemes), establishment of sovereign rights on natural resources, greater partic- ipating of LDCs in the world economic management, and linkage of aid with the issues of special drawing rights (SDRs). After the oil crisis, the confrontation between the North and the South seems to have reached a peak. It is widely recognized that the North-South dispute is one of the most important issues to be solved in order to ensure equitable development of the international society.

In the 1970s, however, the world experienced unprecedented diffi- culties. First, the relative decline of U.S. economic power has been generating unstable effects on the world economy. Secondly, the oil crisis had profound impact on various fields internationally. Uncertainty will persist as recent Iranian events indicate. The struggle for a stable oil supply exacerbates disputes among countries. Thirdly, heterogeneous development and changing competitive positions between countries have been creating unstable conditions, and slower economic growth has intensified trade conflicts and domestic difficulties. The problems the NIEO raises are important because there are urgent and difficult issues to be solved.

The Japanese stance on the NIEO will be affected by several factors: First, Japan as a major economic power has a responsibility in contributing to the achievement of an equilibrated development of the world economy. Japan, therefore, should be keenly interested in the evolution of developing nations. However, Japan has been lagging behind in this respect as indicated by the poor performance in Official Development Aid (ODA). This is partly due to the fact that private capital has been playing an alternative role today in the Japanese case. At the same time, Japan has been so preoccupied with its own economic progress that it has neglected cooperation in the development of other nations.

There are several proposals in the NIEO objectives which Japan cannot easily accept from the viewpoint of a stable functioning of the world economy (for example, indexation). In some cases, the conflicts among developed countries are so serious that compromises and co-ordination become urgent as recent trade issues indicate.

As Japan tackles the NIEO problems,* the Japanese position will be decided after having taken these factors into account. In the following part, the discussion will touch on what kind of obstacles Japan sees for the realization of the NIEO and what kind of measures can be taken to cope with these problems.

MAIN OBSTACLES AND OPPORTUNITIES
FOR THE IMPROVEMENT OF DEVELOPMENT ASSISTANCE

Salient Features of Japanese Aid

Though Japanese development assistance has been expanding rapidly, there is much criticism of the contents and the pattern of this cooperation. As pronounced characteristics of Japanese development aid, several points can be raised: In 1977, the total share of aid was 0.80 percent of GNP. Private capital has been dominant and growing. The ratio of ODA to GNP remains relatively modest compared to that of other developed nations. The grant element is low in the Japanese case and is geographically concentrated on Southeast Asian countries. Furthermore, technical cooperation is lagging behind other developed nations. Poor human resources constitute an obstacle to effective implementation in this field.

The reasons for this situation are manifold. However, one can say that development cooperation has not acquired top priority in postwar foreign policy. Japan has been more involved with its own economic progress than with the development of other nations. Ten years ago, the Japanese balance of payments was still in deficit and neither the

---

*As the NIEO notion has roughly the same content as development cooperation for Japan, in the following part, development cooperation will sometimes be used as an alternative expression for the NIEO.

Japanese nor any foreigners considered Japan a major economic power. In spite of recent efforts, there is a sizable lag in the level of governmental cooperation which major developed nations have undertaken since the 1960s.

Japanese development cooperation began with the payment of war reparations to Asian countries, which is one of the main reasons that the development aid is still concentrated in the Asian region, and private capital has traditionally had an important role. Currently, one can argue that private capital has more networks and more access to development cooperation than the Japanese government. Even if motivated by profit maximization, private capital is more adept at finding projects which are suitable to development cooperation. In contrast with other countries, the research ability of Japanese overseas governmental organizations is extremely poor. Though the network of cooperation has been rapidly expanding, the present capacity of overseas offices is extremely poor. There may be room for further rationalization in administrative arrangements. The unsatisfactory performance of ODA in 1976 was partly due to administrative inertia; however, the small increase in the budgetary appropriation in the first half of the 1970s substantially contributed to this.

Currently, aid projects are screened project by project by the authorized ministries. Although, recently, the approval process has been sizably streamlined, these may remain pending for further rationalization in this field. Furthermore, lack of administrative capability in the recipient countries has caused a drain on the effective implementation of development aid.

Strategies for Improvement

As to the volume of aid, though the ratio remains modest, the absolute level reached third position in the world in 1977 following the United States and France. The government made a strong commitment to double the volume of ODA by 1980 and a further increase is anticipated after that year. The rapid expansion of budgetary appropriation will continue for at least several years. The problem Japan faces in this field is how to translate these quickly expanding financial resources into effective implementation which requires improvement in project research abilities, administrative capacity, and human resources. Japan normally has a huge fiscal deficit (39.6 percent of the central government's revenue was financed by public debt in 1978). One of the most important concerns of the Japanese government is how to reduce this huge deficit which requires an increase in the tax burden. However, there is a reaction against a higher tax rate in Japan as in other developed countries; thus a reshuffling of expenditures will be needed in order to restore fiscal balance in the future. Furthermore, in the 1980s, as the aging problem becomes acute and the social security burden increases substantially, Japan will face critical choices between various competing claims from domestic as well as external sectors.

From the viewpoint of avoiding a fluctuation in the volume of the ODA and preserving the international commitment of the Japanese government, the Nomura Research Institute proposed to prepare a long-term economic cooperation plan which would contain long-term budgetary appropriations for development aid.

Improvement of Absorption Capacity

As stated above, the major problem in the 1980s is how to effectively translate the growing financial resources into development. This will be complicated by the recent proliferation of development assistance strategies. Since industrialization has not succeeded in all countries, and development itself is heterogeneous, economic assistance policies should be carried out according to the conditions in the countries concerned. This implies that the need for establishing aid policy country by country or region by region will increase. This, in turn, will call for sizable enlargement of research facilities in donor countries.

The following are examples of a differentiated approach:

1. For newly industrialized countries, the main form of assistance should be the channeling of private capital flows and the promotion of markets for manufactured products. This would facilitate the industrialization which is now taking place. For countries with inequality in income distribution and poor infrastructure, efforts also should be made to promote the improvement of social progress.
2. For the OPEC countries, the area of main cooperation lies in the technological fields for manufacturing industries as well as for social infrastructure. With the completion of industrial plants currently under construction, marketing of OPEC's products will be of upmost concern.
3. For other resource rich countries, schemes stabilizing export income or commodity prices should be arranged on either a global basis or a regional basis. ODA should be directed to agricultural production as well as to basic needs projects.
4. For least-developed countries, ODA and related technical assistance should be the main part of any aid and allocated to agricultural, educational, health, and rural development.

In order to cope with absolute poverty and to meet basic human needs, development aid should be directed toward the improvement of social progress (for example, enlargement of educational and sanitary facilities and agricultural development). This kind of basic needs approach also requires large research facilities because the projects may be scattered in a wider area than in the case of industrial plants.

Increases in the volume of aid and the differentiated approach call for institutional reinforcement of existing mechanisms. Roughly speaking, the capacity to single out and select suitable projects should be amplified substantially. At the same time, as the Swedish Institute indicates, considerable rationalization is needed in the process of project evaluation and in the delegation of power to lower levels of organization, though these attempts assume an improvement in the capability of the overseas offices.

Reinforcement of the overseas offices is urgent and extremely important in order to supervise implementation of these projects and to assess their achievements in cooperation with recipient countries. However, in view of the poor state of human resources, devices should be created to mobilize experts in private companies to assist the local staffs of developing countries. Cooperation with international organizations and with other developed countries' organizations are also important in this respect.

The Role of Private Capital

Though the ODA will be an important weapon for development cooperation, private capital can also play an important role in the Japanese case, and can partially compensate for the low level of Japanese ODA. Many newly industrialized countries (NICs) may wish to introduce foreign private capital. The number of NICs in the Pacific area suggests the possibility that private firms could have a better opportunity for development assistance in this region by providing technology and capital.

Poor Performance in Technical Cooperation

Though rapidly increasing, the level of technical cooperation is approximately two-thirds of the United States and one-third of Germany in 1978. The most meager performance in comparison with other developed nations is observed in cultural activities. The number of experts who are sent abroad has reached a sizable level, but many of them stay in developing countries for only a short period of time and function as technical consultants, while many engineers from other developed nations work as project leaders and contribute in fostering and educating local staff.

Japan has had unique experiences not only in the industrialization process but also in agricultural development. With regard to infrastructural improvement, regional planning, and administrative services, Japan has a potential to promote technological assistance. The obstacles to this include linguistic barriers. For most Japanese, it takes time before they can communicate with local staffs. There is a need to encourage speaking and comprehension both in formal education and occupational training. The shortness of the stay abroad is partly due to possible further delays in promotions. As most experts are temporarily recruited from the private sector, they are afraid their opportunity for promotion will be taken away while they are abroad. Often, employer evaluations only take into account recent and direct contributions to the performance of the company involved. The life employment system also works to the detriment of technical assistance. Many young people who are engaged in overseas work programs sometimes have difficulties getting jobs when they come back to Japan, because employees usually prefer fresh graduates for life employment.

In view of the urgency of the issue, strengthening government support for technical assistance is of vital importance and the encouragement of consulting businesses is a method to overcome this deficiency. However, it is also essential that social practices and people's attitudes be improved so that the experiences gained in development activities abroad are rated as a promotion factor in private business.

TRADE, INVESTMENT, AND INDUSTRIAL ADJUSTMENT

Though agricultural development and basic needs are important, industrialization still represents a most effective strategy for economic growth in most developing countries. The NIEO proposals also include a series of necessary mechanisms for industrialization. As modern techniques often require large markets and domestic markets remain small in most developing countries, the promotion of exports is a key component of industrialization. Most developing countries are demanding reductions in tariff and nontariff barriers to encourage export of their products.

For industrialization, multinational corporations and private capital in developed countries can offer quicker and more effective opportunities, because they have the technological and financial resources and, above all, easy access to the market. Though many developing countries are cautious about an increase in dependence on multinational corporations, transnational companies have been expanding their investment abroad. Particularly in such industries as electronics and home appliances, dissemination of the production process has been greatly advanced in developing countries. Motivated by profit maximization and by the international division of labor strategy, multinational companies have been redeploying on a worldwide scale. There are many manufacturing firms which are newly established in developing countries. Several developing nations provide incentives for industrial redeployment. Joint ventures have now become the usual formula when foreign capital is introduced in developing countries.

This kind of industrial relocation not only has a manifold impact on international trade and the flow of capital but also on domestic industrial adjustment and employment, in both developed and developing countries. In most cases, labor unions in developed countries strongly oppose this kind of exodus of jobs.

Most developed countries have been facing large-scale industrial adjustment since the oil crisis. As economic growth has slowed down considerably in most developed countries and international competition has intensified, industrial adjustment has become a painful process domestically, resulting in aggravated unemployment. Conflicts of interest grow among developed countries, while imports from developing countries have recently been discouraged in many developed countries.

Against this background, the rise of the so-called neo-protectionist movement is one of the biggest issues to be found in the field of international trade. Contrary to the traditional protectionism, neo-protectionism does not resort to direct trade restrictions. It relies mainly on more indirect measures such as voluntary export restriction and regulation through anti-dumping practices. These protectionist methods are particularly advocated where competition is strong and difficulties of industrial adjustment are great. Sectoral trade restrictions which originated with the Japanese textile issues are now spreading to other products and other countries.

Many developing countries, especially newly industrialized ones, have reacted strongly against the neo-protectionist moves which prevail in developed nations in such sectors as textiles and certain electronic industries. They also express strong opposition to the introduction of preferential safeguards in the GATT (General Agreement on Tariffs and Trade) negotiations.

It is well known that the Japanese trade account has a huge surplus. Many countries complain about their bilateral trade deficit with Japan, as the U.S.-Japanese trade issues typically indicate. Furthermore, there is strong criticism on restrictions imposed in the Japanese domestic market concerning foreign manufactured goods. Criticism is directed toward tariff and nontariff barriers as well as nontrade barriers. This issue is explained by the traditional trade and industrial policies which Japan has pursued since the Meiji Restoration, and the mentality of the Japanese people which was formed during this period. Japan, a resource-poor country, has been accustomed to encouraging the exportation of manufactured goods while imports of manufactured goods have been discouraged. The absence of neighbor industrializing countries in the Asian region has also hindered the development of a horizontal international division of labor. Since the middle 1960s, however, various trade barriers have been removed and tariff rates have been substantially reduced. Preferential treatment has been applied to products from the developing countries. In spite of this progress, a number of nontariff barriers may exist for foreign products. The problem of access, however, may also stem from inadequate marketing efforts to exploit the Japanese market.

The regional pattern and the structure of the balance of payments of Japan are liable to aggravate trade disputes with other nations. Japan has a large deficit in its invisible account and in trade transactions with resource-rich countries such as Canada, Australia, and the OPEC nations. In order to offset this deficit, the trade account should be in surplus with other nations. This policy, however, involves potential tension with other nations in terms of trade policy. Oil price increases could eventually contribute to the decline of the rather substantial surplus that Japan now enjoys. Furthermore, the current surplus fundamentally reflects the competitiveness of the Japanese economy which may continue in the 1980s. Trade policy should involve increase in imports and an increase in ODA to offset the persistent Japanese trade surplus.

In order to promote an adjustment in the balance of trade between Japan and other nations, an opening of the Japanese market is necessary. As trade barriers are removed and tariff rates reduced as a result of the current Tokyo Round of trade negotiations, and as preferential schemes have been expanded for developing countries, the effects will be felt in the near future. Of course, to maintain a steady growth in imports, further efforts will be needed not only by Japanese importers but also by foreign exporters as well. Recently, imports of manufactured goods have been increasing as a result of several factors. These include increases in wage costs in Japan and the growing demand for foreign products.

Developing countries have been extending their exports so quickly that several industries in Japan are now suffering from the boomerang effects caused by a rapid transfer of technologies and active direct investment by Japanese firms since the late 1960s. In 1978, the increase of manufactured goods was nearly 50 percent above its level in 1977. If current trends continue, manufactured goods will dominate a considerable share of Japanese imports.

Though adjustment of its external sector is an urgent and essential task, it is tied to domestic difficulties in Japan. After the oil crisis, economic growth declined and industrial costs increased considerably. Recently, the Japanese economy has roughly recovered in macroeconomic terms, but there remain micro-economic problems. As the number of bankruptcies and the high level of unemployment indicate, Japan still has sizable sectoral imbalances. Looking ahead at the employment situation, while the labor force will not change much, demand for employment will be limited to the manufacturing sector. Thus, the labor situation will not improve even in the medium term and unemployment will be concentrated mostly in the middle and aged working population.

To what extent, and at what speed industrial adjustment can be achieved depends mainly on the capacity of the Japanese economy to absorb unemployment. Recently, the additional labor force has been absorbed by the tertiary sector. Even in the secondary sector, a shift has been taking place from plant workers to administrative and managing areas. So that Japanese firms may have the ability to transfer excess workers from a declining sector to rising sectors within the firm, the need for reeducation will grow. Industrial adjustment will be achieved only in conjunction with active employment policies. Reeducational programs and training activities will be required, which the government could support if such were necessary.

Another trend which affects industrial as well as external adjustments is the export of private capital. Though recently the rate of expansion has decelerated, direct investment abroad from private sources has been expanding. There are push factors in Japan and pull factors in other countries. From the viewpoint of financial and human resources, Japanese firms (particularly the big companies) find promising incentives to build new factories abroad. Sluggish investment activity in Japan produces an accumulation of capital, idle engineering staffs, and saturation in demand for most manufactured goods. Recent trade disputes also work to encourage the exodus of private capital abroad. The strategy of big firms contributes to the redeployment of production processes in developing countries. Pull factors from developing countries are also strong, as many of them want to create new employment opportunities and to explore markets abroad, they provide favorable conditions for foreign firms.

At the same time, there are a number of constraints on the internationalization of industrial activity. Social unrest and the possibility of nationalization by developing countries act as a strong brake on the exodus of private capital to developing areas. Many Japanese firms may prefer the less-developed areas within developed nations, as recent moves in southern Europe indicate. Another constraint is the reaction of the people in the recipient countries. The overpresence of Japanese firms in the Asian region may create opposition to an increased Japanese economic presence. Furthermore, as in other developed nations, trade unions have expressed opposition to the redeployment of production activities abroad. This issue will be exacerbated by any increase in unemployment in Japan.

In order to respond to this situation, various devices have been introduced. There are a number of joint ventures which have already been developed. In some cases, Japanese participation is less than 25 percent of the total amount of stocks. This is a way to avoid Japanese overpresence. (Phase-schemes are other alternatives which compromise the interests or the capitalist owner of the firm with those of the recipient countries.)

Although there are factors that discourage the transfer of private capital to developing countries, industrial adjustment will eventually result in the dissemination of industrial activity among developing countries since many industries want to make use of cheap labor (electronics) and others may be motivated by the desire to participate in the domestic markets of those developing countries as competition among developed nations grows.

Because of growing international interdependence, trade policy as well as industrial adjustment can only be effectively implemented through close international cooperation since conflicts of interest will increase in the future. The policy of Japan will, therefore, be extremely important in this respect. Japan should take the initiative in maintaining free trade principles and preventing rising protectionism. In this connection, one can point to agreements on the various issues in recent trade negotiations among nations. Though the results may not be satisfactory to every nation, such agreements have a great significance in preventing protectionism among major trading partners. In addition to tariff reductions, progress has been made in establishing codes concerning various nontariff barriers, which are regarded as the origin of neo-protectionism. Product standards, anti-dumping practices, and government procurements have a close relationship with recent protectionist measures. The revision of safeguard clauses has not been approved and will be under continuous examination. Japan has made an essential contribution in this area of negotiation and has made large concessions in various fields which may act as stimuli to the advancement of negotiations.

It is important to effectively implement policies in order to prevent protectionism. Furthermore, a great deal of work remains with regard to a compromise among the conflicting interests in several developing countries. Japan should take further initiatives in this area. Earlier tariff reduction and increases in government procurement contracts for foreign producers will be the candidates for these initiatives.

Recent trade friction has created a difficult environment for NICs; some developed countries insist that these countries abolish their export-oriented policies. The argument is made that, in order to avoid excessive competition in the international markets, consultation should be held in several critical industrial sectors (such as iron, steel, shipbuilding) with the newly industrialized countries. Furthermore, there is another argument that, since most advanced technologies are less labor intensive and in conflict with industries in developed countries, there is no reason to encourage the exports of these technologies by providing massive export credits.

It is well known that some developing countries carry out extremely vigorous export policies. These policies, however, may be increasing international competition which facilitates penetration into the market of developed countries and may make NICs "tough competitors" for the remaining developing countries. There is a certain justification for the above assertions which call for a more equal footing for the NICs. However, it should be borne in mind that these countries still have fragile foundations and that a hostile trade environment may be detrimental to them. It should be remembered that, during the sluggish period between 1973 and 1978, the newly industrialized countries made fairly steady economic progress and gave a sizable stimulus to the stagnant world economy. Therefore, newly industrialized countries can be the new frontiers in the future world economy, from which other countries can benefit. Japan should, therefore, act as a brake on protectionist measures against the NICs.

In the above fields, Japan can and should play a leading role through cooperation with other countries. While economic conditions remain competitive, Japan has the responsibility of taking initiatives in order to advance trade liberalization and to promote industrial adjustments, all of which requires an attack on domestic problems caused by growing interdependence.

COOPERATION ON GLOBAL ISSUES

There are several issues which can only be effectively tackled through global cooperation. Cooperation among developed countries with the increased participation of developing countries are indispensable in coping with problems involving energy, foods, commodity, trade, and monetary issues.

The Energy Issue

As for energy, while advances in conservation and development of alternative energy sources have been delayed, demand has been growing with economic growth. The increase is more pronounced in non-oil producing developing countries and consumption is likely to increase more rapidly in these countries than in developed countries in the future. According to several projections, oil production will reach its peak sometime in the late 1980s and the world will face a serious crisis in its energy supply. Developed nations should increase efforts aimed at encouraging energy conservation and developing various alternative energy sources including coal and safe nuclear energy. Furthermore, preparation for crisis management becomes essential. Japan should allocate more resources in these directions through government initiatives. At the same time, developed countries (including Japan) should help developing countries exploit their domestic energy sources. As development of alternative energy sources requires time, the cooperation of OPEC countries is indispensable in coping with uncertainty during the transitional period. There is a proposal involving a preferential price scheme to allocate cheaper oil to non-oil producing developing countries from the OPEC countries. Though effective functioning of this scheme is difficult to achieve, such a scheme would be necessary in case of chronic oil shortages since fast-rising energy prices hinders economic development.

The Food Issue

While demand for food has been increasing, improvement in this situation has been neglected in many countries, as resources are shifted toward industrialization. In addition, too much emphasis has been placed on capital-intensive irrigation projects. Japanese cooperation in agricultural technology should be increased and ODA should be directed more extensively in this direction. As many countries are still vulnerable to domestic and foreign crop failure, further consideration should be given to grain-storage schemes and food aid programs. This is necessary not only for the sake of the developing countries but also for Japan, which itself faces a large deficit in its grain trade.

The Commodity Issue

Japan imports a large volume of commodities and thus has a keen interest in the stabilization of prices. Repetition of the sky-rocketing prices of the early 1970s obviously should be opposed not only by Japan but by other commodity-importing countries. Most developing countries think the widening gap between prices of manufactured products and primary commodities in the 1960s was an important reason for the discrepancy in the economies of developed and developing countries. They argue that ownership of production by multinational corporations contributed to sluggish prices in the 1960s. Encouraged by the success of the OPEC countries, developing countries proposed mechanisms which would ensure reasonable prices for producing countries. After heated discussions in the Conference on International Economic Co-operation, an agreement was reached on setting up a common fund with a buffer stock scheme for a limited number of commodities. Since many commodities are also produced in developed countries, a cartel-type price support system is considered difficult to maintain for a long time. Recently, in conjunction with this kind of price-support arrangement, Lomé convention type of schemes are now under consideration in order to ensure the export earnings of producers of primary commodities. This may also facilitate production stimulated by increasing demand.

The Japanese policies in this area include the following: first, in order to avoid too much price fluctuation, longer-term contracts should be extended as agreed already on several products most of which are, however, produced mainly in developed countries. Second, Japan should participate in the common fund with a buffer stock formula. Japan should be more concerned with a stable supply of commodities than other nations because of poor domestic resources. Third, Japan is examining the creation of a stabex-type scheme in order to ensure ASEAN (Association of Southeast Asian Nations) revenues from the exportation of their primary products. The system can be open to other developed countries by selecting commodities which are of particular interest to the ASEAN countries. Fourth, some countries may prefer to export commodities that require a greater degree of processing. Further cooperation can be developed in this field by increasing imports of processed raw materials.

Monetary and Financial Issues

OPEC countries have been playing an important role in development aid since the early 1970s. Participation in the International Monetary Fund (IMF) has also been increasing. The monetary and financial situation will be strongly affected by the movement of oil prices and by the management of the financial assets of OPEC countries. Accumulation of financial assets by some OPEC countries and economically strong countries, and the debt accumulation of non-oil producing countries remain important issues to be tackled in the future. Though cooperation will be needed to reduce debt burdens, one favorable aspect in this regard is that many debtor countries are resource rich and will have possibilities to pay the debt in the future. But, at the same time, oil price increases are likely to persist, and mechanisms will be needed to aid developing countries who will be harmed by higher oil prices.

REGIONAL COOPERATION

Though many problems should be tackled on a global basis, the importance of a regional approach should not be neglected. Obviously, Japan is interested in Asian development. A regional approach may be more effective as a strategy for development cooperation. For example, recent Japanese cooperation on ASEAN joint projects contributed to the development of manufacturing plants and a regional market for the products. A Japanese initiative in Asian development could serve as in incentive for regional cooperation among nations, and would be a valuable contribution to the world economy as a whole. As the countries in this region are heterogeneous in terms of economic development, cultural heritage, and political systems, it would be an illusion to aim at economic integration in this region. Regional cooperation should be based on those areas in which it is easy to achieve. At the same time, Japan should increase its efforts to promote cultural exchanges with developing countries. Thus, an increase of communications with Asian countries is an important issue and Japan should take a larger initiative in this field.

SOCIAL AND CULTURAL ASPECTS

We have analyzed the obstacles to effective development cooperation in Japan. There are social and cultural factors behind these obstacles, which cause the isolationism of Japanese society. Japan is a closed society which is still difficult to penetrate. This situation is illustrated by the imbalance in cultural exchanges between Japan and other countries. There are interesting statistics concerning translated publications. Foreign publications which are translated into Japanese number more than ten times the number of Japanese books translated into foreign languages. Japan is a large net importer in cultural exchanges, and a large exporter in material transactions. This discrepancy is very pronounced in its relationship with Western developed nations. Concerning developing countries, Japan has less contact in both importation and exportation of information. In any case, the fact that Japanese is not understood well by foreign people remains a reality. Because of this situation, foreign people may think that Japan is a closed society and some people may judge the Japanese to be a silly and selfish people.

Foreigners complain about Japanese nontariff barriers, while the Japanese insist that others have not made an effort to understand the Japanese customs and social arrangements, thus hindering their penetration of the Japanese domestic market. There is a considerable gap between what the Japanese understand of the Americans and Europeans and what the Americans and Europeans understand of the Japanese. This situation stems partly from Japan's cultural heritage as a peripheral nation which always received other nations' cultures and did not export its own. It also is a result of Japanese history since the Meiji

Restoration. Japan has been an industrious student of Western culture. In order to be an equal partner of Western nations, Japan has imported a large amount of information and modern techniques for its development. Since this process lasted a century, its position as a net importer of information cannot be easily changed in a short time in spite of its economic growth. Language barriers, a low profile after the war, and the vagueness of the decision-making process has made the Japanese less understandable for foreign nations.

When Japan was a small power, the discrepancy in mutual understanding worked favorably in terms of economic development, because the Japanese adopted an economic strategy against other nations on the basis of this discrepancy. Now the situation is detrimental to Japanese survival since Japan is an economically powerful country which needs to be understood by foreign nations. The status of mutual understanding is worse with regard to developing nations. Even with Asian nations, the Japanese have a poor communication network. If development cooperation is not backed by mutual understanding between nations, misunderstandings and distrust can develop in both donor and recipient nations. If Japan wants to make a contribution to development in the Asian and Pacific region, it is definitely necessary to encourage cultural exchanges and to increase communication with other nations.

In order to achieve this, Japan should make an effort to advise foreigners about its society and to invite foreigners to Japan as residents so they can understand the real Japan. This scheme calls for considerable changes not only in Japanese administrative arrangements but also in the average citizen's attitude toward the internationalization of Japan. There are few Japanese who eagerly accept foreign students in their homes which is partly a result of poor housing conditions in Japan. But every citizen should make an effort to overcome these barriers. Furthermore, Japan should make a contribution to cultural exchanges between developing countries. For example, Japan can set up a cultural center in the Asian region and assist the projects which aim to make use of Asian customs in order to tackle future problems.

CONCLUDING REMARKS AND POLICY RECOMMENDATIONS

Though Japanese development cooperation has been rapidly increasing since the 1960s, there is much criticism regarding the content and pattern of that cooperation. One typical criticism concerns the smaller share of the GNP for official development in comparison with other developed nations. The grant element is also modest in Japanese aid projects and its geographical distribution indicates a heavy concentration in East and Southeast Asian countries. However, private capital transfers have been rapidly increasing and constitute a large share of development cooperation.

Regarding trade issues, it has been pointed out that imports of raw materials fluctuate too much and have a destabilizing effect on commodity exporting countries. The existence of trade barriers denies manufactured products from developing countries access to the Japanese market.

These criticisms may be justified in many respects but, in several points, they should be complemented or rectified. Roughly speaking, there are three factors which affect cooperation. First, there is a lag in Japanese policymaking, which stems from the fact that Japan emerged abruptly and is not accustomed to being a major power. Second, Japan faces a trade-off between development cooperation and domestic as well as external policy aims, which are sometimes more urgent. Third, there are areas in which Japan has only a limited ability to cope with problems, and these problems can be tackled only through international cooperation with other countries.

Taking account of the criticism and policy constraints mentioned above, the main lines of future policy could be:

1. Concerning the volume and pattern of official development aid, there is a need for further increases in technical assistance which remains at a low level according to international standards. Recently, this situation has been improving with regard to the volume of ODA, regional aid, and the contents of development projects. In view of the commitment the Japanese government currently has, progress will be sizable in terms of financial volume during the coming years. Bottle-necks are likely to be found in human resources including project research capacity, technical staffs, and administrative capacity, but, through increasing volume of financial aid, tangible results in this aspect will be attained. The training of experts and improvements in administration will be key problems. The potential of the private sector should be fostered in this respect and more foreign experts and students should be invited to Japan.

2. In the areas of trade, investment, and industrialization, Japan should mobilize its ability to provide more markets for products from developing countries, and private capital should play a positive role in industrialization in these nations. Devices should be established for further cooperation between Japanese private capitals and recipient countries, as recent forms of joint ventures indicate. In order to promote this strategy, various obstacles must be overcome, including industrial restructuring in Japan and the mitigation of employment problems. Though Japan has common concerns with Western nations in that its industries are facing strong competition from newly industrial-ized countries, Japan should stress the importance of the development of such countries as a new frontier and new pattern in the world economy. Japan should take the initiative in preventing rising protec-tionism. The recent success of multilateral trade negotiations repre-sents progress in setting up a code of conduct for nontariff barriers. Japan should play a leading role in the implementation of such a code.

3. With regard to energy, commodities, food and monetary and financial issues, Japanese cooperation for development can be pursued only with the help of other nations. Since Japan is concerned with the stability of energy, commodity, and food imports, it should play an

active role in the stabilization of supply and prices. Stock building with the Common Fund will be necessary for several products. In addition, the need for larger participation of the developing countries in the settlement of these issues will grow.

4. Parallel to global cooperation, Japan can play a positive role in assisting regional joint projects of the ASEAN countries in promoting Asian cultural communication since it has closer ties with the countries of this region.

5. The promotion of cultural exchanges and the encouragement of mutual understanding between Japan and other nations is extremely important. In order to allow foreigners to better understand today's Japan, Japan should strengthen cultural exchanges and communication in various fields. More funds and human resources should be allocated for this purpose. To invite foreign experts and researchers is an effective way to advance these policies in addition to sending Japanese experts abroad.

3 The Republic of Korea and the New International Economic Order

Jong Youl Yoo

What factors prevent the establishment of a New International Economic Order which have been proposed by the United Nations since 1974? Why has the proposed new global economic system not been realized even after so much effort by so many countries? What are the major reasons for the failure of the proposed NIEO? Is the NIEO an unrealistic, idealistic dream that pursues only the interests of developing nations at the sacrifice of developed nations?

In spite of its many positive global objectives, the NIEO faces many serious difficulties which prevent its early establishment. The Republic of Korea, a rapidly industrializing country, has witnessed many such obstacles in its economic relations with advanced nations. The setbacks that the ROK has suffered are a global phenomenon and, therefore, the analysis of their essential nature and patterns does have international implications.

The objectives and measures proposed by the NIEO are very comprehensive and, in many aspects, very timely and urgent. Nevertheless, their implementation has not been maximized due to external constraints such as the increasing protectionism of developed nations, the aggressive export policy of Japan, and the worsening balance of payments of developed nations. The Republic of Korea is, in spite of its remarkable economic growth, becoming a victim of protective measures which run counter to NIEO proposals. Its experience may not be a model with worldwide applicability since there are many aspects peculiar to the ROK. Still, the systematic analysis of this experience will shed some light on the nature of obstacles to the NIEO.

OBSTACLES TO THE NIEO: THE REPUBLIC OF KOREA EXPERIENCE

The ambitious measures proposed by the NIEO urge advanced nations to help developing nations in promoting economic growth and industrial-

28

ization through greater participation in international trade. The measures are very comprehensive. The increasing protectionism of developed nations, however, has hindered early implementation of the NIEO proposals. Therefore, one can argue that, in the ROK case, increasing protectionism is the prime obstacle to the NIEO. In this chapter, we will examine the patterns of these protectionist trends and analyze why they are increasing.

Increasing Protectionism Vis-à-Vis
the Republic of Korea

Since the 1973 oil crisis, developed nations have progressively strengthened restrictions of imports from developing nations. There are two general types of protectionist measures. One is characterized by tariff barriers and the other by nontariff barriers. Most developing countries impose high tariff rates to curb imports, while advanced nations utilize nontariff measures more frequently. In the 1970s, many industrialized nations reduced tariff rates, while expanding nontariff barriers.

Among nontariff measures, they have chosen quantitative regulation methods. These measures include import license systems, import quotas, and voluntary regulation methods. They are very effective because they do not affect the free price system, yet impose severe curbs on the increase of imports.

Among restricted items, textiles have been the primary target and are still strongly controlled. Ten out of the 23 restrictive measures adopted between January 1977 and February 1978 concern textiles. Specifically, the European Economic Community (EEC) and Sweden strengthened their curbs on textiles by switching from selective to categorical restrictions. The United States has reduced the annual increase of quotas to 6.5 percent from 6.75 percent and has tried to void a previous concession allowing an annual increase of quotas of some merchandise.

Restrictions on iron and steel, shoes, and leather goods have also been progressively increased. Due to lags in the iron and steel industries, developed nations have instituted stricter curbs on foreign iron and steel products. The EEC has adopted the Basic Price System and has imposed anti-dumping duties since March 1978. Each member nation of the EEC focuses on bilateral agreements with South Korea. The United States has used the Trigger Price System since February 1978. This system is very similar to the Basic Price System. It imposes anti-dumping duties on imported steel and iron products whose prices are below the standards established by the U.S. government. If preferential treatment is not given to the products of developing countries, the Republic of Korea will not be able to export any of her iron and steel products to the United States and the EEC.

Sweden, Norway, and Australia took the initiative in restricting the importation of Korean-made shoes in 1974, when the volume of Korean exports to these countries was very small. The Republic of Korea did not suffer much from these measures, but the restrictive measures taken by the United States (the biggest buyer of Korean shoes) and by Canada (the second biggest buyer) represented a great setback. In 1977, the United States forced the Republic of Korea to voluntarily restrict its shoe exports to that country. Canada also implemented restrictive measures against ski boots, rubber shoes, cloth shoes, and waterproof plastic shoes. These measures are to expire in November 1980. In 1978, Finland extended her value added tax to Korean shoes. As a result, those shoes became the second most restricted items after textiles.

With regard to electronic products, the United Kingdom unilaterally imposed an import quota on Korean black-and-white TV sets in violation of GATT regulations. The annual quota was 35,000 sets for 1977 and 1978. The Republic of Korea had already exported 50,000 TV sets to the United Kingdom in 1977 before the unilateral imposition of the quota. In 1978, therefore, the Republic of Korea could sell only 20,000 sets in the British market. Australia started to restrict Korean refrigerators, washing machines, and dryers in 1975, and it seems that country will continue the tariff quota until long-term measures have been worked out.

Norway and Sweden have negotiated voluntary restrictions on the export of leather clothes from the Republic of Korea. Canada has imposed a global quota on foreign leather clothes, thereby fixing import of leather clothes at the 1975 level.

Import licensing measures have been taken by some countries: Japan on brown seaweeds, Finland on specified textiles, Denmark on cassette tape recorders, Australia on manual tools, and New Zealand on major import items from the Republic of Korea.

These protective measures may be concisely summarized in terms of their types and numbers. As shown in table 3.1, 15 protective measures were introduced in 1974. Since then, new measures have been imposed progressively: 12 in 1975, 13 in 1976, and 15 in 1977. In January and February 1978, eight new measures were implemented and two measures were voided. These restrictive measures against Korean products may be illustrated from another aspect, i.e., the restricted items' share of total exports. This is indicated in table 3.2. The eighteen industrialized nations that have imposed restrictions on imports from the ROK are listed in table 3.3.

Patterns of Protective Measures

The protective measures taken by industrialized nations vis-à-vis the Republic of Korea and some other developing nations demonstrate an interesting pattern. It is a pattern completely contradictory to the proposed NIEO measures. The 15 primary measures many of which are listed earlier in this chapter are almost totally ignored. Quota systems are strengthened, "voluntary" restrictions are enforced, import licensing is reinstituted, and heavier duties are levied. This increasing protectionism shows distinct patterns of change: from selective restrictions to categorical control; from a greater to a lesser quota increase per annum; introduction of more stringent regulations; and individual imposition of set-off duties on each exporting company of developing nations.

Table 3.1. Protective Measures of Advanced Nations
against Korean Products

Items	1973 and before	1974	1975	1976	1977	1978	Total
Textile	1	8	5	7	6(1)*	4(2)	31(3)
Iron and Steel	-	-	1	1	-(1)	2	4(1)
Shoes	1	3	-	1	3	-	8
Leather Products	-	-	-	1	2	1	4
Metallic goods Tableware	-	2	-	-	-	1	3
Electronic Manufactures	1	1	2	-	1	-	5
Marine Products	2	-	1	-	1	-	4
Others	3	1	3	3	2(1)	-	12(1)
Accumulated total	8	23	35	48	63(3)	71(5)	

*Numbers in ( ) represent the protective measures that became ineffective during the year.

Source: Korean Trade Association, The Trend of Import Restrictions of Developed Nations and Korean Counter Measures, Seoul, 1978.

These changes in restriction methods may be elaborated as follows:

1. From individual restrictions on a small quantity of items to categorical restrictions on a large quantity of items: examples: a) From

selective to categorical restrictions on textiles (EEC); b) Categorical restrictions on large quantity items of iron and steel (USA).

2. From single-nation to multiple-nation restrictions: examples: a) Shoes: From USA alone to Canada and the EEC; b) Iron and Steel products: From the EEC alone to USA and Canada.

Table 3.2. Korean Exports of Restricted Items*
($ millions)

	1973	1974	1975	1976	1977
Total Export	3,225	4,460	5,427	7,715	10,474
Restricted Items:	451	818	969.6	1,667	2,357
(1) Light Industries	437.5	809.1	961.7	1,637.2	2,321.6
(2) Heavy and Chemical Industries	13.5	8.9	7.9	29.8	35.4

*Amounts are computed at the customs clearance value.

Source: Statistical Yearbook of International Trade, 1978.

Table 3.3. Industrialized Nations that have Imposed Restrictions on Imports from the Republic of Korea

North America
United States
Canada

Europe
   EEC

United Kingdom	Belgium
West Germany	Luxembourg
France	Denmark
Italy	Ireland
Netherlands	

   EFTA

Norway	Finland
Sweden	Austria

Asia
      Japan

Oceania
      Australia
      New Zealand

3. From short-term to long-term restrictions: examples: Iron and steel, textiles.
4. Development of new restriction measures: examples: a) Import Price Reference System (the EEC, UK, West Germany, and Italy); b) The Technical Visa Systems (France); c) The Automatic Licensing System (Italy).

KOREAN DILEMMAS CREATED BY GROWING PROTECTIONISM

The increasing protectionist measures of developed nations have raised many difficult problems for the Republic of Korea. These problems are exacerbated by the structural imbalance in ROK domestic industries. The following 10 problems can be identified:

1. Overconcentration on light industries: Products of light industries represented 62.2 percent of the total exports of the Republic of Korea in 1976. This is in marked contrast to Singapore's 30.8 percent. In Hong Kong and Taiwan these reached 75.5 percent and 60 percent, respectively.
2. Unbalanced industrial structure with heavy concentration on restricted items: The Republic of Korea has as many as 38 restricted items, while Singapore, Hong Kong, and Taiwan have 10, 21, and 25 restricted items, respectively.
3. Heavy reliance on industrialized nations for export markets: In 1976, South Korea exported $4,500 million (58 percent of total exports) to advanced nations, while Singapore exported only $2,316 million (35 percent).
4. Lack of a diversified export market: The big export markets for ROK products are the United States, Japan, the Federal Republic of Germany, the United Kingdom, the Netherlands, Canada, Australia, Saudi Arabia, Iran, Kuwait, and Hong Kong. These 11 countries buy more than 60 percent of all ROK goods. Among these, the seven industrialized countries restrict Korean exports.
5. Ineffective switch of restricted export markets to unrestricted markets: The Republic of Korea has been inflexible in shifting her exports among the 18 industrialized countries including the United States, Japan, and the EEC. Hong Kong, on the other, switched its textile market from Japan to the United States and its shoe market from the United States to the EEC when Japan and the United States intensified curbs on Hong Kong's exports.
6. Lack of regional economic cooperation: ROK does not belong to any regional economic bloc such as the EEC, the ASEAN, or the British Commonwealth of Nations. Therefore, growing protectionism renders the nation nervous and helpless.
7. Underdevelopment of unrestricted items: As was mentioned above, the major components of Korean exports are light industry products. An increasing number of these are becoming the target of restrictions. In 1974, 23 items were restricted; and in 1977,

the number of restricted items increased to 38. Still, the development and export of unrestricted items is very slow.

8. Insufficient production of (GSP) items: The Republic of Korea has not produced enough items subject to the generalized system of tariff preference (GSP). It has developed 625 GSP items, whose total export amounts only to $324,460,000, or 13.6 percent of the total export in 1976; Hong Kong exported 751 GSP items worth $349,917,000 (14.4 percent) and Taiwan 940 items worth $727,987,000 (24.4 percent).

9. Heavy concentration on labor-intensive industries: The Republic of Korea has another structural imbalance: overconcentration on labor-intensive industries. In 1976, ROK exports of textiles reached $1,556 million which is equivalent to 66 percent of the total export of restricted items. Its export of shoes to 17 industrialized nations reached $351 million, 14.9 percent of the total export of restricted items.

10. Large export of everyday commodities which are of major concern to advanced nations: In 1976, the Republic of Korea exported 23 items of everyday commodities to industrialized nations. The protection of these industries, therefore, is a concern of the developed nations. The export of these commodities reaches $2,133 million, 90.5 percent of the total export of restricted items.

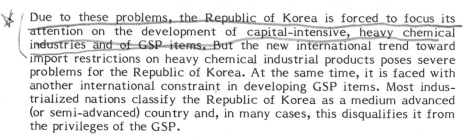

Due to these problems, the Republic of Korea is forced to focus its attention on the development of capital-intensive, heavy chemical industries and of GSP items. But the new international trend toward import restrictions on heavy chemical industrial products poses severe problems for the Republic of Korea. At the same time, it is faced with another international constraint in developing GSP items. Most industrialized nations classify the Republic of Korea as a medium advanced (or semi-advanced) country and, in many cases, this disqualifies it from the privileges of the GSP.

WHY THESE OBSTACLES?

Why, then, did these obstacles arise? Why have industrialized nations begun to impose restrictions on imports, particularly the imports from developing and semi-developed countries? We may provide five direct and five indirect causes for the obstacles. Of course, they are not inclusive, but they are empirically verifiable.

Direct Causes

1. Economic depression and subsequent increases in unemployment in industrialized nations
2. Continuing and growing deficits in the balance of payments of industrialized nations

3. The rapid expansion of exports of developing nations
4. Relative superiority in the developing countries' labor-intensive industries
5. The pressure of labor unions on national trade and employment policies in industrialized nations.

Indirect Causes

1. Protection of weak domestic industries
2. Unstable domestic situations (economic, social, and political)
3. Slow economic growth policies of industrialized nations
4. The weakening of the GATT negotiations
5. The weakening of the international monetary system.

Economic Depression and Subsequent Increase in Unemployment

The most important reasons for the growing protectionism of industrialized nations are economic depression and the subsequent increases in unemployment. During the first half of 1976, industrialized nations showed an economic growth rate of 6.9 percent; in the second half it dropped down to 3.1 percent. The average economic growth rate in 1977 was as low as 3.7 percent. The increase in unemployment rates is very high in these nations as shown in table 3.4. These increases have forced industrialized nations to protect their industries in an effort to absorb the unemployed.

Table 3.4. Unemployment Rates of Major Advanced Nations (in percentages)

Years	USA	Japan	W. Germany	U.K.	Canada	Italy
1965	4.5	1.2	0.3	2.2	3.9	4.0
1970	4.9	1.2	0.8	3.1	5.7	3.5
1974	5.6	1.4	2.6	2.6	5.5	2.9
1977	7.1	2.0	4.5	5.8	8.1	7.2

Source: OECD, Main Economic Indicators, May 1978.

Continuing and Growing Deficit of Balance of Payments

As a result of growing deficits in international trade, industrialized nations are pursuing policies that restrict foreign imports. For example, the United States intensified its import restriction on iron and steel and other big items in 1977 when its balance of payments recorded a big deficit. The United Kingdom and France, which have the biggest deficits among the EEC countries, are most eager to restrict imports. This is indicated in table 3.5.

Table 3.5. Balance of Payments of Major Advanced Nations ($ millions)

	USA	UK	France	W. Germany	Italy
1974	-9,968	-15,503	-7,140	20,349	-10,671
1975	3,173	9,502	2,033	16,001	-3,545
1976	-15,494	-9,714	-8,585	14,276	-6,459

Source: UN, Monthly Bulletin of Statistics.

The Rapid Expansion of Exports of Developing Nations

Since the late 1960s, some developing nations have been successful in their efforts at industrialization and thus have expanded exports to developed nations. In addition, oil-producing countries sold billions of dollars worth of oil to advanced nations. This rapid expansion of developing nations' exports shrunk the relative export volume of the industrialized nations. This is a third factor affecting their protectionism. Table 3.6 indicates the composition of world exports by economic blocs.

Table 3.6. The Composition of World Exports by Economic Blocs (in percentages)

Years	Total	Advanced Nations	Oil producing Countries	Developing Countries	Communist Countries
1970	100	69.2	5.5	12.3	10.5
1972	100	69.0	6.8	11.4	10.2
1974	100	62.8	14.5	11.9	8.6
1975	100	63.8	12.6	11.7	9.7
1976	100	63.0	13.3	12.1	9.6
1977	100	61.9	12.8	12.8	9.6

*Please note these figures do not total 100 percent exactly due to rounding.

Source: GATT, International Trade, 1976-77, Geneva.

Relative Superiority of Developing Nations
in Labor-Intensive Industries

In the areas of textiles, shoes, iron and steel, and electrical appliances, developing countries have enormously improved labor productivity, thereby obtaining relative superiority over industrialized nations. One result has been the expanding export of these items to advanced nations, but the industrialized nations did not restructure their industries to adjust to the change. Rather, they have tended to cope with the new situation simply by introducing import restriction measures.

new situation simply by introducing import restriction measures.

The Pressures of Labor Unions

Labor unions in advanced nations put pressure on their respective governments to impose strict curbs on foreign imports to relieve domestic unemployment. The United States is a model case: the AFL-CIO has 13,540,000 members and the Union of Automobile Workers controls 1,400,000 members. They exercise enormous influence over the White House and the U.S. Congress. For example, a group of shoemakers made demonstrations in New York City shouting for import restrictions of Korean-made leather shoes in 1973. ROK leather goods were subsequently restricted.

CONCLUSION: OPEN INTERNATIONAL TRADE SYSTEM

To establish a new global economic order, we first propose a liberalized trade system which would include a system of balanced adjustment. There would be no protective tariffs, no most-favored-nation clauses, no requirement for certificates of origin designed for discrimination purposes. Every country would have the right and obligation to export and import goods to and from all other countries.

This new trade system carries a great danger: the increasing economic exploitation of the developing nations by the industrialized countries. To offset this danger, the new trade system would institute a system of adjustment for balance of payments. This system would require that a nation with a trade surplus remit it back to the originating nations at the end of each fiscal year in hard currency. This can be illustrated with a hypothetical example: the United States has a trade surplus of $100 million – $50 million vis-à-vis France, $60 million vis-a-vis Africa, and a $10 million deficit vis-à-vis Japan. At the end of the year, the United States would remit $50 million to France, $60 million to the African nations, and receive $10 million from Japan in international currency. Through this measure, international antagonism arising from trade deficits may be resolved and economic neocolonialism avoided. Another positive aspect is that this system will promote a sense of fairness, equity, and cooperation between the South and the North, and among all nations, thus eliminating the danger of politico-military antagonism due to international trade competition. Particularly, this measure will help the world stay aloof from economic depression because maximum business activities would be guaranteed across political borderlines.

Our proposal could easily be institutionalized, in view of the success of various regional economic, cooperative organizations such as the EEC, EFTA, the Latin American Free Trade Association (LAFTA), and the Central American Common Market (CACM). The International Bank for Reconstruction and Development demonstrates the success of joint efforts to meet world economic problems. What we need to create is not a mechanical procedure but, rather, the building of international consensus about joint economic responsibilities, i.e., economic internationalism. Economic internationalism is different from economic nationalism whose prime value is profit maximization. It predicates joint and equal responsibility for world economy and for the economic problems of each nation.

Still, the new international trade system has a flaw: a nation without sufficient natural, technological, and industrial resources would suffer enormously because there is nothing to export. No exports means no capital and technological inflow which, in turn, hinders economic growth. However, under the economic internationalism all nations would be jointly responsible for each individual nation's economy. The U.N. Development Program (UNDP) may be expanded in its function and operation. Each nation would contribute to the development fund in proportion to its GNP per capita. The UNDP would carry out economic development programs by allocating its total fund to needy nations, thus, eventually, more or less equalizing the GNP per capita of all nations.

4 The People's Republic of China and the New International Economic Order: The Strategy of Domestic Development

Paul T.K. Lin

At the beginning of the 1980s, the People's Republic of China (the largest developing country in the world) entered a new stage of development. It has embarked on an immense and complex program to modernize its economy by the end of the century.

The general goals of this program, called the "Four Modernizations" (modernization of industry, agriculture, science and technology, and national defense), were first enunciated by the late Premier Zhou-En lai to the National People's Congress in 1964 and reaffirmed and elaborated in January 1975. But it was not until after the final excision of ultra-left politics in 1976 that the program was revived and gotten underway. By that time, modernization had taken on new meaning and greater urgency due to the loss of a crucial decade during which the PRC's economy fluctuated and marked time while technological progress in the advanced industrial countries moved at an increased pace far exceeding that of previous decades.

Modernization is, of course, a relative concept whose scope and nature are difficult to define. Defined in a narrow sense, it refers primarily to catching up with the global "state of the art" in science and production processes. The objectives envisaged for China were defined by Vice-Premier Deng Xiaoping to the Fifth National People's Congress in these terms:

By the end of this century, the output of major agricultural products is expected to reach or surpass advanced world levels and the output of major industrial products to approach, equal or outstrip that of the most developed capitalist countries. In agricultural production, the highest possible degree of mechanization, electrification and irrigation will be achieved. There will be automation in the main industrial processes, a major increase in rapid transport and communications services and a considerable rise in labor productivity. We must apply the results of

39

modern science and technology on a broad scale, make extensive use of new materials and sources of energy, and modernize our major products and the process of production. Our economic and technical norms must approach, equal or surpass advanced world levels.

An ambitious program – all the more so because it has been delayed for so long. The two "modernization decades" ahead can, in fact, be regarded as a major Chinese effort to span a "modernity lag" that should be measured from at least the late 1950s. Indeed, on Mao Zedong's agenda, the technological revolution, as the main propellant of modernization, was to have begun as far back as 1958, after he was reasonably satisfied that the sweeping changeover to public ownership of the means of production (and the political and ideological support for it) had largely been effected. In his programmatic "Sixty Points on Methods of Work," written in January 1958, Mao said:

> What we need now is a technological revolution so that we can catch up with or surpass Britain in 15 years or a little longer. . . . From this year on, while continuing to complete the socialist revolution on the political and ideological fronts, we should shift the emphasis in our Party's work to the technological revolution.

Almost unbelievably, the shift of emphasis failed to materialize for a full 20 years. The delay involved many complex factors on which future historians will no doubt expend much effort in order to unravel them. Of overriding significance was the growing division within the Party leadership on the assessment of the domestic political situation and the need for continuing the class struggle. The Eighth Party Congress (1956) had taken the position that, with the socialist transformation of agriculture, industry, and commerce, the bourgeoisie had been vanquished in the economic and political realm. The main, large-scale contest of classes was over, and there should now be an all-out effort to build up the economy.(1)

In the ensuing years, Mao Zedong became more and more disenchanted with Soviet politics and the Soviet model of development which the PRC had followed in the First Five-Year Plan. Domestically, two concerns began to dominate his thinking: the prevention of an emergence in the PRC of a bureaucratic stratum alienated from the people; and the establishment of a self-reliant and autonomous path of development for the PRC, untrammeled by dependence, conceptually or in practice, on an increasingly hostile Soviet Union. The politics of the first concern tended to radicalize the economics of the second concern, and vice versa, in an escalating process.

In this atmosphere, it was inevitable that political opportunists would enter the stage to capitalize on Mao's revived concern about the class struggle. Their tactics were to magnify differences of viewpoint into class antagonisms, wielding every available device of sloganeering demagoguery, including a false concept of egalitarianism that had nothing in common with progressive social change. Critics of economic excesses and errors began to be stigmatized as class foes opposed to the whole political and strategic orientation of the new policies. This atmosphere was hardly conducive to longe-range planning and stable economic growth.

The problems of the Great Leap Forward of 1958-59 illustrate this point. This was a bold and imaginative attempt to make an economic breakthrough. The conceptual approach was to inject at least three new variables into the development process in order to propel it at a faster pace and to overcome hampering imbalances: (1) maximum mobilization of the full potential of the PRC's own human and material resources to effect a spurt in capital formation; (2) the adoption of new technologies wherever possible; and (3) institutional innovations to facilitate the operation of these two factors. For a country like the PRC, this self-reliant, people-oriented approach might conceivably have been most effective in activating vast numbers of people and achieving important results, provided revolutionary enthusiasm was combined with rigorous science. Unfortunately, just prior to the Great Leap Forward, an "Anti-Rightist" campaign, aimed at combating the influence of elements considered to be regressive, had snowballed out of all proportion into a sweeping denigration of intellectuals, in effect leaving politically suspect the highly-educated stratum who possessed the skills and experience for modernization. As a result, the Great Leap Forward was deprived of its sobering contribution, and no technological revolution took place.

As an experience in the use of mass movements to accelerate economic development, the record of the Great Leap Forward was a mixture of success and failure. Where successes were gained, they were notably in areas which involved indigenous or intermediate but labor-intensive technology: the construction of numerous water conservation and land reclamation projects, small hydroelectric plants and village factories, the expansion of transportation networks, the creation of rural health systems based on local paramedics (the famous "barefoot doctors"), and other additions to the "social overhead." The fiascos were of two kinds: (a) attempts to use indigenous technology to develop high-technology production processes, such as the nationwide "all-out for steel" campaign using "backyard steel furnances," the precipitate program to achieve immediate and spectacular increases in foodgrain production per unit area; and (b) attempts to alter the institutional structure of production and distribution before productivity had risen to a level which warranted such structural changes. Examples include the oversized and managerially unwieldy structure of the original people's communes, which attenuated their advantages for accommodating more efficient economies of scale; the premature attempts to equalize the allocation of resources among rich and poor production units; the excessive limitation or outright abolution of private plots, cottage industries, village markets and so on. These actions did not help to increase either production or consumption.

If lessons of hindsight are to be drawn, it is perhaps not idle to speculate what advances might have been gained had the Great Leap Forward confined itself to types of technology reasonably within reach of the people and had institutional change been more gradually introduced in keeping with both objective needs and possibilities, taking carefully into account the level of productivity and the level of consciousness.

The Great Leap Forward was followed by a severe economic slump caused by natural disaster and human error, compounded by the abrupt withdrawal of Soviet experts which left key industrial projects in shambles. But from 1962 to 1966, the economy rebounded and even attained a higher rate of growth as a consequence of stringent government measures. These included selective retrenchment in capital construction, correction of imbalances in the economy, and consolidation and improvement in all sectors.

These measures, by their very success, reinforced the mood of dissent from the earlier policies. Mao Zedong began to see a dangerous trend toward "revisionism" and a grave threat to his whole strategy of development. Since the danger seemed to emanate from the top echelons of Party and government, he saw no recourse but to make a direct appeal to the people to counter the danger. What ensued was one of the most extraordinary episodes in human history – the Cultural Revolution, undoubtedly the largest, sustained mass movement of all time, launched by the supreme leader of the country calling on the people to rebel. Originally targeted at high-handed, bureaucratic power-holders "taking the capitalist road," the attack, spearheaded by young people, quickly took on a momentum of its own and broadened to strike at all authority, good and bad. The exercise of "mass" democracy deteriorated at times in virtual anarchism.

The Cultural Revolution was originally conceived as another propulsive movement in Mao's concept of continuing revolution, and no doubt, it succeeded, as no other previous movement, in involving ordinary citizens in the assessment of public issues and the supervision of public leaders on a gigantic scale. But it also differed from all past movements in two other, less positive, respects: First, in the turmoil caused by the shattering of the apparatus of authority, the movement fell under the control of a complex cabal, later dubbed by Mao as the "Gang of Four." The social and ideological roots, outlook, and style of this group can only be described as premodern (if not feudal), for they demagogically espoused ultraradical lines of policy in an unbridled struggle for power. Their ascendancy to power brought with an unparalleled reign of terror, a kind of reverse McCarthyism on a grand scale that was only cut short by their summary arrest in September 1976. Second, the Cultural Revolution, partly under manipulation and partly out of control, veered off course and spawned social and economic disorder. This disorder turned out to be far longer in duration, broader in scope, and more disruptive in effect than any previous upheaval. It generated unnecessary social tensions that vitiated the struggle against the real regressive forces, who were, more often than not, camouflaged behind the facade of militant dogmatism.

The havoc that resulted was appalling – in human suffering for millions of pilloried officeholders, in the loss of schooling for a generation of young people, and in economic chaos whose effects are still being felt today. A special kind of damage was inflicted on the minds of people who fell captive to ultra-left sophistry in the genuine believe that it was in keeping with the revolutionary spirit of "politics in command." A plethora of specious polemics disseminated such notions as these: that to pursue science and technical expertise was to risk bourgeoisification, while good "politics" was all that was necessary to solve problems; that raising standards of living was a contaminating bourgeois value, whereas production should be pushed as an end in itself; that any form of commodity production and of the market was bound to be capitalist-prone and should be eliminated as soon as possible; that income differentials as well as the principle "to each according to his work" held the germs of capitalism and that, by implication, the socialist principle of distribution should really be "equal pay for unequal as well as equal work"; that foreign trade was tantamount to national betrayal, while self-reliance meant reinventing the wheel behind closed doors. It is no accident that every peak in ultra-left extremism, such as in 1967-68, 1974, and 1976, was marked by a sharp downturn in the economy.

The deterioration of the Cultural Revolution into such a serious travesty of its original goals requires an explanation which still awaits much more analysis. That matters would not have gone so far had it not been for the Gang of Four seems indisputable. But to attribute all the problem to this small political cabal would be both superficial and unconvincing. Even the very fact of their long stay in power is itself an issue demanding explanation and analysis. Such an analysis compels one, of necessity, to examine the historical, political, social, and ideologicial antecedents of contemporary Chinese society and the problems they pose for modernization and development.

If modernization is an imperative of history for China, it cannot be undertood simply as a straightforward effort to span the technology gap or to build, within a generation or two, the industrial infrastructure which took Europe centuries to achieve. The task of telescoping history is even more complex and challenging. To regain perspective, it is helpful to recall that China was for many centuries ahead of Europe in technology, institutions, and even standards of living, and it was the transfer of technology from China to Europe – including breakthroughs in paper, printing, the compass, gunpowder, the sternpost rudder – which helped make possible the modernization of Europe. Sometime during the fifteenth or sixteenth centuries, Europe spurted ahead, largely because of technological and systemic changes which, for various reasons, did not begin to take place in China until the present century. Yet, today, China has chosen to undertake the building of socialism, a "post-capitalist" society. Thus, if Western Europe is to be taken as the paradigm of "modern" social and economic change, moving in the last few centuries from premodern feudalism to modern capitalism, China's contemporary transition to "post-modern" socialism can be said to start further back and is an attempt to leap further forward than the modern societies of the West, without tranversing the full course of the capitalist stage. Historically, in Marx' general historical scheme, capitalism was supposed to have provided the prior productive capacity as well as the matured social contradictions, for the emergence of socialism. By contrast, the PRC is attempting, in one continuous, integral process, to transform her low-productivity agrarian economy, burdened by survivals of "feudal" values and institutions, into a high-productivity industrial society in which the technology is "modern" and the values and institutions are nonexploitative and nonoppressive, i.e. "post-modern." An extraordinary feat indeed.

It cannot be expected that such a leap in history can be achieved without upheavals and tensions. For an extended period, the old and the new, the traditional and the modern, will coexist in the PRC, some aspects in sympathetic symbiosis, others in antithetical symbiosis. From the perspective of socialist development, selective rejection as well as selective acceptance is called for, with regard both to tradition as well as to modernity. But because Chinese socialism emerged, not out of the highest development of capitalism, but out of a hybrid society of semi-feudalism and stunted capitalism, any regression in the process of socialist development is not likely to assume the form of full-fledged capitalism, but that of a fedual-type reaction, mixed with strong, small-producer or petit-bourgeois propensities. This would seem to account for some aspects of behavior of the Gang of Four and their adherents.

It is fair to remind ourselves at this point that what still prevails in the PRC is the integrative power of the revolutionary values that Mao and other Chinese leaders have tried for three decades to develop — service to the people, human equality (as distinguished from illusive egalitarianism), democratic behavior and closeness to the masses, hard work and frugality, and mutual help and social responsibility. But the recent trauma of living under the imperious authoritarianism and divisive machinations of a Jian Qing has shocked China into a realization of the feudal characteristics still inherent in the new society.

These are not confined to the Gang of Four. On a lesser scale, they continue to hamper modernization and development in many ways. A case in point is the yamen style of bureaucratic decision making — a kind of "holding court" in which a responsible official "wills" something to be done, or pronounces judgment on complex matters at his own discretion instead of finding rational solutions through systematic and objective studies. Yet the bureaucrat is not entirely to blame for the persistence of this style since, for so long, society has seemed to accept it as a matter of course.

At great cost, the PRC has drawn a number of profound lessons from the recent past that form the basis for a comprehensive, critical rethinking and for reuniting the country behind a renewed development push. But, while the widespread revulsion against ultra-left politics has aided rejection of the more glaring absurdities of policy, it has proven to be a difficult task to unshackle people's minds from the conceptual confusion that the ultra-left disseminated. Important headway was made in a recent, nationwide debate around the issue "What is the criterion of truth?" which appears to have been widely successful in helping many cadres break out of the mental cages of ideational dogmatism.(2) If it is firmly held that the only test of truth is practice, there should emerge, on the basis of critical revaluation of the successes and failures of the past three decades, a broad consensus on a development path that fits the PRC's specific conditions – a "Chinese Road to Modernization."

The most fundamental lesson for China is that it must make a decisive shift of emphasis to economic development. This should be aimed at raising productivity and the living standards of the people as rapidly as possible. To ignore or downgrade this central task would be to court disaster in all other fields. This requires, simultaneously, a new stability and unity and a revitalized democratic system undergirded by law.

Is modernization needed for this purpose? The notion of "development without modernization" can only be afforded by comfortable romantics. In the PRC's circumstances, it would be inconceivable to accomplish the central task of economic development without a sweeping program of modernization. But such a program must proceed from the actual needs and possibilities of the country, rather than from the wholesale transplantation of "modernity." This merits the most careful analysis.

The present structure of the PRC's economy evolved over a long period of isolation inflicted on it in the early years by the United States and then by the Soviet Union. In the decade prior to 1977, it was self-inflicted under the aegis of the Gang of Four. It can, therefore, be said that the policy of self-reliance was partly a principle of proud self-discipline, and partly a virtue born out of necessity. Thus, historically, the maximum mobilization of China's human and material resources was conducted in the context of both self-reliance and self-seclusion, though seclusion was not a choice demanded by China's socialist values.

Despite errors and setbacks, the PRC has achieved some remarkable results in the course of 30 years. It attained an average aggregate growth rate for industrial and agricultural production officially put at 9.5 percent per annum, although Western economists, while acknowledging a high rate of growth, place the rate at a lower figure.(3) The PRC also achieved a drastic change in the structure of its economy – the ratio of industry to agriculture in the total product being reversed from 10 versus 90 percent before liberation, to 75 versus 25 percent today.(4) An industrial infrastructure was built up which now comprises some 350,000 enterprises, big and small, and the country now possesses a work force of 50 million in urban and rural industry.(5) Though still poor in terms of per capita wealth, the PRC is already first in the world in aggregate output of cotton cloth, second in foodgrains, third in coal, and fifth in steel, while a rich and diversified resource base still waits to be fully tapped. It is, thus, now without a sound industrial base on which to modernize.

But these large advantages must be weighed against serious constraints. An excessive rate of population growth (a cumulative 66.7 percent in the 25 years from 1953 to 1978) has slowed the improvement of living standards, the rate of capital accumulation, and the satisfaction of employment and educational needs. This continues to be a major problem, despite the government's success in reducing the growth rate to 1.2 percent and its determination to achieve zero growth by the year 2000.(6) The long hiatus in formal schooling during the Cultural Revolution has handicapped a whole generation which now requires retraining to fit it for the tasks of modernization. An enormous civil service, endowed with permanent tenure (enjoying "iron rice bowls," as the saying goes in China) responds with uneven speed to the new requirements of proficiency and efficiency. Above all, serious problems of imbalance or disproportionality continue to act as a brake on overall growth. It is the constant correction of these imbalances that will shape the necessary matrix for rapid modernization and development.

It may be useful here to identify briefly some of the imbalances that are perceived to have strategic significance, and to delineate the corresponding problem of how to achieve a better balance.

1. For years, there has been a lack of congruence, at times acute and at times less so, between the level of productive forces and the institutional framework in which production and distribution is carried out. The problem for PRC cadres has been to accept the fact that the PRC is a poor country in the very earliest stage of socialist development and that, hence, it might be ineffectual if not counterproductive to adopt inappropriate advanced forms of public ownership and control (e.g., overcurtailment of individual enterprise in some service trades, overextension of government authority in the collective economy) or premature transitions to "egalitarian" distributional principles ("eating out of the common pot," the "iron rice bowl" syndrome[7]) in place of the socialist principle, "to each according to his work." Such approaches inhibit production and delay the process of modernization.

2. There exists an imbalance in resource allocation between the satisfaction of consumer needs and the maintenance of a healthy rate of capital formation. In 1949, the new regime inherited a subsistence economy in shambles, with little in the nature of an industrial infrastructure. This necessitated a high rate of capital accumulation which could only be achieved through hard work and rigorous frugality. But, if this rate became too high (as it did during the Cultural Revolution), it would squeeze out improvement in living standards and affect worker morale. Wages and amenities must be increased on the basis of rising productivity, but not in accordance with some sort of socialist "Say's Law" that higher production will generate its own consumption. The premise to start with must be the need to meet the rising cultural and material requirements of the people. The optimum rate of capital formation should be determined by the criterion of what makes development move faster. In the PRC's own experience, overall growth was quickened when the rate was set at a little over 20 percent in the

First Five-Year Plan period and in the readjustment period of the early 1960s, while development was slowed in other periods when there was a higher rate of capital accumulation.(8)

3. Experience has taught the PRC that major problems can arise from any serious disproportionality in the relative development pace of the heavy industry, light industry, and agriculture sectors. The salient factor is the economic role of agriculture. Eight hundred million out of one billion Chinese live on the country's farms, and any talk of stability and progress would be meaningless without first and foremost solving their problems of production and livelihood. Furthermore, in the PRC's present stage, agriculture plays a special role as the base for the whole economy. Only when it is on a sound footing can food, raw materials, capital, and an adequate market be provided for industry. Although the PRC has always paid more attention to agriculture, even during the First Five-Year Plan, than the Soviet Union, growth in the rural sector still lagged behind that of industry, retarding overall growth. The consumer goods industry also found itself in a low priority position. It was hampered in making full use of its advantages of small investment, quick turnover, and ready adaptation to the export market.

The underlying problem was a scale of priorities that, in effect, placed heavy industry first, light industry next, and agriculture last in the allocation of resources. This is not a new problem. As early as 1956, Mao Zedong had called for resolute action to reverse the priorities. Aware of strong resistance from industrial planners who feared that a shift of investment priorities to agriculture with its high capital-output ratio would retard the capital goods sector in the short run, Mao argued:

> Is your desire to develop heavy industry genuine or feigned, strong or weak? If your desire is feigned or weak, then you will hit agriculture and light industry and invest less in them. If your desire is genuine or strong, then you will attach importance to agriculture and light industry so that there will be more grain and more raw materials for light industry and a greater accumulation of capital. And there will be more funds in the future to invest in heavy industry.(9)

There appears to be wider acceptance of this argument today, and much effort is being put into the firm implementation of the agriculture-light industry-heavy industry scale of priorities. There remains the concrete problem of finding the optimum balance at any given juncture.

4. Another long-standing issue has been the problem of proper balance between the role of state planning and that of the socialist market. In the past, economic planners, by shunning the market as an allocating mechanism, have complicated their own lives with impossible self-imposed tasks, and allowed rigidities of central control to produce irrationalities and waste in the allocation of resources. This is especially conspicuous in the production of capital goods (which until now have not been considered commodities) and in the state procurement of

staples. The continuance of earlier measures which have served their purpose, such as unified purchase arrangements and procurement quotas, can no longer meet the needs of the far more complex and fast-moving demand-supply realities of today. The limitations of over-centralized, overbureaucratized planning are also only too evident in directing the collective economy. The problem is a serious one because this sector involves agriculture and 80 percent of the population. Here the focus is not only on the efficiency of the system, but also the violation of the autonomy and self-management principles of the communes and other collective enterprises.

The constraints on centralized planning arise from the fact that the PRC socialism started from a fragmented economic base with under-developed commodity production and a weak economic planning and information apparatus. As modernization progresses, the scale and diversity of decision-making will mushroom, and the tendency of a bureaucracy to inflate itself with more and more (often underskilled) economic managers will spiral. If left unchecked, this could have a debilitating effect on development. As presently structured, planning leads to overplanning with production determining the market, rather than the market determining production. Expanding the role of the socialist market is an antidote. This does not necessarily mean, however, that government planners will be denied access to economic means to enforce social policy. They would still be able to resort to a variety of fiscal means – e.g., differential taxes on wanted and unwanted goods, price policy, and control of credit. What is clearly needed is an optimum relationship between plan and market to allow the commodity economy to expand within the guidelines of the state plan. In the end, restoring the legitimacy of the law of values as a stimulus and mediator in the economy does not mean weakening, but rationalizing and strengthening the leading role of central planning.

A separate but related problem concerns the relationship between the jurisdictional scope of the central government on the one hand and that of lower echelons of government and individual enterprises on the other. Here, what must be taken into account is the vastness and diversity of China, with many different and complex problems, many of which can best be handled locally. The tendency in the past has been to put too much under central control, even the accounting of income and expenditure of individual enterprises. Central organs could even institute interregional equalization formulas which often had a counter-productive effect on development. Today, it is increasingly emphasized that the narrowing of regional disparities must not be accomplished by a leveling process, but by nurturing affluence where favorable conditions exist in order to help less favorably endowed regions. An optimal devolution of economic authority would enhance initiative, efficiency, and a vital sense of responsibility without weakening central planning.

5. Difficult choices are also faced in trying to strike a balance between the import of technology and the fuller utilization of existing technological and plant capacity. The spotty and outdated nature of the

PRC's technology requires it to bring in advanced technology and managerial techniques if it is to modernize at a speed which would narrow rather than widen the gap with the advanced industrial countries. The principal constraints on this process are scarcity of hard currency reserves and a still limited capacity to assimilate new technology. Furthermore, the PRC has, in 30 years, built a considerable industrial plant with much capacity still unused or waiting to be upgraded.   Strong directives have been issued by the State Council warning against succumbing to the temptation to launch new projects, especially those requiring payment in foreign currencies, without very thorough planning on the local level and careful policy consideration on the national level. Partly because of the excessive zeal of certain heavy industry branches which led to serious losses in 1978, a temporary moratorium on new large-scale projects was declared in the spring of 1979, which is to last, with few exceptions, through the three-year period of readjustment. In the logic of using trade as a means of improving self-reliance, the PRC's order of preferences is to favor importing selected equipment over complete plants, and technology over equipment, whenever possible. This is consistent with the principle that imported technology is to supplement and fill out rather than to be a substitute for existing capabilities.

    6. Finally, we come to the crucial human problem – the discrepancy betwen the development of human resources and the demands of modernization. The launching of the "Four Modernizations" has focused attention on the continuing paucity of skilled manpower in almost every field. The ten-year interregnum of the ultra-left aggravated the problem in two ways: a whole generation was deprived of adequate schooling while it was exposed to an avalanche of misguided norms of thought and behavior. Thus, the PRC is faced now with the dual task of educating and reeducating. In a sense, a fifth modernization – the most crucial of all – should be added to the "Four Modernizations":   the modernization of the modernizers. Here I refer to the upgrading not only of scientific-technological capacities, but also of qualities of the human spirit.   In the socialist perspective, "modernity" includes advanced human values.   The modernizers themselves must transcend self-serving careerism and embrace attitudes of dedication to the people's interests, to ideals of human equality and cooperation, to the struggle against exploitation, and to unyielding intellectual and moral integrity. If the new generation were to scorn these norms in an overreaction to the hollow hypocrisy of the Gang of Four, the great promise of the future would be in danger of vanishing into thin air.

    Because of the scale and complexity of the modernization effort, the government has instituted policies aimed at bringing into play all available human resources – workers, peasants, intellectuals, businessmen, the one million college students, as well as the 17 million government cadres. This will surely require the creation of new and imaginative training programs which embrace the two dimensions of technical expertise and human values.

The six problems I have listed above are not, of course, exhaustive. But they may be of sufficient significance to illustrate the fact that future development in the PRC will be energized in large measure by a process of overcoming the imbalances and disproportionalities that impede modernization. The new policies are aimed at performing this task. There is, in my opinion, no evidence that these new policies represent a change in China's basic strategy of development.

All development strategies which have any practical meaning are little more than attempts to conceptualize the basic dynamics of a long and complex process. These conceptions must be tested and corrected by practice at every stage. This would appear to be especially true of the path the PRC has taken, since it is in many respects a pioneering one. Its basic postulates do not fit into the experience of most of the industrialized countries. The strategic postulate is that it is possible in the long term to achieve rapid, self-reliant economic growth at the same time as key socioeconomic disparities (including the classic ones – the urban-rural, mental-manual labor, industry-agriculture gaps) are gradually narrowed. The tactical postulate is that, at any given stage, it is possible to find the optimal, interactive relationship between the pace of progressive social change and the pace of economic growth in such a way as to spur both processes. This implies that, even if it is necessary sometimes to go one step backward in order to make a correction of balance, this should be done in order to move two steps forward.

A final word about the PRC's relation to the world economy. It is that the PRC has rejoined the world market, and that its foreign trade is on the verge of a very large expansion.(10) There is no evidence, however, that the PRC will allow this expansion to become a decisive proportion of GNP or to make it excessively vulnerable to fluctuations and disturbances in the international economic situation. In the long term, the purpose of engaging in foreign trade is to reduce China's dependence by introducing the equipment and technologies it needs but does not yet have, to create new industries or to expand and upgrade present productive capacities. Its exports are primarily aimed at generating foreign exchange to pay for its imports.

Although the PRC has again begun to accept foreign credit facilities to finance its enormous capital construction program, the government has moved cautiously in order to keep the aggregate level of indebtedness to modest levels, giving preference to "pay as you go" transactions whenever possible. As the new patterns of trade develop, it is becoming increasingly clear that the PRC will try to channel trade to the types of ventures which would at once help to solve shortages of funds, generate new export capacity to pay for imports, or create import substitution industries.

The potential for international trade in a market of one billion people is staggering. Yet, there is little evidence that the PRC will allow the vagaries and uncertainities of the world market to play a disruptive role in its economy or to veer it off course. Its first concern has consistently been to build up its own strength and, on that basis, work for the most favorable international environment possible.

It is the autonomous and self-reliant nature of the PRC's economy, added to its potental sympathies as a developing country identified with the Third World, that determine its attitude to the global economic structure and to the whole orientation and program of the New International Economic Order. The scale of its own needs and problems will probably place severe constraints on the PRC's ability to increase direct aid to other developing countries for some years to come. But it has endorsed and subscribed to the Common Fund. It has given firm support to the Arusha Programme for Collective Self-Reliance, the Integrated Programme of Commodities, the proposed International Code of Conduct on the Transfer of Technology, and other component positions and projects of the NIEO. Its representatives have repeatedly taken the view that building up the collective strength of the developing countries is a necessary factor in improving their negotiating positions for a restructuring of the world economic order. In this regard, the PRC has seen much promise in the formation of the various regional systems of economic cooperation.

In the final analysis, the prime issue for the People's Republic of China is whether it can successfully solve its own problems of development by discovering their inherent laws of change and shaping an effective strategy suited to Chinese conditions. One-third of the population of the developing world lives in the PRC, and the lessons of success and error in its efforts will be of wide international concern. Above all, if the PRC succeeds in its modernization goals by the end of the century, the result can only be a crucial shift in the world balance of economic forces that is bound to make a profound difference in the realization of NIEO goals.

NOTES

(1) See especially Liu Shaoqi, "Political Report of the Central Committee of the Communist Party of China," Sept. 15, 1956. For English text, see Eighth National Congress of the Communist Party of China (Peking, Foreign Language Press, 1956).

(2) An editorial in the Renmin Ribao (People's Daily) on May 12, 1978, entitled "Practice is the Sole Criterion of Truth," gave much impetus to the debate. In its Communique of December 22, 1978, the Third Plenum of the CCCPC (the Soviet Party Congress) noted the historic significance of the debate for emancipating the minds of people, warning of the danger of intellectual atrophy if blind rote-learning of written doctrince were not abandoned in favor of critical learning, with practice as its guide.

(3) Professor Dwight Perkins of Harvard University estimates that China's average annual rate of economic growth between 1952 and 1974 was about 6 percent.

(4) Ma Hung, "Shixian Si Hua yu Wo Guo Jingji Jiegou de Gaige" (Realizing the Four Modernizations and the Reform of China's Economic Structure), in Jingji Guanli (Economic Management) IX (1979).

(5) Ibid.

(6) An authoritative discussion of the population issue is contained in an article by Vice-Premier Chen Muhua, entitled "Controlling Population Growth in a Planned Way," Peking Review, Nov. 16, 1979.

(7) "Chi Da Guo Fan" (eating out of the common pot) and "Tie Fan Wan" (iron rice bowl) are denigratory phrases of much currency in the PRC today, referring to the system of remuneration and permanent tenure with little relation to performance.

(8) An article by Liu Suinien and Zhou Ying in Vol. IV, 1979 of the authoritative party journal Hung Qi (Red Flag) deals with the relationship between rates of accumulation and consumption. The authors attack as fallacious the view that favors excessive rates of accumulation as a means to force the pace of development, and recommend a rate not exceeding 30 percent.

(9) Mao Zedong, "On the Ten Major Relationships," Selected Works (Peking: Foreign Language Press, 1977), p. 286.

(10) The Japanese External Trade Organization (JETRO) estimates that China's total foreign trade volume for 1979 rose to a record level of between $28.5 billion and $29 billion, compared with $21.6 billion the previous year.

5 The People's Republic of China and the New International Economic Order: Relations With the Third World

Eugenio Anguiano

Since its establishment in 1949, the People's Republic of China has carried out an active foreign policy unequaled by any of the Third World countries. In matters of foreign economic relations, the PRC has displayed intense activity in granting financial aid and loans to more than 55 countries on the five continents. This role of aid donor has been continuously played for more than two decades by the PRC which, in turn, received economic aid during the 1949-1959 period, when the Soviet Union helped to develop several industrialization projects. Since then, the PRC of Mao Zedong achieved moderate but sustained economic development without imports of capital and without any foreign debt. It even became a net exporter of capital.

These characteristics, however, began to change recently, when the post-Mao PRC leadership took the decision to accept foreign debt in principle. Even before 1976, the Beijing government operated with a low profile in the external credit market through suppliers' credits and deferred payments in the purchase of its capital equipment and turn-keys industrial plants. Later on, the PRC reestablished reciprocal bank deposits with several foreign banks. According to statistics of the Bank for International Settlements, the PRC's borrowing on foreign bank deposits in 1978 amounted to about $500 million.

This characteristic of the Chinese economy (being a developing one and at the same time a net supplier of aid abroad) can be better understood if we analyze the behavior of Beijing's diplomacy in an integral way, and view it as a result of some specific, theoretical, and practical conceptions. It is evident that Beijing's activism in granting economic and military help to other countries responds to that integral conception which, in its turn, is closely related to the very particular ideas of the leaders themselves on the stability, consolidation, and safeguarding of their own socio-political system. In other words, the study of the PRC's relations with other developing countries, particularly in terms of economic cooperation, must be seen in the context of that nation's ideology and "praxis."

In evaluating Chinese participation in the necessary although yet unobtained New International Economic Order, it is necessary to survey the changes in Maoist foreign policy and briefly recall the main internal and external factors that have motivated those changes. The PRC's ultimate objective, and that of any other society, is one of preserving national interests and the values of the society. For this task, various instruments such as foreign policy are employed, which, for a developed nation or for a military and political power, is a way of influencing the rest of the world. In the case of the People's Republic of China, we can observe variants related to its condition as a developing nation, simultaneously pursuing ideological goals and state interests. Coinciding with this (at least until very recently) is the PRC's economic strategy of self-reliance which has kept its big population free from the need for foreign credits and foreign capital. Again, this last element seems to be on the verge of changing and, if that happens, it will have enormous repercussions in the international markets.

In this chapter, the evolution of PRC foreign policy is first outlined. There follows an analysis of the visible reasons which induce that country's leaders to help other developing countries, which also involves the question of the type and scope of that aid. Finally, there are some conclusions about the role the PRC might play in the NIEO.

IDEOLOGY AND DIPLOMACY

PRC foreign policy has been very closely linked to an ideology based on its interpretation of Marxist-Leninist tradition. The Chinese adaptations of Marxism have undergone changes which, when related to matters such as diplomacy, give rise to oscillations in the conduct of the Beijing government in the international arena. An analysis of such conduct must begin with a retrospective review of events of almost the last three decades.

Bearing in mind the excessive simplifications made in attempting to establish historical periods, as well as subsequent arbitrary subdivisions, we believe it convenient to define the epoch corresponding to the years 1949 to 1952 as that in which PRC diplomacy began to be defined. During these years, the political ideology of the Chinese socialists was nourished by the United States' aggressive attitude toward the new Beijing regime and by the latter's need to be fully recognized as a legitimate state. The exclusion of the regime from the United Nations' system, and the fact that Washington's supremacy within that organization was the cause of such an exclusion provoked a politico-military alliance between Moscow and Beijing. Compounding this was the PRC stubbornness in diplomatic affairs. With the Korean War, this behavior was further accentuated, and Mao Zedong ratified the alignment of his government toward "only one lane,"(1) i.e., the socialist bloc, with the Soviet Union as its leading country.

The inclusion of the PRC in the Soviet sphere plus the bipolarism of the cold war prevented the Beijing government in its early years from developing any policy oriented toward neutrality. Neither did it accept the possibility of a third path. This conception of a mortal struggle between two mutually exclusive political systems in the world differed from the idea of the "unified front" policy with which the Chinese socialists initially conducted campaigns against "United States imperialism." When Mao argued that his country would participate in an international "united front" (made up of the Soviet Union and other socialist states, as well as the "large revolutionary masses of other countries" where socialism did not prevail[2]) with the aim of promoting a world revolutionary struggle, he left untouched the orthodox conception of a "united front" (an alliance with political forces different from those of the communists, but sufficiently progressive as to unite around a nationalist and anti-imperialist struggle).

It was only when the Korean conflict began to show signs of a political solution and the new Beijing regime headed toward a clearer consolidation by launching their first five year economic development plan and by promulgating the first political constitution for the nation, that a new, more "flexible" stage in Beijing diplomacy started. From 1953 to 1956, the PRC opened up somewhat and began relations with developing countries outside the socialist bloc,(3) (i.e., with governments not dominated by communist parties). (See table 5.1 for a list of countries with whom Beijing has diplomatic relations.) At the same time as Beijing put less emphasis on armed struggle and sought agreement with the nonaligned countries of Asia and Africa, a formula for coexistence was being introduced into Beijing's diplomatic semantics, which has been used since then in establishing relations with governments which have no ideological affinity with China. This formula deals with the five known principles first stated in the Sino-Indian agreement of Pancha Shila(4) held in June 1954, and later incorporated in the resolutions of the First Conference of Afro-Asiatic countries as an ideal framework for the development of relations among countries with different political systems.

The so-called Spirit of Bandung, where the Afro-Asiatic conference was held, prevailed in Beijing's diplomacy. Thus, it came closer to the classical concept of a united front, with its concepts of revolutionary social change, opposition to one sole common enemy, and the possibility of an alliance between united heterogeneous political forces to achieve the common goal of obtaining complete political and economic independence for the respective countries.   The PRC affirmed that unity among marginal or peripheral countries is characterized by a symbiosis of peace and national unity, or, in their own words: "peace and national independence are so closely linked as to be indistinguishable."(5)

With this type of approach to the Afro-Asiatic countries, Beijing sought to improve her international position and to avoid conflicts with its border neighbors, as well as to counteract the regional military alliances the United States belonged to such as ANZUS (Australia, New Zealand, and the United States) and SEATO (Southeast Asia Treaty Organization), the latter being promoted by Secretary of State John F. Dulles, to fill the power vacuum which, in his opinion, the French left in

Indochina. What is more, the Beijing government began to diversify its foreign relationships — diplomatically, economically, and politically — a policy in conflict with the political line adopted by the XX Congress of the Communist Party of the Soviet Union (CPSU).

Table 5.1. Diplomatic Relations of the People's Republic
of China by Regions and Countries (March 1979)

Africa (44)	Algeria, Benin, Botswana, Burundi, Cape Verde Is., Cameroon, Central Africa Republic, Comoro Is., Congo, Chad, Djibuti, Egypt, Equatorial Guinea, Ethiopia, Gabon, Gambia, Ghana, Guinea, Guinea-Bissau, Kenya, Liberia, Libya, Madagascar, Mali, Mauritania, Mauritius, Morocco, Mozambique, Niger, Nigeria, Rwanda, São Tomé and Principe, Senegal, Sierra Leone, Somalia, Sudan, Seychelles, Tanzania, Togo, Tunisia, Uganda, Upper Volta, Zaire, and Zambia.
The Americas (14)	Argentina, Barbados, Brazil, Canada, Chile, Cuba, Guyana, Jamaica, Mexico, Peru, Surinam, Trinidad and Tobago, United States, and Venezuela.
Asia (28)	Afghanistan, Bangladesh, Burma, Cyprus, Korea (Democratic People's Republic), India, Iran, Iraq, Japan, Jordan, Kampuchea (Democratic), Kuwait, Laos, Lebanon, Malaysia, Maldives, Mongolia, Nepal, Oman, Pakistan, Philippines, Sri-Lanka, Syria, Thailand, Turkey, Vietnam, Yemen (Arab Republic), Yemen (People's Democratic Republic), and a liaison office with the Palestine Liberation Organization.
Europe (28)	Albania, Austria, Belgium, Bulgaria, Czechoslovakia, Denmark, Germany (Federal Republic), Germany (Democratic Republic), Finland, France, Greece, Hungary, Iceland, Italy, Luxembourg, Malta, Netherlands, Norway, Poland, Portugal, Romania, San Marino, Spain, Sweden, Switzerland, Union of Soviet Socialist Republics, United Kingdom, and Yugoslavia.
Oceania (5)	Australia, Fiji, New Zealand, Papua New Guinea, and Western Samoa.
TOTAL:	119 Countries 1 Liaison Office

The last years of the 1950s brought about profound changes for the PRC in its internal situation as well as abroad. This is also naturally reflected in important changes in China's diplomatic policy and conduct. In the national sphere, alterations were made in government policy in order to confront the economic problems left by the "Great Leap Forward" campaign and the accelerated collectivization of the land. Within the Communist Party of China (CCP), differences between Mao and other leaders arose provoking political purges which would be of great significance in the mid-1960s.

In the international field, what was most remarkable was the breakdown in the Sino-Soviet Alliance,(6) as China's dispute with the United States continued. The virtual cancellation of any Soviet aid to the PRC, including economic assistance which was suspended totally in 1960, weakened Beijing's capacity to respond to what were considered serious threats to her stability and territorial sovereignty. Nonetheless, this did not deter the PRC leadership from its continual confrontation with the United States, nor did it impede the beginning of a long period of open conflict with Moscow.

A new stage of retraction and hard-line policies in Chinese diplomacy was seen between 1956 and 1965, affecting relations with the other underdeveloped countries. These relations were particularly clouded by the conflict between the PRC and India, in which one aspect of the doctrine of the five principles failed: that of resolving frontier differences through peaceful negotiations and in a spirit of mutual equality, respect, and benefit. The PRC's attitude toward the rest of the Third World focused primarily on the "unity and struggle" strategy; that is to say, cooperation with governments and allied political parties in resisting imperialism and, at the same time, preparing conditions suitable for a revolutionary situation in the poor nations of Latin America, Asia, and Africa, in particular those which had recently obtained their political independence.

An outline of a period so rich in events as the second half of the 1950s and the first half of the 1960s has serious limitations since it simplifies to an extreme a variety of events not easily placed in the historical period arbitrarily adopted here. For instance, there was the shift of PRC diplomacy in 1956-65 toward a more revolutionary approach. This was evidenced by the tour of Zhou Enlai through various African countries(7) to ratify the "Spirit of Bandung" regardless of ideological differences. Nevertheless, the dominant tone of that period was one of support for national liberation movements and rejection of the thesis of a pacific coexistence between capitalism and socialism. The fact that Mao claimed that the "East wind prevails over the West wind" was more than a play of words; its purpose was to push PRC foreign policy toward a more militant position and to show that the Chinese model of communism was to be the only valid one for all underdeveloped regions of the world.

Besides the ideological reasons for imposing a hard line, there were concrete facts that were deemed threats by the PRC leaders. The United States' intervention in the Vietnam war increased to unacceptable proportions, and, as a result, the PRC's border situation deteriorated. It no longer depended on any nuclear umbrella, nor did it yet have the capacity which could serve as a deterrence against the NATO nations.(8) The regional military alliances excluded the PRC or were prepared to confront it. In the United Nations, the pro-Taiwan lobby blocked any initiative in favor of Beijing. Given such circumstances, the only way of preserving national security, in the PRC's view, was to strengthen one's forces and to seek revolutionary alliances with governments or social sectors of countries experiencing explosive situations. In this context, aid given abroad was directed to governments in serious disagreement with the developed capitalist countries. In these governments, actual or potential revolutionary movements could be found, whether in Southeast Asia, the Middle East, Africa, or Latin America.

A period of retraction and isolation with respect to the outside world was accentuated in the PRC from 1965 to the summer of 1967, when the fervor of the Cultural Revolution drove the Red Guards and other demonstrators in Beijing to demonstrate against several embassies, to insult foreign diplomats, and to burn part of the facilities belonging to the British delegation. The moderate position that called for a certain degree of coexistence with other nations was overcome by the radicalism of the "popular war" which advocated the rising up of the peripheral areas against the metropolitan areas, an allusion to the way the PRC peasant revolution had shifted power from rural bases to provincial cities and urban centers of national importance.(9)

The PRC's failure to obtain a second meeting of Afro-Asiatic countries where the Soviet Union would be excluded, and other unfavorable events (such as the annihilation of the Communist Party of Indonesia, the overthrow of President Nkrumah of Ghana while he was on an official visit to the PRC, and the predominance of Moscow in the international communist movement) contributed to the development of a policy of extreme radicalism, which abandoned any idea of an adjustment to reality. The Chinese perceived a struggle on two fronts — the United States being the main enemy, followed by the USSR — and they aided materially, politically, and morally all guerilla forces in developing countries.(10)

At the same time that the unstabilizing effects of the Cultural Revolution were being controlled and a new internal order was emerging, Beijing foreign policy changed its orientation from a "united front among nations" to one of cooperation with governments of countries that did not necessarily share the same ideology. The international opposition and criticism faced by PRC diplomacy and the serious border confrontations with the Soviet Union that took place in 1969 evidently alarmed the leadership that arose from the 9th Congress of China's Communist Party, in respect of the vulnerability of their country and the danger of being isolated from the exterior.

International channels of communication were gradually restored, in the light of events such as President Nixon's suggestion to President Charles DeGaulle that he would be prepared to visit China. Even before this, from the middle of 1968 on, the ambassadors recalled during the Cultural Revolution,(11) began to return to their posts abroad, and the following year, talks on the ambassadorial level were taken up again between the Chinese and the Americans in Warsaw. By October 1970, diplomatic relations between the PRC and 30 developed and Third World countries had been established. Finally, a new conflict within the PRC – which led to the split in the so-called "Cultural Revolution Group," with the surprising downfall of important figures such as Chen Boda and later Lin Biao himself – facilitated the predominance of a pragmatic and moderate faction which sought the rehabilitation of power organs and the broad participation of the PRC in the world through an increased number of political, economic, and technological relations with other countries, regardless of immediate ideological questions.

A new stage in Chinese foreign policy began at the end of 1971, with the PRC's entry into the United Nations, with full rights restored and an initial understanding with the main adversary of the first 22 years of the regime set up by Mao Zedong. This stage has prevailed until the present day, with some important changes which will be referred to later. Under the obvious orientation of Zhou Enlai and with the approval of Mao, who always defended a doctrine of continuous revolution, a change of emphasis occurred with regard to friends and foes. The Soviet Union now became Beijing's main adversary, and, in practical terms, the only threat to the security of China's regime in the opinion of its leaders. To counteract this threat, the Chinese have attempted to set up international opposition to what they consider "the hegemonic ambitions of the two superpowers," which compete with such ferocity between themselves to obtain world hegemony that, sooner or later, they will provoke a new war. Zhou Enlai argued that "the factors for both revolution and war are increasing. Whether war gives rise to revolution or revolution prevents war, in either case the international situation will develop in the direction favourable to the people." He added, "The Third World is the main force in combating colonialism, imperialism and hegemonism. China is a developing socialist country belonging to the Third World, but we also support the countries and people of the Second World in their struggle against superpower control, threats and bullying."(12)

The preceding outline corresponds to the well known scheme of the three worlds or spheres, sketched by the Chinese leaders: the first of these worlds refers to the superpowers; the second includes the economically developed countries which, nonetheless, depend politically on one of the two hegemonic centers of power; and the third is made up of the developing nations.(13)

In abandoning the concept of a world divided between socialism and capitalism, the fundamental goal of which was opposition to United States' dominance and support for revolutionary movements, the PRC shifted to a concept that emphasizes the existence of an international community of interests that are not strictly ideological, but of a nationalistic nature. The slogan repeated over and over by the Beijing leaders that "countries want independence, nations want liberation, and the people want revolution" reflects the order in which the PRC perceived the hierarchical order of its international interests.(14)

The present doctrinal conception has been widely disseminated through the PRC's communication system(15) and has given rise to numerous international polemics. Having outlined the basic elements of that doctrine, we must now look into other "realpolitik" aspects. The first one to be considered is the Sino-Soviet dispute, undoubtedly crucial for the PRC, since it is in the light of such a conflict that one can explain a large part of Beijing's international behavior. It must be pointed out that the main questions of this dispute — frontiers, politics, and ideology — have been unsolved since before the Cultural Revolution, and that any significant changes within the Beijing leadership have not in any way altered the differences with Moscow (differences that have, in fact, increased).

The fact that the Chinese consider their old socialist ally the main threat to their national security has given rise to a series of tactical measures to counteract that risk — real or perceived, it does not matter, the effect is the same. These measures have caused dramatic changes in alliances and forces in confrontation throughout the world as well as in Asia. The first change has been the effort of the Beijing regime to consolidate a greater number of states against the two great superpowers. This was the trend in the first half of the 1970s. Gradually, such diplomacy moved toward a clearer emphasis on the promotion of unity among nations of the Second and Third Worlds in withstanding the peril of Soviet hegemony.

After Mao Zedong's death and the events of 1976, which culminated in the arrest and political demise of those considered the highest representatives of the extreme left wing of the Cultural Revolution,(16) the convictions of the PRC socialists with respect to the USSR, far from being moderated or opening up some kind of coexistence with the Soviets, were reaffirmed and gave rise to even more drastic measures: the rupture of the close relations with Albania; intensification of economic, technological, and political cooperation with the West; a conclusion of a peace treaty with Japan and the establishment of full diplomatic relations with the United States; the search for foreign technology to modernize the economy and military structure; and open hostility and recently war against Vietnam.

It is not our intention here to deal with the causes of the Sino-Soviet difference and less still to raise our opinions on this matter. We simply point out the significance of specific attitudes of the PRC in its diplomatic dealings. Before ending our analysis of the evolution of PRC foreign policy, we consider it relevant to point out that, like any other modern state, the Chinese adopt specific attitudes toward the rest of the world in terms of their own national interests. Today, those interests are related to their capacity to respond to the Soviet threat, and to the objective of speeding up the PRC's economic development and modernization. For this, the PRC is prepared to intensify cooperation with developed capitalist countries and, to a lesser extent, with the underdeveloped ones. This does not mean that the latter have lost importance for Chinese diplomacy. On the contrary, a major concern of the Beijing regime is the improvement of relations with the Third World, so far as there is a competition with the Soviet Union and its allies for gaining the confidence, support, and sympathy of the governments of these countries. But, if the PRC is going to succeed in fulfilling the ambitious goals of the so-called "four modernizations" (agriculture, industry, science and technology, and national defense), the Second World and the United States are going to play a more crucial role than the Third World as sources of foreign support.

POLICY OF AID AND COOPERATION WITH THE DEVELOPING COUNTRIES

In the previous section, we outlined the outstanding elements at work in PRC foreign policy, as well as the most important changes that have taken place in this policy during the last 30 years. These elements must be taken into consideration when studying the Beijing government's cooperation and economic aid policy with respect to developing nations, since these factors influence the country's different periods of isolation and internationalism which, in their turn, affect the aid flow abroad and its orientation.

In spite of these fluctuations, Chinese aid to the Third World has been characterized by its continuity over 20 years, by the widespread diversification of such aid, and by the favorable conditions granted to the recipient countries. Notwithstanding obvious propagandist or ideological motives, aid from Beijing has been directed to countries with very diverse socio-political systems and with very different per capita income levels, some of them with levels even higher than those reached by the Chinese themselves.

In decision-making with respect to foreign aid, at least three kinds of factors have influenced Chinese policy: the dispute with the United States and later with the Soviet Union; China's geographical situation; and internal ideological, political, and economic considerations.

With regard to the first factor, it is enough to add to what has been said before, that the PRC, through its aid to other countries, has sought to break its isolation; in addition to gaining influence and international recognition in order to counteract the threat posed by the two superpowers. When this action was motivated by American pressure on the Beijing regime, the PRC granted aid to other socialist or neutral countries in order to strengthen such alliances and, at the same time, to break the embargo, isolation, and strategy of "containment" imposed by Washington. At the same time that Sino-Soviet differences increased, the Chinese sought to win the sympathy of socialist governments in disagreement with the USSR, as in the case of Albania and Yugoslavia, with those states that tried to follow an independent path from the Moscow diplomatic line (Romania) and with those attempting to maintain their neutrality in the Sino-Soviet rift. In a wider context, China has also appealed for the support of nations in Africa and Latin America whose relations with the Soviet bloc were not particularly close, or which even underwent a period of rigidity.

The geographical factor, with respect to the granting of foreign aid, has been important since the foundation of the PRC. Initially, the emphasis of aid was placed on Asia, and on countries in other regions of the world prepared to begin diplomatic relations with Beijing. Later, there was correlation between aid and the rise of new states in Africa and the Middle East which, on obtaining their independence, saw in the Beijing regime a source of help separate from the two poles of world influence. Yet another element employed by the PRC in an effort to influence others within its geographical sphere was the promotion of specific international events (such as the thwarted Second Conference of Afro-Asiatic Nations). The PRC also sought the backing of the developing countries in its attempts to recover its full rights in the United Nations (simultaneously with its efforts to isolate the Taiwan regime)(17). In any event, the aid granted by the PRC has expanded from a regional and almost border focus (North Korea, Mongolia, and Vietnam), to a global one, with greater concentration of interests in Sub-Saharan Africa, North Africa, the Middle East, Asia, and Southeast Asia.

With respect to the internal factors, it is sufficient to point out, for the purposes of this study, that internal and external economic conditions have not been of a determining nature in the choice of countries to receive aid from Beijing. This is affirmed by the fact that such aid, in many cases, has been granted to countries with a higher per capita income than that estimated for the PRC. Another example is the fact that, during the critical moments in the PRC's economy, such as the 1959-1962 period, the flow of aid to the exterior was not suspended.

The cooperation granted by the PRC has been of two kinds: military and economic. This aid has gone to other socialist states as well as to developing nations with political systems different from that of China and fairly heterogeneous themselves. With respect to the level of capital exports, there are no officials statistics available, and we only estimate this through the information from the recipient countries and from the press communiques on bilateral agreements between Beijing and other governments. Little is known, for example, of the extent of the PRC's aid to Vietnam or Albania, although judging from what was revealed by both of these parties in the recent conflicts which resulted in the suspension of all Beijing cooperation with Hanoi and Tirana, its amount was considerable, regardless of whether one of the parties tried to exaggerate such an amount and the other to minimize it.

Various institutions and persons have been trying to determine with greater precision the flow of PRC aid to the rest of the world. However, it will not be until the government of that nation decides to make public such information that we can be sure of the facts. Meanwhile, an approximate idea of PRC foreign aid may be found in table 5.2. Both sections of the table cover the same period and their results do not greatly differ with regard to the amount of financial

Table 5.2. People's Republic of China: Total Aid
by Area to December 1975
(in millions of U.S. dollars)

"A"

| Area | Aid Promised | | Aid Delivered | | | |
| | | | Low Estimate | | High Estimate | |
	($)	(%)	($)	(%)	($)	(%)
Communist Bloc	1,352.25	30.1	3,110.0	76.1	6,340.0	67.2
Developing Nations of which:	3,102.40	69.0	970.0	23.8	3,070.0	32.5
Asian Nations	933.70	20.8	440.0	10.8	1,600.0	17.0
Middle East Nations	518.20	11.5	120.0	2.9	420.0	4.4
African Nations	1,488.50	33.1	400.0	9.8	1,000.0	10.6
Latin American Nations	162.00	3.6	10.0	0.3	50.0	0.5
European Nations	40.00	0.9	5.0	0.1	25.0	0.3
TOTAL	4,494.65	100.0	4,085.0	100.0	9,435.0	100.0

People's Republic of China: Economic and Military Aid
to Less Developed Countries, 1955-1975
(in millions of U.S. dollars)

"B"

| Total | | Economic Aid | | Military Aid | |
| Committed | Dispersed | Committed | Dispersed | Committed | Dispersed |
$	%	$	%	$	%	$	%	$	%	$	%
4,415	100	2,185	100	3,840	87	1,660	76	575	13	525	24

Source: Elaborated from statistics presented by John Franklin
Cooper, China's Foreign Aid (Lexington, Mass.: Lexington
Books, 1976), p. 23; and CIA, Communist Aid to Less Devel-
oped Countries of the Free World, 1954-1976, Washington,
D.C., October 1976, pp. 1 and 5.

resources granted by the PRC to other Third World Countries: $3,102.4 million of committed aid and $3,070 million of aid disbursed (in the high calculation of Cooper),(18) and $4,415 million committed against $2,185 million disbursed (according to the CIA's calculations). Many other estimates exist, which mostly fluctuate around $5,000 million in Chinese promised financial aid to developing countries.

Comparisons of the above figures with the transfer of resources by capitalist developed countries to the underdeveloped regions give a very disproportionate picture in absolute terms and is of relatively little use. The fact is that, although the PRC is a country with world political influence, its present resources and stage of economic development are much lower than those of the OECD countries. Moreover, if we take into consideration the amount of foreign aid given by the PRC in relation to its own economy (statistics are not available to calculate the relation between foreign aid and GNP in the case of the PRC), the least that can be affirmed is that very few donor nations in the world show a greater effort than that made by the PRC in giving aid. Furthermore, it must be remembered that the estimated amount of PRC foreign aid is most probably below the actual amount, particularly when the cooperation in nonmonetary terms (training of foreigners in the PRC and assigning technicians and workers abroad, for example) is taken into consideration, as well as the aid granted to other socialist regimes such as North Korea, Vietnam, Kampuchea, Laos, and Albania, for which we do not have exact information.

However, with the somewhat fragmentary data available, we can draw some conclusions as to the characteristics of PRC aid. One of these is that more than three quarters of the cooperation designated for developing nations is of an economic nature and only a small percentage is earmarked for military purposes. This is partly explained by the PRC's limited capacity for developing modern and sophisticated weaponry. Another characteristic is that, with regard to the level of committed aid, the Third World would receive twice as much as other communist countries. However, when the comparison is made with regard to delivered aid levels, the proportion is inverted (see table 5.2). This is probably due to the greater capacity of the communist regimes to absorb the resources placed at their disposal by Beijing, given the similarity in organizational systems, standardization, and the way in which the factors of production are allocated. Finally, we can observe greater importance given to the African nations within the group of developing countries when it is a question of promised aid; and the relative greater importance of the Asian states, in terms of aid delivered. Again, geographical and cultural "distance" explains those differences.

During Zhoe Enlai's visit to Mali in 1964, he gave a speech in which, among other things, eight principles for granting aid to other nations were defined. Such principles are still officially invoked and they can be summarized as follows:

1. In offering aid, the Chinese government bases its ideas on the concept of mutual equality and benefit, and never considers such

action as an expression of unilateral goodwill but, rather, as something which is bilaterally useful and which will promote economic cooperation;

2. The Beijing government strictly respects the sovereignty and independence of the recipient nations, without attempting to impose conditions or privileges;

3. The PRC provides foreign aid in the form of loans free of interest or with a low interest rate, and is prepared to extend the amortization periods of such credits whenever this is necessary to alleviate the burden of debtor countries;

4. The objective of granting aid is not to make the recipient countries dependent on the PRC, but to help them to progress toward self-reliance and independence;

5. The purpose is to aid debtor countries in developing specific projects which require as little investment as possible and which are designed to yield positive results in the shortest possible period;

6. The Chinese must supply equipment and material of the best quality available in internal production at the current prices of the domestic market and, whenever necessary, such products may be substituted by others from internal production that may have better specifications or quality;

7. On granting a particular kind of technical assistance, the Beijing government will make sure that the personnel of the country receiving that assistance is totally familiar with the use of the technology involved;

8. When it is necessary for the PRC to send technical personnel to those countries to which aid is given, such personnel will strictly adjust to the standard of living in those countries, without demanding any special treatment or facilities.(19)

Much of this might seem to be pure rhetoric. However, the empirical evidence available and the experience of various governments that have negotiated economic cooperation agreements with the PRC show that the official PRC institutions apply this doctrine in a fairly extensive way.

Based on the above, some conclusions can be drawn with regard to the fundamental characteristics of economic aid granted by Beijing. To begin with, such aid is generally given for short or middle-term activities. It is directed to projects rather than programs, and is granted in a very selective way to those countries that are facing critical economic and political conditions, and as a gesture of goodwill. Taken together, these elements coincide with the criteria enunciated and they aim to obtain positive results in the shortest possible period, as well as to avoid prolonged intervention by the PRC in the economic affairs of its debtors.

Another important aspect of PRC economic aid is the favorable conditions under which it is granted, which undoubtedly fit the definition of "official development assistance" as conceived in the framework of the NIEO. Nevertheless, the application of those loans to the objectives outlined is largely carried out by acquiring PRC products, so the aid is very conditional or of a tied-character. In addition, we should point out the bilateral nature of Chinese aid, which is largely explained by the official nonparticipation of that nation's government in the regional and international institutions or agencies in charge of distributing economic cooperation multilaterally. This is also a result of the close link existing between the granting of aid and political objectives that could not be obtained in the same way were they to go through the multilateral mechanism.

In general, all countries concede that foreign economic aid imposes certain implicit or explicit conditions on the respective cooperation programs; for example, there is the determination of exclusive areas in which aid is to be given, norms of economic conduct and provision of information to be applied, as well as the requirements of the donors that a friendly attitude exist on the part of the receivers. This conception has been criticized several times by PRC officials for its colonialist nature and it is not explicitly adopted in any form by the Chinese themselves in their agreements. Nevertheless, to give aid, there are many ways of imposing conditions on cooperation without spelling them out in any contract.

It has been mentioned that a large part of PRC aid takes the form of goods and services which must be delivered with certain norms of quality and volume, and at prices prevailing in the PRC domestic market. These elements can be regulated by the authorities of that country, without such regulation being understood abroad. It is very probable that, due to certain manipulation, a sizable proportion of officially announced aid is never carried out due to unavailability of one particular product at a given moment, or because the price at which the product is offered is not suitable for the buying country (see Table 5.2). On the other hand, economic cooperation agreements are usually negotiated by Beijing in conjunction with other scientific and technological bilateral trade agreements, or with political agreements of nonaggression or a solution of border conflicts. The smallest financial negotiation entails the gathering of very high officials from the countries interested in obtaining aid, with their PRC counterparts and, on many occasions, that level involves heads of state or government.

Finally, it is obvious that the Beijing government is very sensitive to the status of its diplomatic relations with another government or to the possibility of establishing such relations when it is decided that aid will be granted to a certain developing nation. What is more, that sensitivity is often increased when it is a question of the level at which relations between concerned countries and the Soviet Union are closed. Examples of this are the recent cases of Chile, Zaire, Egypt, Pakistan, and Somalia, where Beijing speeded up its material aid to the respective leaders of these countries in times of serious difficulties or a split with Moscow. Another recent example is the suspension of aid to Vietnam for its identification with the Soviet position as well as for its specific attitude toward the PRC.

Before concluding this part of the study, it is necessary to review the PRC's situation with respect to trade relations with the Third World nations. Again, we find here a lack of official statistics on PRC foreign trade, and we need to have access to those foreign sources which, based on the data of third party countries, calculate the magnitude and regional distribution of such trade. In table 5.3, the PRC's trade balance from 1950 to 1977 is analyzed. The years are divided into four periods, and a distinction is made between trade carried out with communist countries on the one hand, and with noncommunist countries on the other.

The PRC's foreign trade was highly dynamic from 1950 to 1957 — a period during which the reconstruction of the country began, the Korean War took place, and the first five-year plan was carried out. In this stage, imports of capital goods and strategic inputs for production played an important role in growth strategy. To finance the trade deficit accumulated in those eight years — $855 million — the PRC had to make use of foreign loans, borrowing mainly from the Soviet Union. The loans, obtained through a series of bilateral agreements with the Soviet Union, have been estimated at $1.4 billion, of which $1 billion was economic aid.(20) With these external resources it was possible to carry out a period of intense industrialization which was supposed to promote enough exports to pay for foreign economic and technical assistance.(21)

The average annual growth rate of foreign trade was then 12.3 percent, in spite of the fact that, during the first two years of the period analyzed, production capacity was very seriously affected by the recently-ended civil war. More than three-fifths of the PRC's trade was carried out with communist countries, particularly with the USSR, and the remaining 36 percent was with the noncommunist countries, both developed and less developed. The PRC's economy was quite open with respect to the communist bloc; thus, the country accumulated an overall deficit, at least in terms of balance of trade. (There is not enough information of the other items to estimate balance of payments.) Such a deficit was, for the whole period 1950-57, $885 million, of which 72 percent was the imbalance vis-à-vis communist countries.

Another period, 1958 to 1965, was characterized by a severe decrease in PRC foreign trade. During 1962-63, trade fell below the levels of the previous seven years (see table 5.3). The suspension of Soviet aid and the political divergences with that country, along with the "Great Leap Forward," affected adversely the economy and the composition of foreign trade; exchanges with communist and noncommunist countries were almost in a similar proportion with only a small margin of predominance of the former bloc. The lack of external support and the recession that the domestic economy suffered forced the leadership in Beijing to develop a different policy of development. Economic growth would be achieved with nationally available resources; and, although this policy of self-reliance did not imply full autarky, imports of capital goods and other requirements were to be limited by the capacity of export earnings — without resorting to any foreign debt.

Table 5.3. People's Republic of China: Balance of Trade
(in millions of U.S. dollars)[1]

	1950 – 1957		1958 – 1965		1966 – 1970		1971 – 1977	
	$	%	$	%	$	%	$	%
1. Total Trade[1]	18,855		27,605		20,165		78,095	
Exports	9,000	100.0	14,535	100.0	10,270	100.0	39,775	100.0
Imports	9,855	100.0	13,070	100.0	9,845	100.0	37,310	100.0
Balance	-855		1,465		425		2,465	
2. Communist Countries	12,200	64.7	14,590	52.8	4,405	21.8	13,760	17.6
Exports	5,795	64.4	8,290	57.0	2,540	24.7	7,245	19.5
Imports	6,410	65.0	6,290	48.1	1,865	18.1	6,020	15.7
Balance	-615		2,000		675		1,725	
3. Noncommunist Countries	6,650	35.3	13,025	47.2	15,760	78.2	64,330	82.4
Exports	3,205	35.6	6,245	43.0	7,730	75.3	32,035	80.5
Imports	3,445	35.0	6,780	51.9	8,030	81.1	32,295	84.3
Balance	-240		-535		-300		-260	
Average[2] Annual Rate of Growth of Total Trade		12.3		0.4		0.4		17.7

[1]Data were reorganized from a yearly basis into the periods shown in the Table, therefore the components may not add to the correct totals.

[2]Figures were calculated from the yearly figures – initial and final values – and according to the usual method of calculating the average annual rate of growth.

68

In table 5.3 it can be seen that part of this shift in economic strategy is evidenced by the accumulated trade surplus of 1958-65, obtained primarily from the exchange with other communist countries.

The last two periods are not comparable with the previous ones. However, these divisions are significant since they include important political events. The first period (1966-70), during which the Sino-Soviet dispute was accentuated and the old confrontation with the United States persisted, was one of isolation from the exterior, people's war diplomacy, and inward concerns. The average yearly rate of growth of total foreign trade from 1966 to 1970 was similar to the 1958-65 period (table 5.3), but without the drastic reductions in absolute figures from year to year. During that time, the percentage of trade with communist and noncommunist nations continued to be modified, favoring the latter (78 percent of the total and an accumulated deficit of $300 million).

The second period, from 1971 to 1977, refers to the opening up of the PRC to the West – more precisely, to the noncommunist countries, both developed and developing. The average annual monetary rate of growth to total trade was 17.7 percent; and, although the PRC incurred an accumulated deficit of $260 million with the noncommunist countries, her favorable balance with the communist nations overcame this.

During the period 1973-1977, the PRC had unfavorable trade balances with Japan, Western Europe, the United States, and Canada. Only with Australia and New Zealand did it register a considerable surplus. However, altogether, the PRC bought more from the capitalist developed markets of the world than it sold to them. With the Soviet Union, there was fairly balanced trade, although with Eastern Europe as a whole the PRC had a favorable balance, and also a surplus of 3 to 1 with communist countries in the Far East. Overall, the PRC is a net exporter of goods to developing countries, except those in Latin America where it had a deficit in the years considered. The main buyers of PRC products are Southeast Asia, South Asia, Africa, and the Middle East.

The probable trend of PRC trade in the near future, in the light of the 1977 and 1978 trade and financial agreements, is for a rapid growth of commercial exchanges with Japan and Western Europe and with the United States. The ambitious targets of the "Four Modernizations" which would place the PRC among the economic world powers by the end of the century, as well as Beijing's rift with the Soviet Union and the communist bloc (with the exception of Romania), make it possible to assume that the economic interdependence of the PRC may be increasing with respect to the capitalist developed countries. Somehow, Beijing will continue expanding its ties with the less developed nations of the Third World, given the crucial role that the PRC leadership still assigns to Asia, Latin America, and Africa, the perceived need to counterbalance Soviet political and ideological influence, and the PRC tradition of activism in the Third World.

To substantiate this belief, we only have to recall the medium-term trade agreement (eight years) finalized in 1980 between China and

Japan, to exchange US$20,000 million of products, which will even further accentuate the PRC's economic interdependence with a country which now represents a major market. It is obvious that the capital goods and advanced technology sought by Beijing will not be found in the developing countries, nor for political reasons, in selected advanced communist countries.

It is worth pointing out that, in accordance with the data available, from 1950 to 1977, the People's Republic of China generally had a favorable trade balance of approximately $1,475 million, while the economic aid granted by this country is estimated $9,435 million of which $1,800 to $2,200 million has been allotted to the noncommunist developing countries (round figures taken from tables 5.2, parts A and B, and 5.3). Even when this calculation is only an approximation, it gives us an idea of the strength of the Chinese regime when participating in world economic relations as net contributor of financial cooperation, in competition with other, more developed states which count on capital surplus. It is very possible that other aspects of the PRC's balance of payments (such as income for remittances from abroad, services, etc.) show positive balances. Otherwise, we could not explain the origin of the resources which the PRC transfers abroad in the form of aid.

Keeping aside the political considerations of the PRC's strategy of strong cooperation with other developing countries, as well as the impact that the recent "punitive" military action of Beijing against its former close "comrade-in-arms" – the Socialist Republic of Vietnam – might have on such strategy, it is necessary to say something about the economic potential for the PRC to maintain in the future its unique role of being a developing country as well as net exporter of aid.

In his report to the Fifth National People's Congress (February 1978) Mr. Hua Quofeng, Chairman of the CCP's Central Committee and Prime Minister of the State Council, outlined the 10-year economic plan (1976-1985) to accomplish the first step of the modernization and development of the PRC which is a "gigantic task"(22) laid down by Zhou Enlai "acting on Chairman Mao's instructions" shortly before the death of both leaders. The long-run goal is to put the PRC economy "in the front ranks of the world" by the end of the twentieth century.

The basic goals of such a plan are to increase the value of the agricultural output by 4 to 5 percent a year and of industrial output by over 10 percent. The former sector should achieve 85 percent mechanization and an output of 400 million tons of grain by 1985 – among other things. In industry, 120 large-scale projects in iron and steel, nonferrous metal complexes, coal, oil, gas, utilities, and others should be completed.

Leaving aside the discussion of the possibilities for the PRC to succeed in accomplishing the plan, it is important for the purposes of this chapter to say something about the impact of rapid growth and modernization of the PRC economy upon the traditional concept of "self-reliance" and upon the PRC foreign trade-financial relations.

Although neither the Prime Minister's speech nor the PRC press are explicitly abandoning the principle of "self-reliance," there have been practical decisions and theoretical discussions that indicate important changes in the meaning and implementation of the policy of "self-reliance." It is true that such a concept does not suggest that autarky has to be the way in which China should develop its economy; it has, rather, been a concept that literally means "regeneration through one's own efforts."(23) This implies that the process of economic trans-formation should be done basically with domestic resources and without foreign debt, or at least without a big one. (In fact, the Beijing government emphasized until recently that the economic development was achieved with no external debt.)

But once the main goal of economic policy becomes to increase the rate of growth and to promote modernization of the country, the option to return to certain levels of foreign indebtedness becomes more attractive. It is clear that the PRC leadership is ready to "make the foreign things to serve national interest,"(24) especially when China's import capacity is limited by its export earnings which, in turn, will continue to be dominated by the export of oil, other raw materials, and light manufactures. In order to avoid foreign trade becoming a severe bottleneck in the desired future economic development, the PRC has to accept a certain limit on capital inflows (foreign debt).

So far, the Beijing government has concluded agreements involving direct borrowing for longer terms than usually preferred, as well as barter and other similar agreements. There are even indications that Beijing is ready to negotiate some forms of joint venture agreements with foreign firms, but these intentions have been only vaguely voiced.

In the period 1971 to 1977, the PRC's trade surplus was $1.5 billion. This figure gives only an approximation of reality since nothing is said about aid commitments abroad, or payments abroad for capital and other services (conversely, there is nothing said of income from the same issues). In view of the lack of official data, it is necessary to work with figures given by "third-party" sources and to depend on incomplete information. Bearing in mind these constraints, it is worth noticing that, in spite of the above-mentioned eight-year surplus, the PRC had to incur some indebtedness, according to a recent study. The PRC had an outstanding debt of $1.3 billion for 1977, which represented a "ratio of debt service to hard currency of only 8 percent," a light burden if it is compared with the accumulated trade surplus of 1971-77, or with the ratios found for other developing nations.(25)

Nevertheless, if at present the PRC appears to have no serious troubles with international liquidity, the future trend seems to be a more pessimistic one. The PRC has concluded several long-term trade agreements, and has contracted for the purchase of complete or "turn-key" projects which require increasing amounts of hard currency – provided by either major exports of goods and services or foreign credits. To give an idea of these requirements, take the following cases: The eight-year agreement with Japan(26) calls for an exchange of $20 billion divided into an equal amount of PRC exports (mainly coal and oil) and Japanese sales of plants and equipment. There are similar long-term agreements for the PRC to supply oil to Brazil and to the

Philippines; and, between 1973 and 1977, the PRC signed an agreement with eight capitalist developed countries (see table 5.4) for the purchase of plants in an amount of $3.6 billion, and for a variety of products. All this may affect the capacity of China to maintain a level of credit and aid of other developing nations.

Looking at the future, the situation appears more complex not only in relation to the PRC's role as an aid-donor nation, but also in the expectations that it will be be a big borrower in the international capital market. According to a forecast for the PRC economy for 1975-85 (and assuming that there will be no dramatic changes in the "current [PRC] policy regarding foreign borrowing or investments and the desired level of self-dependency")(27) the PRC's exports and imports will grow at an annual rate of 5 to 6 percent. This coincides with the trend of the last 25 years. If this should happen, then no important change should be expected in the PRC dual position as a moderate borrower and moderate capital lender. But if the PRC really wants to achieve all or the majority of its development targets, then the picture will be different because of the requirements of foreign capital.

There have been many figures and speculations of the most likely total capital required for the PRC to fulfill its economic plan, but Japanese experts have recently estimated the cost of the ten-year economic program of the PRC to be around $250 billion for the entire period.(28) The foreign trade figures have also been revised. Some more optimistic analysts believe that the PRC's exports will expand at an average annual rate of 20 percent, requiring the country to borrow only $25 to $50 billion which is a practical figure in terms of policy. If this late forecast is accurate, the PRC will be an active borrower in the international capital market but, eventually, may maintain some marginal activities as an aid giver. Furthermore, the main part of the PRC's economic interdependence (trade, capital, and technology) will be with the developed countries.

CHINA AND THE NIEO

Since its entry into the United Nations, the People's Republic of China has rhetorically supported all the initiatives coming from developing countries, particularly when these involve the majority of such nations. In its capacity as a permanent member of the Security Council, Beijing has censured the regimes of South Africa and Rhodesia for segregationist policies; backed the Arab countries and the Palestine Liberation Organization in their dispute with Israel; and, above all, actively promoted the formation of a common parliamentary front to oppose the "hegemony of the big powers."

These political positions have led to some contradictions which are derived from the Sino-Soviet dispute and the way in which some Third World countries are involved in it. Occasionally, PRC policy has had to opt for one particular side in detriment to the other when conflicts between developing nations have arisen. An example of the first case is

Table 5.4. People's Republic of China: Contracts
for Whole Plant Imports. January 1973–
September 1978

Nation/Firm	Type	Value in Millions of U.S. $	Con- tract Signed	Com- ple- tion	Comments
JAPAN					
Toyo Engineering	Ethylene + butadiene	50	2/73	1978	Japan Ex-Im/ Comm. bank financing
Toyo Engineering + Mitsui	Urea and Ammonia	42	4/73	N.A.	Japan Ex-Im/ Comm. bank financing
Toyo Engineering + Mitsui-Toatsu	Urea and Ammonia	43	9/73	N.A.	Japan Ex-Im/ Comm. bank financing
Mitsubishi	Ethylene + poval	34	2/73	N.A.	Japan Ex-Im/ Comm. bank financing
Mitsubishi	Polyethylene low pressure	22	7/73	1975	Japan Ex-Im/ Comm. bank financing
Mitsubishi	Friction materials	15	12/75	N.A.	Japan Ex-Im/ Comm. bank financing
Mitsubishi	Ethylene plant	10	6/78	N.A.	Japan Ex-Im/ Comm. bank financing
Asahi Chemical	Acrylonitrile monomer	30	3/73	N.A.	Japan Ex-Im/ Comm. bank financing
Asahi Glass	Brown glass plant	68	6/78	1981	for color TV tube plant
Kuraray	Vinyl acetate and poval	26	3/73	1976	Japan Ex-Im/ Comm. bank financing

Table 5.4. (Cont.)

Nation/Firm	Type	Value in Millions of U.S. $	Con-tract Signed	Com-ple-tion	Comments
Kuraray	Polyvinyl alcohol	19	2/74	1976	Japan Ex-Im/ Comm. bank financing
Kuraray	Steel mill technology	32	5/78	1982	
Toray + Mitsui Shipbuilding	Polyster chips	50	5/73	1976	Japan Ex-Im/ Comm. bank financing
Sumitomo	Benzene, toluene + xylene	5	5/73	N.A.	Cash deal
Sumitomo	Polyethelene high pressure	47	8/73	1976	Japan Ex-Im/ Comm. bank financing
Hitachi Ltd.	2 thermal electric power plants	72	9/73	1975	Japan Ex-Im/ Comm. bank financing
Hitachi Ltd.	Color TV tube plant	75	7/78	1981	
Nippon Steel and Hitachi Ltd.	Hot strip rolling mill + silicon steel plate	299	6/74	1977	Demag supplying other part of the complex
Nippon Steel	Ancillary equip- ment for steel plate	65	10/74	1977	for prehot strip mill
Nippon Seiko	Spherical bearings	3	4/75	1976	Progress payments
Nippon Steel	Desulfurization plant	26	6/76	N.A.	
Nippon Steel	Steel mill technology	78	5/78	1980	

Table 5.4. (Cont.)

Nation/Firm	Type	Value in Millions of U.S. $	Con-tract Signed	Com-ple-tion	Comments
Mitsui	Cinder pelletizing	14	8/76	N.A.	
Nisso Petrochemical	Ethylene glycol	15	12/73	1977	Japan Ex-Im/ Comm. bank financing
Mitsui Petrochemical + Mitsui Ship-building	Polypropylene	25	10/73	1977	Japan Ex-Im/ Comm. bank financing
Nisso Petrochemical	Synthetic fiber	14	3/74	1976	
Teijin	Polyester spinning	16	1/74	N.A.	Japan Ex-Im/ Comm. bank financing
Teijin	Polyester/ polymer	40	3/76	N.A.	Teijin + Nissho-niwai 5-yr. Japan Ex-Im Comm. bank financing; 80,000 ton/yr capacity
Toho Titanium	Polypropylene catalyst	5	1/74	N.A.	catalyst for Mitsui poly-propylene plant
Toyo Seiko	Cylindrical bearings	8	4/75	1976	Progress payment
Ibigawa	Laminated board	1	7/75	N.A.	
Ataka	Air separation	11	11/75	1977	Progress payment 35,000 cc.mts/ hour capacity
Japan Gasoline	Aromatic complex	36	12/75	N.A.	
Japan Synthetic Rubber	Styrene-butadiene rubber	27	2/76	N.A.	With Mitsubishi and Japan gasoline, 5-yrs Japan Ex-Im/Comm. bank financing; 240,000 tons/yr capacity

Table 5.4. (Cont.)

Nation/Firm	Type	Value in Millions of U.S. $	Con- tract Signed	Com- ple- tion	Comments
Maruberi + Japan Gasoline	Ethylene plant	200	7/78	1981	
Kyokuto Boeki Kaisha	Hot scafer/ kilm	10	3/76	N.A.	
Makajima Seiki	Wallpaper plant	1	4/76	N.A.	With Kumiai Boeki Company
Chiyoda	Natural gas refining	20	11/77	1980	5-yrs Japan Ex-Im/Comm. bank financing
Dainippon Tokyo	Phosphorous plant	10	6/78	1981	for color TV tube plant
Dainippon Screen	Shadow mask plant	11	6/78	1981	Color TV tube plant
Toshiba + Hitachi	Integrated circuit plant	53	8/78	1981	Color TV tube plant
Tokyo Electric Power Services	Thermal power plant	2	8/78	1980	Design and construction contract
Nikki Engineering + Nippon Polyrethane	Synthetic leather base materials	37	9/78	1981	
TOTAL (Japan)		1667			
FRANCE					
Alsthom	Hydroelectrical turbines (2)	10	2/73	N.A.	
Speichem	Vinylacetate	90	5/73	1976	Consortium of France, W. Ger. and U.K.
Technip + Speichem	Petrochemical complex	300	9/73	N.A.	probably involving other W. Europe firms

Table 5.4. (Cont.)

Nation/Firm	Type	Value in Millions of U.S. $	Con-tract Signed	Com-ple-tion	Comments
Heurtey	Ammonia + urea complex (2)	120	2/74	1977	5-yrs credit financing
Electromechanique	Thermal electric plant	41	4/74	1976	
Rhone Poylene	Nylon spinning	10	8/74	1977	progress payments
TOTAL (France)		571			
WEST GERMANY					
Friedrich Uhde + Hoechst	Acetaldehyde	4	7/73	N.A.	
Uhde	Vinyl chlori-monomer	19	1/74	1976	
Uhde	Polyethylene	15	3/74	1976	
Uhde	Ethanol	20	1/76	N.A.	100,000 metric tons/yr
Uhde	Petrochemical plants (5)	105	4/78	N.A.	
Demag	Cold rolling mill	200	3/74	1977	Consortium of European firms led by Demag
Demag	Continuous casting mill	57	8/74	1977	Part of steel complex purchased from Japan and Germany. Progress payments
Brown Boveri	Electrical Sub station	5	8/74	1977	
Linde	Benzene	20	7/75	N.A.	

Table 5.4. (Cont.)

Nation/Firm	Type	Value in Millions of U.S. $	Con-tract Signed	Com-ple-tion	Comments
Krupp	Dimethylther-ephthalate	50	12/75	N.A.	Progress payments, 90,000 metric tons/yr
Siemens	Turbine	6	12/75	N.A.	
BASF	Diethylhexonol	24	3/76	N.A.	50,000 metric tons/year
Kraus Maffei	High reactive lime	7	8/76	N.A.	
Zimmer	Polyester fiber and film	12	6/77	1980	
Lurgi	Terephthalic acid	27	6/77	1980	U.S. technology from Amoco
TOTAL (West Germany)		571			
UNITED KINGDOM					
Technicolor Ltd.	Motion picture processing	8	7/73	N.A.	cash deal
Rolls Royce	Jet engine plant	200	12/75	1980	50 jet engines plus manufacturing facilities and equip.
Davy Powergas	Oxoalcohol plants (2)	68	8/78	1981	
Dowty	Coal fence equipment	133	9/78	N.A.	
TOTAL (United Kingdom)		409			
UNITED STATES					
M.W. Kellogg	Ammonia plants (3)	75	3/73	1976	probable feedstock plants for Dutch urea plant

Table 5.4. (Cont.)

Nation/Firm	Type	Value in Millions of U.S. $	Con- tract Signed	Com- ple- tion	Comments
M.W. Kellogg	Ammonia plants (5)	130	11/73	76-77	
Kaiser	Iron ore mines	5	9/78	N.A.	Developmental contract
TOTAL (United States)		210			
ITALY					
G.I.E.	Electrical thermal power plants (2)	79	11/73	N.A.	5-yrs financing
SNAM Progretti	Polypropylene	16	1/74	N.A.	Progress payments
Mechaniche Moderne	Detergent	1	9/75	N.A.	Progress payments
Eurotechnica	Detergent alkalation	35	10/75	N.A.	Deferred payment
Nuovo Pignone	Centrifugal compressor technology	8	7/76	N.A.	
TOTAL (Italy)		139			
NETHERLANDS					
Kellogg Continental	Urea plants (3)	34	2/73	1976	Subsidiary of M.W. Kellogg
Kellogg Continental	Urea plants (5)	55	9/73	1977	Subsidiary of M.W. Kellogg
TOTAL (Netherlands)		89			
DENMARK					
Haldor Topsoe	Ammonia catalyst	13	12/73	N.A.	
TOTAL (Denmark)		13			

Table 5.4. (Cont.)

Nation/Firm	Type	Value in Millions of U.S. $	Con- tract Signed	Com- ple- tion	Comments
FINLAND					
Tamglass	Automobile glass plant	N.A.	N.A.	N.A.	
GRAND TOTAL		3530			

N.A. Not Available

Source: Data collected by National Foreign Assessment Center (CIA), China: International Trade, issues Dec. 1976, 1977, and 1978 (this reference refers to an annual report — not a book).

the PRC's political attitude to Cuba's participation in specific African countries, while an example of the second is the PRC's veto of Bangladesh's entry into the United Nations in 1972.

In spite of such situations, the image which the People's Republic of China has attempted to project, that of a solid ally of the causes of Third World countries, has not been greatly impaired and, in general, the PRC enjoys support and prestige among most of the Third World countries. Recent events, such as the controversy of the present Beijing leadership with the government of Albania (an apparently steadfast ally) or the more serious conflict and "punitive" border war against Vietnam, have provoked unrest, principally among the political parties and left wing movements in various countries of the developing regions. Nevertheless, at the governmental level, there does not seem to be a decline in PRC popularity. Greater participation in the international economy and the recent opening up abroad are indications that state interests will prevail over ideological considerations in that country's relations with the rest of the world.

With respect to economic questions, the Beijing government's official position continues to be the same as that defined by leaders who are no longer in office. In his speech before the 33rd Session of the United Nations General Assembly, China's Minister of Foreign Affairs ratified the line of conduct followed by his country in recent years, one of support for the principles established in the Sixth Special Session of the General Assembly in 1974; and he explicitly reaffirmed that

The Chinese government decidedly supports . . . the reasonable proposals . . . formulated by the developing countries, such as the integrated commodities programme and their common fund, the reduction or cancellation of debts, the increase in funds for development and the improvement of the conditions for technology transfer, with a view to promoting the development of production and the scientific and technological progress of these countries.(29)

An additional policy statement on the NIEO can be found in the speech by Han Nianlong (chairman of the Chinese Delegation to the 34th Session of the General Assembly). That speech was given on September 27, 1979, and the relevant excerpt has been placed in the Appendix to this chapter.

An important gap exists between the support which the PRC gives to the Third World countries, and the adoption of specific measures that will help to speed up progress toward a more equitable and just international economic order. This does not mean that Beijing has not done anything concrete in this respect. It is sufficient to recall the financial aid granted to different developing countries under conditions with regard to the cost of aid, its extension, flexibility of payments, no direct political imposition, etc., which equal or go beyond the goals announced within the framework of the NIEO. On a multilaterial level, the positive role of the Beijing officials must be considered in their participating in UNCTAD III, UNCTAD IV, and the Sixth Special Session of the U.N. General Assembly.

The PRC's contribution to the NIEO has been, until now, only one of moral support for the reforms proposed, and not specific support measures. This is largely explained by the fact that the main resolutions adopted up to now, with respect to the world economy and development, deal primarily with the relations between noncommunist developing countries and capitalist developed ones. Such is the case with regard to the Generalized System of Preferences, or of the annulment of foreign debt, and the proposal that the rich nations should transfer at least 0.75 percent of their GNP to the poor ones, in the form of official development assistance.

However, as the PRC is a nondeveloped socialist community, its capacity to influence world trends in financial and technological transfer is limited in relation to other countries.(30) What is more, its foreign trade is directed more and more toward Japan, Western Europe, Canada, Australia, and New Zealand, and, of course, the United States. In addition, a rapid shift in policy is taking place from the stance in which domestic resources alone were relied on for economic development (regardless of the speed at which development took place), to the present attitude under which the PRC is speeding up its economic development. It is very probable – as was mentioned before – that the PRC will, in the future, receive a growing amount of capital from abroad. Thus, the case of the PRC becomes more complex and is, of course, different from that of other aid exporting countries.

Bearing in mind the economic constraints on the behavior of the Beijing government in relation to the NIEO, it is reasonable to assume that the PRC will continue to follow the same line in the future, that is, giving moral support for the principles of the NIEO, while having a limited concrete capacity to effect the reforms adopted by the United Nations. Even within these limits, the participation of the PRC in the parliamentary debates on NIEO is of great importance, due to the political role that the PRC plays in the international system as a whole; a role that the present Beijing leadership wants to enhance.

Though the PRC is considered a developing nation, it is of interest to note its decision not to formally enter the Group of 77, to which it was invited at UNCTAD III (1972). This policy has been explained by Beijing representatives on the grounds of convenience for the 116 state members of the Group, since the PRC can strongly support the goals of the Group without attaching itself to their collective decisions. Since the entry of the PRC to the United Nations was a matter of representation rather than admission,(31) it was simply considered a member of Group A in UNCTAD in place of Taiwan. Yet the Beijing delegation has always played, since it became a member of UNCTAD, a separate and independent role, yet one that is supportive of the Group of 77.(32)

The division into groups does not strictly correspond to the concept of economic blocs — the mere existence of these blocs would be contrary to the spirit of a more just and dependable international economic order. Rather, the division represents a separation between economically developed areas and the less developed ones. At the same time, it takes into account the existence of different economic and social systems. Futhermore, Groups B and D represent other homogeneous characteristics; Group B is made up of the OECD developed countries, many of which are part of a common military alliance (NATO), or of the EEC. In Group D we have the countries which participate in the Warsaw Pact and in COMECON. Under these circumstances, it is understandable why the PRC has remained an entity apart and unassimilable by any of the other groups, in spite of the fact that, regionally, it is part of Asia, as well as being a socialist developing country.

In any case, what is important for the developing nations is that the PRC actively contributes to the discussions and negotiations on the NIEO, just as it did in concrete cases in the Declaration on Environment (Conference of Stockholm), or in the elaboration of the Charter of Economic Rights and Duties of States. Its moral support will be much more useful in finding future solutions to the prevailing problems of the international economic system, provided such support is expressed by the participation of Beijing delegations in the different commissions and work groups, in which specific aspects of the NIEO are discussed.

We must not forget, however, the increasing participation by the PRC in world economic activities, since this will have repercussions in one form or another on the whole system. One can cite as an example the situation of the world market of capital and international aid flows. Until Beijing obtains access to official foreign loans for its development, or to credits from the specialized international organizations — e.g., World Bank, IMF, Asian Bank of Development — its position will continue to be that of a net giver of foreign aid, which signifies a favorable attitude toward the NIEO goals in matters of international aid.

The Beijing government is beginning to receive foreign capital from private sources as a result of its excellent credit rating and numerous foreign investors are turning to the new and promising PRC market. This has important significance for other developing countries, in that the PRC's presence, as a national receiver of private trade credits, could have repercussions on the availability of funds for loans, and on their cost. There are, as yet, no signs that this has taken place; but there is the possibility that the interests of various Third World nations and those of the PRC will diverge and compete on questions as concrete as the cost of world credits, their accessibility, the qualitative conditions on which these credits are granted, and other such factors. Thus, the PRC's participation in regional and international discussions will be fundamental as the Third World finds more favorable receptivity from the private suppliers of credit for their objectives of reform and rationalization.

This example can be extended to the transfer of technology, to international trade flows, to developing countries' more favorable access to the markets of developed countries, to sea freights, etc. On all these issues, active collaboration is required from the PRC and not just the sympathy of a nation which harbors almost a quarter of the world's population and whose government plays an outstanding role in world politics.

CONCLUSION

The main conclusion that can be drawn from this chapter is that the PRC plays so important a political and economic role in the world that all efforts made by the international community to change economic relations between rich and poor counrtries have to take into account the participation of the PRC if they are to succeed.

So far, the Beijing government has played an active role in strongly supporting the principles, programs, and codified behavioral norms embodied in the NIEO. Although the Beijing government has never submitted any written proposal or draft resolution for the NIEO, its representatives have taken an active part in the three basic elements of the NIEO in plenary sessions, committees, and special groups.(33)

In many respects, the PRC has projected its general political principles, such as self-reliance and independent development of national economies, through the resolutions of NIEO. This has developed into a kind of mutual legitimization of the Beijing conceptualization and participation in efforts to reshape the world economic order, and the conceptualization that the nations of the Third World have in this regard.

There are clear indications that Beijing is moving toward a period of intensive economic growth which will require foreign capital and technology. This opening of the PRC economy is obviously oriented toward the developed nations with whom there will be increase interdependence. This, in turn, will necessitate changes in the nature of the

PRC's relations with the Third World and also in connection with the future negotiations on the NIEO.

One example may aid in understanding the implications of this change. The PRC is increasingly active in the international capital market, particularly in the private capital market. At the end of March 1979, the Bank of China concluded its first loan not connected to any specific investment project or bilateral trade deal. It was a syndicated private bank credit of about $875 million. Only a few other developing nations, the so-called intermediate developed ones, are able to enter the commercial credit network, and probably none has the present credit capacity of the PRC. Yet, this country is not yet a member of the World Bank or the IMF, and it is also an important aid donor entity. Under such conditions, the participation of the PRC in the next negotiations on international finance, aid, and assistance issues in the NIEO has to be more specific than the general support given to the resolutions already adopted on these matters.

Something more could be said on other issues such as international trade, industrialization, and technology transfer, but it is better to wait until the coming UNCTAD V, to see specifically what the PRC's position will be in order to reach more objective conclusions.

NOTES

(1) See Mao Tse-tung "On the People's Democratic Dictatorship," Selected Works (Peking: Foreign Language Press, 1973), Vol. 4, p. 415.

(2) Ibid.

(3) In 1949, only one developing country (Burma) recognized and established relations with Beijing. In 1950 another four countries did the same (Afghanistan, Pakistan, Indonesia, and Sri Lanka). North Vietnam and Israel (the first Middle East state to recognize Mao's China) recognized the Beijing government, but without establishing diplomatic relations with it. In 1955, Nepal joined the list of relations; Egypt, Syria, and Yemen followed in 1956.

(4) These are: mutual respect for territorial integrity and sovereignty; no aggression; no interference in the internal affairs of each country; equality and mutual benefits; and peaceful coexistence. In the conference of the 29 Afro-Asiatic nations in Bandung, two more principles were added: the right of peoples to freely choose their own politico-economic-social systems; and the right to abstain from inflicting injury upon nations.

(5) Quoted in B.D. Armstrong, "People's China," Revolutionary Diplomacy: Chinese Foreign Policy and the United Front Doctrine (Los Angeles: University of California Press, 1977), p. 73.

(6) The Treaty of Friendship, Alliance and Mutual Assistance between the People's Republic of China and the Union of Soviet Socialist Republics, signed in 1950 and with a duration period of 30 years, has been, in the last years, only a dead letter; but it is still technically in force. On April 3, 1979, the PRC announced officially that it will not ask for an extension of the pact beyond April 11, 1980, when it will formally expire.

(7) Between December 1963, and February 1964, Zhou Enlai accompanied by the then Minister for Foreign Affairs, Chen Yi, and other high officials, visited the following countries: Egypt, Algiers, Morocco, Tunisia, Ghana, Mali, Guinea, Sudan, Ethiopia, and Somalia.

(8) In October 1964, the first nuclear test was carried out in the PRC; in June 1967, the first explosion of a hydrogen bomb took place.

(9) See extracts from Lin Biao's speech, "Long Live the Victory of People's War," quoted in Alan Lawrence, China's Foreign Relations Since 1949 (London and Boston: Routledge and Kegan Paul, 1975), pp. 181-85.

(10) For a history of China's aid to revolutionary movements, see Peter Van Ness, Revolution and Chinese Foreign Policy (Berkeley: University of California Press, 1970); and Jay Taylor, China and Southeast Asia, exp. ed. (New York: Praeger, 1974).

(11) During a brief period the PRC had only one active ambassador abroad, in Cairo.

(12) Report on the Work of the Government presented by Zhou Enlai to the Fourth National People's Congress on January 13, 1975.

(13) In 1964, the Chinese talked of four spheres: United States' imperialism and Soviet revisionism as one extreme; the true socialist countries as another. Two intermediate spheres remain, one made up of the underdeveloped countries and another of the developed ones. Ten years later, Deng Xiaoping explained the theory of the three worlds in his speech before the Sixth Special Session of the United Nations General Assembly.

(14) Zhou Enlai consistently used this slogan which was preserved by Hua Guonfeng in his reports to the 11th National Congress of the CCP and the 5th National People's Congress.

(15) See, for example, the speech of Huang Hua, China's Minister of Foreign Affairs, at the 33rd session of the U.N. General Assembly. Peking Review No. 41, October 18, 1978.

(16) Madame Jiang Qing, widow of Chairman Mao; Wang Hongwen, Zhang Chungiao, and Yao Wenyuan.

(17) No automatic relationship exists between foreign aid and recognition of a determined international power. Nevertheless, this tendency can be seen: of 34 socialist and Third World countries that had received aid from the PRC until 1971, only four voted in favor of considering the PRC's entry into the U.N. and Taiwan's exclusion as an important matter, and two of these countries (Lon Nol's Cambodia regime and the Central African Republic) voted against the Albanian Resolution. On the other hand, 18 countries received initial Chinese aid during that same year or in the two subsequent years, on recognizing and establishing official relations with Beijing. (See John F. Cooper, China's Foreign Aid, Lexington, Mass.: Lexington Books, 1976, particularly tables 1-3 & 1-4, pp. 12-13.)

(18) John Franklin Cooper, China's Foreign Aid (Lexington, Mass.: Lexington Books, 1976).

(19) See Peking Review, No. 7, February 14, 1964, pp. 6-8.

(20) ". . . The loan program was phased so that between 1950 and 1955, China was a net recipient of Soviet credit; thereafter, repayments exceed new credits. The loans were finally paid off in 1965." Christopher Howe, China's Economy: A Basic Guide, (New York: Basic Books, 1978), p. 134.

(21) According to Howe, ibid., of the 291 large-scale production projects that were to be finished by 1967, only 130 were completed when Soviet economic cooperation was cancelled in 1959. The total value of these projects is estimated at $3.3 billion and what was, in fact, delivered was the sum of $1.35 billion.

(22) Published in the English Language Version by Peking Review, No. 10, March 10, 1978, pp. 7-40.

(23) See Samuel S. Kim, China, The United Nations, and World Order, (Princeton, N.J.: Princeton University Press, 1979), p. 227.

(24) For a comprehensive view of the economic strategy of the present leadership, see Hu Chiao-mu, "Observe Economic Laws, Speed up the Four Modernizations," Peking Review 21 (45) (November 10, 1978): 7-11; (46) (November 17, 1978): 15-23; (47) (November 24, 1978): 13-21.

(25) See China: International Trade, 1977-78, National Foreign Assessment Center (CIA), Washington, D.C., Dec. 1978, p. 5 and Tables A-12, A-13, (pp. 22-23).

(26) Concluded in Feb. 1978 and later extended for an additional five years.

(27) See China Economy Post-Mao: A Compendium of Papers, Vol. 1 "Policy and Performance," Joint Economic Committee, Congress of the United States – 95th Congress, Washington, D.C., November 1978, p. 32.

(28) A good synthesis of this prognosis is reported in Business Week, January 15, 1979, p. 48.

(29) See Huang Hua's speech, cited in note 15.

(30) Until 1965, according to some calculations, the United States had contributed approximately half of the aid granted – $30,000 million in economic aid and $33,000 million in military aid – while the socialist countries had contributed $8,000 million in economic aid and $3,500 million in military aid. In the same period, the PRC had contributed less than $1,000 million in economic cooperation.   Quoted by John F. Cooper, China's Foreign Aid (Lexington, Mass.: Lexington Books, 1976), p. 131.

(31) When UNCTAD was first established, the participant countries were divided into four categories: Group A, representing all countries of Asia (except Japan, plus Yugoslavia) and all African nations; Group B representing all the capitalist or so-called developed market economy countries; Group C integrated all Latin American and Caribbean countries; and Group D, USSR and all communist countries of Eastern Europe. Groups A & C formed the 77 bloc.

(32) For a detailed analysis of the PRC's role in the NIEO see Kim, China, the United Nations, and World Order, p. 37; and Samuel Kim, "Behavioral Dimensions of Chinese Multilateral Policy," The China Quarterly, no. 72, Dec. 1977, pp. 713-42.

(33) These elements, which were achieved after a long and complex process of negotiations, are: Declaration on the Establishment of the NIEO, The Programme of Action, and the Charter of Economic Rights and Duties of States.

APPENDIX TO CHAPTER FIVE

International Economic Problem*

The steady deterioration of international economic situation is one of the important factors making for international turbulence. Some developed countries, especially the superpowers, have used various means to shift the consequences of their economic crises and difficulties onto the developing countries so that the latter face worsening trading terms, mounting foreign debts and great difficulties in their economic development. The energy problem is an increasing concern of most countries. Many developing countries have pointed out that the root cause for all evils of the present international economy lies in the existing inequitable and irrational international economic order. Therefore, they strongly demand a fundamental restructuring of the international economic system. This demand is entirely just, being in the interest of the overwhelming majority of the people of the world.

Five years ago, thanks to the efforts of the developing countries, the Sixth Special Session of the General Assembly adopted The Declaration and Programme of Action on the Establishment of a New International Economic Order, which constitutes a basic document guiding economic negotiations and dialogues. Five years have passed, but how much progress has been made in these negotiations and dialogues? Very limited. They are mostly in an impasse. The reasons are clear to all. The most important reason is that the two superpowers have set up obstacles of all kinds. The obstacles have multiplied especially since the beginning of this year. At the Fifth Session of the UNCTAD and other international economic forums, many reasonable proposals made by the developing countries on changing the outdated international economic relations have thus been stalled. This unreasonable state of affairs cannot be allowed to continue. The developing countries have come to realize more and more that in order to achieve progress in the negotiations for the establishment of a new international economic order, they must strengthen their unity, uphold principles, persevere in struggle and energetically promote mutual economic assistance and cooperation. The Arusha Programme for Collective Self-Reliance and Framework for Negotiations adopted at the Ministerial Meeting of the Group of 77 held last February and the economic documents adopted at the recent Conference of the Heads of State and Government of the Non-Aligned Countries provide clear guidelines for promoting the economic co-operation among the developing countries and strengthening their negotiating positions with the developed countries, and they give expression to the common will and desire of the third

---

*Source: Speech by Mr. Han Nianlong, Chairman of the Chinese delegation to the 34th Plenary Session of the General Assembly, September 27, 1979, reprinted in Peking Review, no. 41 (October 12, 1979), pp. 19-20.

world countries. Thanks to the efforts of the developing countries, the recent U.N. Conference of Science and Technology for Development registered some preliminary results. We believe that the united struggle of the third world countries will secure continuous progress for the just cause of establishment of a new international economic order.

In order to bring about effective solutions to the international economic problems, recognition of the developing countries' full rights and true equality in decision-making in international economic affairs is essential. The correct way to settle pressing economic problems is for the developed countries and the developing countries to sit together for all-around consultation, break the present impasse, explore and adopt effective measures to narrow down the gap between the rich and poor countries and establish a new international economic relationship that is equitable, rational and based on equality and mutual benefit.

Having realized the importance of a constructive dialogue with the third world countries, a number of developed countries have in their bilateral or multilateral relations adopted positive measures, such as increasing their economic and scientific-technical aid and supporting the establishment of an integrated programme for commodities and its common fund. These measures are welcome. It is in the interest of the developed countries themselves to strengthen their co-operation with third world countries on the basis of respect for independence and sovereignty and genuine equality. Moreover, this will help advance the common cause of world peace and stability. We hope that more developed countries will understand the situation and favourably respond to the demands of the developing countries.

The Chinese Government sincerely hopes that the Special Session of the General Assembly scheduled to be held in 1980 at the suggestion of developing countries will make an important contribution in helping the economic development of the developing countries, establishing a new international economic order and formulating a new international strategy for development. The Chinese Government will work together with the other developing countries to that end.

6 The New International Economic Order and Industrialization in India
Nirmal K. Chandra

The New International Economic Order is generally recognized as a declaration for altering the existing balance of economic power between the industrialized countries and the Third World. By whittling down structures of dominance as exemplified by the transnational corporations (TNC), by negotiating for improved terms of trade for their exports of primary and other low-priced goods, and by increased technical and economic assistance through multinational agencies, the Third World countries hope to create a new world order which will enable their economies, particularly their industries, to develop at a much faster pace.

As long as the present structure of international economic relations continues, the vicious circle of low income, high unemployment, specialization in a narrow range of primary goods, and chronic shortages of foreign exchange – in short, all the characteristics of underdevelopment – will remain unchanged. It follows that any partial success in breaking one or more of the weaker links in the chain of dominance, e.g., the victory of the OPEC nations in raising the price of oil, should be welcomed.

Yet the very success of OPEC underlines the limitations of such a strategy. For it is by now well-known that the poorer sectors in these countries have not benefited to any appreciable extent and the lion's share of their revenues is either going back to the advanced countries for the supply of arms, capital goods, or consumer luxuries, or the unutilized funds are reinvested in government securities, private bonds, and assets through the intermediary of transnational banks. Many of the industries recently set up with Western know-how run at a low capacity, often lack domestic markets, and are unable to generate surpluses for self-propelled growth. In other words, a kind of enclave industrialization has started, which is only tenuously linked with the social, technological, and economic environments of these countries. As a result, the long-term dependence of these countries on Western imperialist powers has not materially declined.

To a considerable extent, this dependence syndrome is internalized by Third World countries. It pervades nearly every facet of the dominated country's culture, interspersed though it may be with the rhetoric of strident nationalism, religious dogma, distinctiveness of social institutions, or economic self-reliance. At the level of material culture – what goods are to be produced, by whom, in what manner, and how or by whom these will be appropriated – most of the Third World elite seem to be abjectly dependent on the latest ideas prevalent in developed countries. Much of this is reflected in the realm of technological policy.

In most of the literature, whether in the Third World or in the West, development is taken to be synonymous with modernization, i.e., adoption of up-to-date technologies in ever wider sectors of the national economy. By common consent, the know-how for these remains exclusively with the rich countries. Generally, it is available on payment which is not only for the know-how, but also for associated capital goods, intermediates, and sometimes even raw materials.

PER CAPITAL INCOME IN INDIA, 1900-1975

Since the end of the 1960s, Indian economists have been discussing the problems of stagnation in the national economy. Many economists believe that stagnation is rooted in some structural factors leading to a persistent demand recession. Previously, the sluggishness in growth was attributed in government publications to a whole host of extraneous factors, e.g., the unusual droughts of 1965-66 and 1966-67, the step-up in defense spending owing to the Indo-Pakistani War of 1965, the crisis over Bangladesh in 1971-72, or inadequacy of net foreign aid. Here, we shall present further data in support of the structuralist hypothesis.

In table 6.1 are data on per capita net material product (NMP) for the years 1900 to 1975. Not only Marxists, but many other perceptive scholars have felt that the standard Western practice of including the tertiary sector in the computation of national income is misleading, at least for less developed countries (LDCs). V.K.R.V. Rao, India's leading scholar in the field of national income studies, argued that

> whereas this   rise in the service sector's share   would be an indication of economic progress in the case of countries which record a sharp rise in the per capita figure of national income at constant prices, it is not equally a matter of satisfaction in the case of countries like India which show practically no change over two decades   between 1931-32 and 1951-52   in their per capita figure of national income at constant prices.(1)

Indeed, Sivasubramonian's study(2) indicated a rise of 163 percent in tertiary income between the five-yearly average levels of 1900-01 to 1904-05 and 1942-43 to 1946-47; over the same period the NMP (which may be defined as the sum of the net outputs of the primary and of the secondary factors) increased by a mere 39 percent.

Table 6.1. Per Capita Net Material Product of India,
1900-1975

Years	1938-39 constant Price (in rupees)	1960-61 constant Price (in rupees)
1900-01	39	206
1903-04	41	217
1910-11	43	227
1916-17	45	238
1924-25	43	227
1929-30	43	227
1930-31	43	227
1940-41	40	211
1946-47	38	201
1950-51	166	186
1956-57	183	204
1960-61	196	219
1964-65		232
1970-71		242
1975-76		241

Source: S. Sivasubramonian, "National Income of India, 1900-01 to
1946-47," Ph.D. dissertation, Delhi School of Economics,
1965; and various issues of the Economic Survey for the years
1950-51 onwards.

As indicated in table 6.1, there exist separate series for the years
1900-01 to 1946-47 according to Sivasubramonian, and the official
series for the years 1950-51 onwards. How does one link them? For
agriculture, we have used the Index Numbers of Harvest Prices of
Principal Crops in India.(3) For 1950-51, the index with 1938-39=100
stood at 558. For mining, manufacturing, electricity, gas, and water
supply, we were obilged to use the Economic Adviser's Index of
Wholesale Prices, assigning to semimanufactures and manufacturers the
same relative weight as in that index, i.e., 36 and 64 percent,
respectively.(4) Thus, at current prices, per capita NMP in 1950-51 was
177 rupees, which was equivalent to 35 rupees at 1938-39 prices or 186
rupees at 1960-61 prices. The ratio between the last two figures has
been used to link the prewar and postwar figures. In table 6.2, we have
chosen the peak year in each decade and the terminal years in each
series. Finally, it should be noted that the figures up to 1946-47 refer to
British India, while those from 1950-51 onward refer to postpartition
India.

If our procedure is correct, it follows that there is practically no
increase in per capita NMP over the period as a whole. The postwar
peak was reached in 1970-71 when the level was less than 2 percent
above that of 1916-17.(5)

Table 6.2. Per Capita Production of Foodgrains
and Consumption of Selected Articles,
1893-1975

			Consumption of Selected Articles				
Annual average for the years	Foodgrains production (kg)	Average Year	Cotton piece goods/ cloth (metres)	Manmade fibres (metres)	Kerosene (litres)	Sugar (kg)	Tea (kg)
	1		2	3	4	5	6
1891-92 to 1899-1900	214	1921-22	10.7	-	2.4	-	0.05
1900-01 to 1909-10	221	1929-30	14.6	-	3.5	3.8	0.09
1910-11 to 1919-20	221	1932-33	15.1	-	2.8	2.8	0.08
1920-21 to 1929-30	205	1938-39	15.0	-	2.7	2.9	0.12
1930-31 to 1939-40	171						
1955-56 to 1959-60	175						
1960-61 to 1964-65	183	1955-56	14.4	-	-	5.0	0.26
1965-66 to 1969-70	172	1964-65	15.2	1.6	-	5.1	0.31
1970-71 to 1974-75	183	1970-71	13.6	1.7	-	7.3	0.39
		1975-76	12.6	1.4	-	6.1	0.45

Table 6.2. (Cont.)

Source: For foodgrains production in col.(1): Calculated from G. Blyn,
           Agricultural Trends in India 1891-1947: Output, Availability
           and Productivity (Philadelphia: 1966), Appendix 3A; and for
           1955 onwards various issues of the Economic Survey were
           used. For the consumption figures in columns (2) to (6):
           Sivasubramonian, p. 351; and various issues of the Economic
           Survey.

Note: Blyn's foodgrains series does not include small millets or
           pulses other than gram. The post-independence figures would
           have to be reduced by about 10 percent to make them
           comparable with those calculated from Blyn's figures.

As a further check, table 6.2 refers to the production of foodgrains
and consumption of some important articles, both on a per capita basis.
The foodgrains data are the averages of the three initial years of the
Blyn study, the subsequent decade, and the last decades of the same
study. In the postindependence period, five-yearly averages are given
from the mid-1950s to the mid-1970s. The consumption figures, both
before and after independence, refer to the peak years only. These
figures in table 6.2 are too eloquent to need further comment; they
corroborate the plausibility of the stagnation in per capita real income
revealed in table 6.1.

It may not be out of place to cite another study by A.K. Bagchi(6)
seeking to show that the per capita gross domestic material product in
Bengal and Bihar around 1794 was 15.8 rupees or 47.4 rupees at 1900
prices, whereas Sivasubramonian's estimate of NMP per capita for
British India in 1900-01 at current prices was only 32.6 rupees. Thus,
there was a decline of nearly a third over the hundred odd years. Given
the possibilities of large year-to-year fluctuations, we cannot rely too
much on the one-point estimate for 1794. In all probability, there was a
significant decline in the nineteenth century due to the extensive
destruction of handicrafts admirably chronicled above all by R.C.
Dutt.(7) To be on the safe side, we merely assert that there was no
upward trend over that period. Thus, stagnation in per capita income
extends from the end of the eighteenth century to the present day.

EMPLOYMENT AND UNEMPLOYMENT IN INDIA, 1900-75

One notable feature of the Indian economy is the more or less
continuous decline in the labor force participation rates, i.e., the
proportion of total workers in the whole population from 1911 onward.
Data shown in table 6.3 pertain to the present borders of the country. It
is important to note that the concept of "work" underwent a number of
changes over the years. A more or less identical concept was used
between 1901 to 1921 and 1931 to 1951. As compared to the previous

census, there were significant changes in 1931, 1961, and 1971. It is believed by B.R. Kalra, one of those in charge of the 1961 census operation, that "unpaid family workers" were better represented in 1901-21 than in 1931-51. It follows that a comparison between 1921 and 1931 or between 1951 and 1961 is not fully justified. Kalra was, indeed, aware of the objection that the 1961 definition of work was a little too liberal, but thought that it was the right one to adopt for a country like India.(8) In our view, it is rather futile to chase after the correct definition; it is much more important to maintain comparability over time so that one can determine any trends. From this point of view, one cannot defend the fairly important changes introduced in 1961 nor the apparent reversal in 1971. Fortunately, a resurvey carried out in late 1971 and early 1972 enabled a two-way comparison over 1961-71, one by using the 1961 approach and the other by adopting the 1971 methodology. Both these are shown in table 6.3.

Table 6.3. Employment Rates in India, 1901-71
(Percentage)

	1971	1961	1951	1931	1921	1911	1901
Persons	32.9 (36.0)	43.0 (39.9)	39.1	43.3	46.9	48.1	46.6
Males	52.5 (55.9)	57.1 (55.9)	54.0	58.3	60.5	61.9	61.1
Females	11.9 (22.9)	28.0 (22.9)	23.3	27.6	32.7	33.7	31.7

Sources: (1)   For 1901-61: Census of India 1961, Vol. I India, Part II-B(iii) General Economic Tables, Delhi, 1965, pp. 26-27.

(2)   For 1971: Census of India, Series-I-India, Miscellaneous Studies Paper 1 of 1974; Report on Resurvey on Economic Questions - Some Results, New Delhi, undated, table 5, pp. 18-19. The figures in parentheses for 1971 are the results of a resurvey using the same concepts and methodology as those of the 1961 census; similarly, the figures for 1961 in parentheses correspond to the concepts and methodology of the 1971 census.

From table 6.3 it would appear that the 1971 concept of work bears a family resemblance to that used for 1931 and 1951 insofar as one gets a smooth time-trend. Throughout the period 1931-71 there was a gradual decline in the participation rates except for a mild upturn in 1951-61 with respect to "persons" and males; for women, however, the fall is continuous. This is corroborated by the fact that economic growth was somewhat more rapid in the 1950s than in the 1960s. Even if one were to take the 1961 approach, one can still see a fall in the rates in 1961-71. Bearing in mind all these data limitations, one may conclude that the participation rates: (a) rose slightly in 1901-11; (b) fell in 1911-21, the 1921 rates being a little higher than the 1901 levels; (c) fell quite sharply in 1931-51; and (d) fell again quite significantly in 1961-71. About the periods 1921-31 and 1951-61 the evidence in inconclusive. However, comparing 1901 or 1921 with 1961 or 1971 leaves no doubt that there was a definite and perceptible fall irrespective of whether one opts for the 1961 approach or the 1971 approach for those last two censuses.

The fall in the participation rate, one might argue, is not unusual at all.   In Western Europe as well as in North America, a similar development took place from sometime between 1920 and 1930, and continued up to 1960; in Japan, too, the same thing happened from 1900, though an upturn occurred between 1950 and 1960.(9) To neo-classical economists, all this might be a vindication of the theory of diminishing marginal utility of income, a proof of the common man's preference for leisure instead of work. But this cannot explain the Japanese case from 1950 to 1960, i.e., precisely the period when the Japanese workers were approaching a state of affluence. As Sweezy and Magdoff remarked, such flucuations merely reflect those in the demand for labor-power in a capitalist society; a drop in the rate means growing unemployment, although such drop-outs may not actively search for work in order to be officially counted as unemployed.(10) We have no doubt that this argument is a fortiori true for a country like India with a stagnant per capita NMP. To say that people, especially those below the subsistence level, opt for idleness and hunger is grotesque.

Many scholars would like to leave women out of the picture for the simple reason that, in census after census in India, the responsible officials have noted the lack of precision regarding the data for women; the borderline between household chores and work in household industry or agriculture is rather thin. It mirrors the ambiguities of women's role in a male dominated pre-industrial society. As a rule, the male heads of household responding to the interviewer may have neither correctly understood the questions about the activity status of women nor replied accurately to the same.   Hence, a sudden change noticed between any two consecutive consensus may raise doubts about the authenticity of the data. But, if the same trend is observed over a fairly long period, one cannot dismiss it.   To do so would imply a growing bias in the same direction – a thesis that needs further justification in the light of other kinds of evidence extraneous to the census. Thus, we feel that, when Thorner and Krishnamurthy rejected the data for women spanning several decades, they were not very convincing. Indeed, as it is well-known, when jobs get scarce in capitalist countries, the axe falls first on actual or potential women workers along with the young.(11) In India, the steady decline in the participation rate for women is intimately linked to the gradual extinction of many cottage industries, especially in the villages.(12)

However, there are two serious difficulties in using crude participation rates of the type given in table 6.3. If the age-composition of the population undergoes a major change, as in times of rapid population expansion, or if there is a substantial increase in the proportion of young people engaged in full-time education, the crude rate might change in response to these exogenous factors. None of these factors was important to India up to 1921, but the same cannot be said of the postindependence years. To eliminate these deficiencies, we have considered only the population aged 15 years or more, less the number of full-time students in these age brackets. This truncated population may be called the potential labor force (PLF). However, all those categorized as workers remain so in our estimates since the age-structure of the working population is not available for all the census.

Table 6.4 reinforces our earlier contention regarding the declining trends in 1931-51 and 1961-71, and the upturn of 1951-61. The intercensal rates of change are accentuated (as compared to table 6.3) up to 1961; on the other hand, the decline in 1961-71 is moderated.

Table 6.4. Workers as a Percentage of the Potential
Labor Force, 1931-71

	1931	1951	1961	1971
Persons	66.0	59.0	69.4 (64.4)	55.0 (60.0)
Male	88.2	82.5	93.5 (91.5)	90.0 (92.0)
Female	42.7	34.5	44.4 (36.3)	19.3 (27.3)

Source: (1)   The same as in table 6.3.

(2)   The data on the age-structure and full-time students have been obtained from various censuses.

Note: Figures in parentheses have the same meaning as in table 6.3.

Finally, we may note some absolute figures for 1961 and 1971. While the PLF rose from 272 to 338 million, workers increased from 189 to 197 million (according to the 1961 definition) or from 175 to 180 million (according to the 1971 definition). The fall in the activity rate can be attributed entirely to women. Though the PLF for women increased by 28 million over 1961-71, the number of workers declined by 15 to 17 million, depending on the choice of the 1961 or the 1971 definition; unadjusted census figures, however, show a much higher (and rather improbable) fall by as much as 28 million.

It would be erroneous to jump to the conclusion that the difference between the PLF and the actual workers, i.e., 45 percent of the PLF as per the 1971 census, constitutes the pool of unemployed in any meaningful sense. Many of them, especially women from upper income groups, do not generally engage in a gainful occupation. Moreover, many poor women find work only occasionally during agricultural seasons, and may have been counted as non-workers since such part-time workers are only partly employed.

The National Sample Survey (NSS) has been organizing periodical surveys on the employment situation. According to the latest one of 1972-73, the unemployment rates were barely above 1 percent in urban areas and 5 percent in rural areas. (13) Hence, concludes Krishna-murthy, the situation is no different from that in advanced capitalist countries. As for the urban unemployment rate, he finds comfort in the fact that it is high among younger age groups (under 30 years) and negligible for the older people, and calls urban unemployment a "transient" phenomenon.(14) This last argument is patently false. Nearly everywhere in the world, unemployment rates among the youth are higher than those for the older groups. The experience of involuntary unemployment may be "transient" (though the length of it may stretch up to 5 years or more) for the individuals concerned; but, for the society as a whole, it is a perpetual problem insofar as a substantial part of its younger people cannot be provided with jobs. Basically, unemployment is a macro-economic concept, while Krishnamurthy turns it into a micro-economic one.

Fortunately, even the government of India is nowhere as complacent as scholars like Krishnamurthy. If the NSS rates were true, and if one used the 1971 census figures on the number of persons in the labor force, unemployment would be around 3 million in 1971, evenly divided between the rural and urban areas. The Draft Five Year Plan 1978-83, however, put the employment gap in March 1978 at 20.6 million, of which about four-fifths were in the rural areas. This higher figure is arrived at by considering not only the unemployed, as above, but also those who work only seasonally. Other serious scholars put the employment gap at much higher levels still. If S.K. Rao's calculation for the 1960s were accepted, the total gap in 1971 would be 54 million for rural India;(15) A.K. Sen, using a different approach, put it at 42 million in the early 1970s.(16)

Employment exchange data for urban India presents a truly alarming picture. The number of unemployed rose from 3.0 million in 1968 to 6.9 million in 1972 to 10.8 million in October 1977.(17) It has been found that many who are on the active registers are actually employed or engaged in full-time studies; on the other hand, many of the un-employed do not bother to register as rather few vacancies are filled through the employment exchanges. However, these data may not be too unreliable.(18)

The unemployment problem is by no means peculiar to India. Barnet and Müller have compiled some evidence to back this argument. Thus, a U.N. estimate for 1960 found that 27 percent of the labor force in the Third World had no work. Eric Thorbecke calculated that 43 percent of the Peruvian labor force was "not needed in the production of that nation's national product." The percentage of unemployment in 1960 ranged from 20 percent in Argentina, Brazil, and Mexico to 42 percent in the poorer countries of Central America and the Caribbean. According to another estimate by J.P. Grant of the Overseas Development Council, Washington, the number of fully unemployed in the under-developed countries nearly tripled between 1950 and 1960.(19) Finally, an official ILO (International Labor Organization) report gave sectoral and overall unemployment rates which are reproduced in table 6.5. The figures speak for themselves and need no further commentary.

Table 6.5. Unemployment in Selected Latin
American Countries (Percentage)

	Chile	Peru	Para-guay	Uru-guay	Vene-zuela	Colombia	Central American States
Agriculture	30	13	40	20	-	30	25
Nonagriculture	28	29	-	-	-	-	14
Total	-	-	-	20	30	0	-

Sources: E. Lederman, quoted in the World Employment Programme, Report of the Director-General to the International Labour Conference, Geneva, 1969.

GROWTH AND STAGNATION OF THE SECONDARY SECTOR, 1900-75

Although per capita income from material production has shown no further tendency to rise, there is little doubt that manufacturing accounts for a growing share in the national output. Only over the long term is this statement true, for there are none-too-brief stretches when this share remained constant or even fell.

For the sake of comparability with Sivasubramonian's data, mining and quarrying are included in the secondary sector. On the other hand, electricity, gas, and water supply (often included along with manufac-turing in postwar official statistics) have been taken out. In order to emphasize the variation over time, we have indicated the range for each subperiod.

In table 6.6 it can be seen that the proportion of mining and manufacturing was definitely low at the beginning of this century. The 1920s and 1930s were marked by a slow upward shift. This tempo was not maintained in the 1950s. Similarly, a rise in the 1960s was followed by a fall in the 1970s. Indeed, the ratio in 1975-80 was only a shade above that reached during World War II. It may further be noted that the ratio is highly sensitive to agricultural conditions; in a good crop year it may decline in spite of buoyant industrial conditions and, conversely, for a bad agricultural year it may rise. Most important, the rise in the ratio from the beginning of the century reflects not so much a sustained thrust on the industrial front as the depressed conditions in agriculture.

Table 6.6. Share of Mining and Manufacturing in Net
Nation Income or Net Domestic Product

Period	Percentage	Period	Percentage
1900-01 to 1913-14	11.7 to 14.1	1954-55 to 1960-61	16.8 to 19.6
1914-15 to 1929-30	11.8 to 15.4	1961-62 to 1969-70	20.2 to 23.0
1930-31 to 1946-47	15.4 to 18.1	1970-71 to 1975-76	19.1 to 20.4

Sources: (1) Figures up to 1946-47 calculated from Sivasubramanian, op. cit, p. 338; and relate to the net national income at constant 1938-39 prices.

(2) Figures from 1954-55 to 1969-70 are taken from CSO, Estimates of National Product 1960-61 - 1969-70, New Delhi, 1971; and relate to the NDP at constant 1960-61 prices.

(3) Figures for 1970-71 to 1975-76 are taken from CSO, National Accounts Statistics 1970-77 - 1975-76, New Delhi, 1978; and relate to NDP at constant 1970-71 prices.

Next, let us examine the occupational structure of the population. The data are presented in table 6.7. "Cultivators," "agricultural laborers" and "unclassified and general laborers" are included under the agricultural heading. Following Thorner, we believe that most of the last category probably consists of agricultural workers who may earn a substantial part of their incomes from other activities. Under the heading of industrial workers are all those in household and non-household manufacturing. Once again, for 1961 and 1971 two sets of figures are given to enable a comparison over this decade. While the resurvey indicated the occupational categories "cultivators" and "agri-cultural workers," the remainder was grouped under "other workers"; we have assumed that industrial workers would form the same proportion of "other workers" in the resurvey as in the census for the two years.

On the whole, the percentages for the entire period 1911-71 are quite stable, for both agriculture and industry. However, among women, the shift away from industry and the consequent dependence on agriculture is quite marked; in view of the decreasing proportion of women in the work force this is not reflected in the columns for "persons."

In order to throw some further light on the question of deindustrialization in India, let us first recall that there is no disagreement among scholars about the declining ratio of industrial to total workers during the years 1901 to 1931. In order to develop a picture of the overall pattern of work or idleness, forced or voluntary, we prefer to relate industrial workers to the potential labor force (PLF) defined earlier. The data given in table 6.8 show that: (a) for the male workers, there was a gradual rise until 1961 and a slight fall thereafter; (b) for the females, there was a sharp decline in 1961-71 which more than neutralized the rise in 1951-61; and (c) for the two sexes together, the ratio was fairly steady, and in 1971 was marginally below that in 1931. In view of the fairly small movements, it would be a little too rash to talk about deindustrialization.(20)

Table 6.7. Agricultural and Industrial Workers
in the Total Work Force, 1911-71 (Percentages)

	1911	1921	1931	1951	1961	1971
Agricultural Workers Persons	71.6	73.4	71.5	73.0	73.6 (68.7)	69.7 (70.5)
Male	69.8	71.5	70.9	69.9	69.0 (65.0)	67.5 (67.3)
Female	75.1	76.9	72.8	80.4	83.6 (78.4)	80.1 (81.3)
Industrial Workers Persons	9.5	8.7	8.2	9.3	9.5 (11.3)	9.5 (9.3)
Male	9.2	8.8	8.3	10.1	10.1 (11.4)	10.0 (10.1)
Female	10.0	8.6	7.8	7.6	8.2 (10.8)	7.0 (6.6)

Sources: Up to 1961:   Census of India 1961, Paper No. 1 of 1967
           1971:   Census of India 1971, Series I India, Part II-
                        B (ii), General Economic Tables, Tables B III
                        Part A and Part B.

           Figures in parentheses under 1961 and 1971
           are according to the resurvey of 1971-72.
           The source is cited under Table 6.3 where
           explanations are also given.

Table 6.8. Industrial Workers as a Proportion
of the Potential Labor Force (Percentage)

	1931	1951	1961	1971
Persons	5.4	5.5	6.6 (7.3)	5.2 (5.6)
Male	7.3	8.3	9.4 (10.4)	9.0 (9.3)
Female	3.3	2.6	3.6 (3.8)	1.4 (1.8)

Sources and explanation: See tables 6.4 and 6.7.

However, comparing the trends from 1901 onward in the shares of mining and manufacturing in national income and industrial workers to total workers or the PLF, one is struck by the asymmetry. While the first ratio has somewhat increased, the second has fallen by a small amount. It follows that labor productivity in the new industries is significantly above that for the economy as a whole. Further, tables 6.6 to 6.8 indicate that, to a certain extent, female workers are being replaced by male workers, thereby supporting the view of many observers that the slow decay of many household industries is throwing more and more women out of the labor market.

THE PATTERN OF INDUSTRIES

In the preindependence period, small and household industries dominated the industrial scene in terms of employment; but factory employment grew, whereas agricultural employment either stagnated or declined slightly. Thus, in the early years of the century, the small industry sector(21) provided work for over 13 million persons which fell to 12 million by the end of World War II. In 1971 there were 6.4 million in the household industry, and 5.5 million in the small industry sector.(22) Factory employment, however, expanded from 0.6 to 2.6 million until the end of World War II and stood at 5.2 million in 1971.(23)

What were the main types of factory industry in the earlier half of the twentieth century? In terms of employment, jute and cotton textiles accounted for almost two-thirds during the first few years, but gradually fell to between a third and two-fifths toward the close of this period. Their share in the net output was somewhat less since these industries are typically those with low value-added. Thus, in 1945-46 they accounted for a quarter of the net product of the factory sector. Between the two, cotton textiles was far more important than jute textiles.

Sugar was another major industry which went through a big expansion in the 1920s, but its contribution to total factory sector output reached a peak of 3 to 4 percent. The iron and steel industries were perhaps a little more important, but the data are available only for the Tate Iron and Steel Company, the contribution of which reached a maximum of 3 percent. In general, metals and mineral processing industries were well-developed, employing more than 150,000 workers (over 10 percent of the total) in 1919; at its height there were nearly 450,000 workers in 1945-46, over 14 percent of the total. In terms of value-added, its share should have been considerably higher. Other major industries in terms of employment were chemicals, food and beverages, and tobacco; government-owned factories also employed substantial numbers. Once again, information on output is scanty. Other less important industries were cement, paper, and matches.

Industrial growth in the colonial period was expedited in the wake of a series of protective measures enacted during the early 1920s.(24) Hence, a process of import-substitution industrialization was started, although the extent of tariff protection was much smaller than present-day levels. Nor was protection granted easily. Moreover, the colonial government relied on British supplies rather than domestic production for its purchases; in the period after World War I, it gave partial support to domestic industries. The growth of the jute industry, however, was primarily export-oriented, exports accounting for 70 to 80 percent of the production; in addition, raw jute was sent out in considerable quantities, the value of which fluctuated at around one-half of jute manufacturing exports in the interwar years.(25) For cotton piecegoods in the first few years of this century, exports were nearly a quarter of the very low level of domestic production in the factory sector; by the latter half of the 1930s, production had increased 6 to 8-fold, and exports amounted to under 5 percent.(26)

Other characteristics of industrial growth may also be noted briefly. First, agro-based industries, i.e., those using cash crops as their main raw materials, dominated the scene. Textiles, tobacco, and edible oils are some examples. Second, with the exception of jute, nearly every industry was geared to the domestic market. Third, in view of the low and stagnant per capita incomes, very few industries really catered to the consumption needs of the masses. Cotton textiles would be an exception; but, even here, the growth was of an import-substitution type. Fourth, this import-substitution, even for simple items like cotton textiles, did not go far enough, for the country's imports were still nearly 21 percent of the domestic production by the mill sector.(27) Fifth, although British India was among the top countries in the world in terms of the absolute magnitude of its industrial output, practically no machinery sector developed. Finally, the industrial pattern was such that average labor productivity in the factory sector as a whole remained fairly static; employment and net output (at constant 1938-39 prices) both increased about fourfold.

Table 6.9 shows annual growth rates for different subperiods of overall industrial output as well as for groups of industries classified in more than one manner. Now one can see more clearly the changing growth rates over time. The following conclusions may be drawn from the table: (1) There was an acceleration in industrial growth up to 1965, followed by a sharp, though not continuous, deceleration in 1965-66.(28) (2) The same tendencies prevail for practically all the subgroups. (3) Under the input-based classification, the metal industries had the highest rates up to 1965, but then fell drastically; the fall was quite meager for chemicals which have since become the leading growth industry. Agro-based industries never had a high growth rate, but have fallen below 2 percent since 1965. (4) In the consumer goods sector, durable items have had a much faster growth than nondurable ones.

Table 6.9. Annual Growth Rate in Industry,
1947-76 (Percentages)

	1947 to 1951	1951 to 1955	1955 to 1960	1960 to 1965	1965 to 1970	1970 to 1976	1965 to 1976
I. Use-based classification							
1. Basic goods	-	4.7	12.0	10.4	6.2	6.8	6.5
2. Capital goods	-	9.8	13.1	19.6	(-)1.4	6.0	2.6
3. Intermediate goods	-	7.8	6.4	6.9	2.6	3.3	3.0
4. Consumer goods	-	4.8	4.4	4.9	4.1	2.9	3.4
a) Durables	-	-	-	11.0	8.5	4.3	6.2
b) Nondurables	-	-	-	-	2.8	2.9	2.8
II. Input-based classification							
1. Agro-Industries	0.3	4.0	3.8	4.0	1.7	1.8	1.7
2. Metal Industries	4.5	7.5	14.1	18.2	0.7	5.1	3.1
3. Chemicals	26.2	8.5	12.2	9.0	9.8	7.3	8.4
III. Electricity & allied	-	10.4	14.7	14.4	11.8	6.8	9.1
IV. Overall Industrial output	4.8	5.7	7.2	9.0	3.3	4.7	4.1

Source: K.N. Raj, "Growth and Stagnation in Industrial Development," Economic and Political Weekly, Annual Number, Feb. 1976, and S.L. Shotty, "Structural Retrogression in the Indian Economy since the Mid-sixties," Economic and Political Weekly, Annual Number, Feb. 1978.

What accounts for the slowing down? Without going deeply into the question that has engaged the attention of many Indian economists,(29) we would like to emphasize that the lack of purchasing power among the masses has been the main obstacle.(30) The real wage rates have not been increasing in line with the rise in labor productivity so that wages represent a smaller and smaller part of the value-added in the factory sector. As in the developed capitalist economies, in India, too, industrial growth has a strong labor-saving bias. As a result of a number of complex factors, per capita consumption of industrial goods has been rather static.

For the period since 1960-61, official statistics are available on the per capita consumption of major items. Excluding cereals and cereal substitutes entirely, and part of some other items, we have computed an overall measure of per capita consumption of industrial goods(31) at constant 1960-61 prices for the years 1960-61 to 1974-75 which are given in table 6.10. There appears to be a very mild rise in the 1970s, but not sufficient to merit serious attention; and there has been a fall since 1971-72. This finding is corroborated by the data given earlier in table 6.2 on the per capita consumption of selected articles.

Table 6.10 Per Capita Consumption Expenditure
on "Industrial" Goods, 1960-74
(Rupees at constant 1960-61 prices)

	Rupees		Rupees		Rupees
1960-61	102	1965-66	103	1970-71	110
1961-62	96	1966-67	103	1971-72	112
1962-63	97	1967-68	103	1972-73	108
1963-64	98	1968-69	105	1973-74	108
1964-65	104	1969-70	105	1974-75	108

Source: CSO, National Accounts Statistics 1960-61 - 1974-75, Delhi, 1976.

As for real wages, unfortunately, the data are not quite usable. Statistics on money wages have been collected since 1960 for workers earning 400 rupees or less per month. In a period of rapid inflation, an unknown percentage of workers should have crossed the threshold of 400 rupees; thus the average for those who remained inside that class is devoid of any interest.(32) Had the ceiling been raised from time to time, or, if data had been collected on such categories as unskilled, semi-skilled, or skilled workers, one could make meaningful statements on earnings. Further, the cost of living index is widely suspected to have a downward bias; in fact, in June 1977, the government appointed a review committee to examine these issues. Nevertheless, no serious scholar has argued that real wages, except in a few isolated pockets, have increased by more than a small amount in the last two or three decades; on the other hand, labor productivity has increased quite significantly.

On the share of wages in the value-added in manufacturing, the National Commission on Labour found that it declined almost continuously from 53.3 percent in 1949 to 36.5 percent in 1964; the share of salary, though, went up from 10.6 to 13.7 percent over the same period.(33) Available data for the later years do not segregate wages from salaries. Thus, in the National Accounts Statistics for the years since 1960-61, the information pertaining to the compensation of employees as a proportion of total income in registered manufacturing (i.e., the factory sector), increased from 55 percent in 1960-61 to 64 percent in 1967-68 and 1968-69, but then fell to 60 percent in 1973-74 and 1974-75. In view of the widely observed tendency for salaries in the private sector to rise faster than wages, and in view of the recent trend toward the so-called "professionalization of management" (which, in reality, amounts to creating more jobs at higher pay for the executive cadre), one cannot make any inference about movement in the share of wages from the statistics on employees' compensation. Even though no solid information is available, to the best of our knowledge, there is a widespread belief that the wage-share is falling in the factory sector.

Of the remarkable rise in labor productivity in this sector, there is little doubt. Between 1951 and 1975, factory employment rose by a mere 78 percent, while industrial output expanded by 292 percent at 1960-61 prices. Hence, labor productivity more than doubled in a quarter of a century; this rate of progress is comparable to that in most advanced capitalist countries.

The rapid rise in average levels of labor productivity is intimately linked to the growing capital-intensity of production. A Reserve Bank study found that fixed investments required to create a new job in the organized industries and mines were as high as 23,000 rupees during the First Five Year Plan (1951-52 to 1955-56), 27,000 rupees during the Second Plan, and 39,000 rupees during the Third Plan.(34) Even allowing for the modest inflation in 1951-65, the increase was quite marked. In the mid-1970s, the level should have reached at least 50,000 rupees.

Tables 6.11 and 6.12 illustrate the lopsidedness of the Indian industrial structure as well as further trends in the same direction. The disparity between the high productivity industries and the average for all industry is greater in India than in the industrialized countries; the same is true for other underdeveloped countries. Further, in India as well as in Brazil, and to a lesser extent in Mexico, there was a shift toward high productivity industries. These trends are likely to have not only continued, but perhaps accentuated after 1963 in view of the rise of petrochemicals, fertilizers, and other highly capital intensive industries.

Table 6.11. Indexes of Capital-Intensity
in Different Industries, 1963

| | All Manufacturing | Extremely low | Levels of value-added in different industries | | | | |
			Low	Inter-mediate	High	Extremely high	Mining
Industrialized Countries	100	50	60	100	150	200	140
Nonindustrialized Countries	100	40	50	130	300	380	520
India	100	40	70	130	290	300	180

Source: D. Turnham, The Employment Problem in Less Developed
Countries (OECD, Paris, 1971), p. 95.

Table 6.12. Output Shares of Different
Manufacturing Industries, 1949-63
(Percentages)

| | India | | Brazil | | Mexico | |
	1953	1962	1949	1963	1950	1960
Low productivity industries	52	33	30	19	22	18
High productivity industries	26	25	29	51	31	30
Unclassified	22	42	41	30	47	52
All manufacturing	100	100	100	100	100	100

Source: D. Turnham, The Employment Problem in Less Developed
Countries (OECD, Paris, 1971), p. 96.

It is now recognized widely by persons professing different ideologies that, unless industries become more labor-intensive in the Third
World countries, development cannot be sustained nor the unemployment problem alleviated. Frances Stewart, for instance, observed that,
even by raising the national savings rate to, say, about 20 percent of
the income, one can barely absorb 1 percent of the labor force into
industry every year at the currently observed levels of capital-intensity
for India; however, the potential labor force expands at a faster rate
than 1 percent.

The main problem with high capital-intensity is not, in our view, the lack of savings. As we saw earlier, India today does not know what to do with her savings and many OPEC countries can see no better alternatives for their liquid funds than to invest them in Western banks or treasury bonds.

Excessive capital-intensity should ceteris paribus lead to large-scale underutilization of capacity in a typical Third World country like India. To simplify the argument, let us suppose that India adopts the same industrial technology as the United States in every single branch so that labor productivity is the same in the two countries, although wages are several times lower in India. For this hypothetical case, it is assumed that in the United States there is a high level equilibrium, i.e., full employment and full utilization of capacity. In view of the relative wages and productivities, the wage-share in net output will be far lower in India than in the United States. This shortfall in the workers' effective demand could be made up by a step-up (as compared to the corresponding U.S. levels) either in the capitalists' consumption or in sales outside the domestic capitalist system, e.g., government expenditure on arms or welfare, peasants' purchases, destruction of whatever handicrafts that survive, exports, and so on. Since there are fairly narrow limits to all these options, the most likely consequence is a sharp cutback in production and employment with a multiplier effect.

There is a great deal of evidence regarding the low rate of capacity-utilization in highly capital-intensive import-substitution industries that are established in the Third World. A study for India indicates utilization rates ranging from 12 to 69 percent for a broad spectrum of 45 different sectors. The Reserve Bank also found that capacity utilization in all industries taken together was, in the last couple of years, well below 80 percent of the peaks attained in the past.(35)

THE DRAIN OF RESOURCES

Nineteenth century Indian nationalists with Dadabhai Naoroji(36) in the forefront, formulated the celebrated "drain theory," showing the various ways in which resources were pumped out of that poor country by the colonial masters.   Defenders of imperialism, e.g., Vera Anstey,(37) though they quibbled about one item or another, did not deny the existence of such a drain. Nevertheless, it was regarded as the necessary price the Indians had to pay for "enjoying" the benefits of Pax Britannica; moreover, the drain was only a tiny fraction of India's national output so could not be considered an onerous burden.

In contemporary discussions about foreign aid, capital, and technology, there are strong echoes of this earlier debate. If one replaces the words "imperialism" and "Pax Britannica" by "neocolonialism" and "foreign capital," one will find that most economists, even many from the Third World, are today repeating what the Vera Ansteys said decades ago.

It is important, therefore, to restate the basic nationalist axiom: foreign rule, even if it may be "progressive" in some ways, is essentially predatory in nature and can never be a substitute for self-rule. It is an axiom, because one cannot prove it one way or the other. Similarly, given the contemporary situation, we start with the axiom that, in general, foreign private capital is not essential for the development of a Third World country. There can be exceptions to this rule. Thus, Japan at the end of World War II was obliged to allow foreign oil companies to set up refineries, which was a desired alternative to continuing imports of refined products. But the same argument does not apply to India. India had cheap and abundant reserves of an alternative fuel (coal) which Japan did not have. As the Japanese experience shows, concession in one area need not necessarily lead to concessions in other areas. Conversely, a general ban on foreign capital need not deter particular foreign capitalists from entering a country.

Let us return to the second counterargument against Naoroji, namely, that the drain was a tiny fraction of the national income and therefore not a burden. Indeed, the fraction was small. By using the more detailed estimates of A.K. Banerji and others, Sivasubramonian found that in the present century "net factor incomes going abroad" as a percentage of net national income at current prices ranged between 1.00 and 2.35 from 1900-01 to 1940-41, the simple average being 1.69 over the whole period.(38) The drain was rather low in buoyant times (i.e., good crop years), but much higher (over 2 percent) for most of the depressed 1930s.(39)

Is it meaningful to compare the drain with the national income? As Paul Baran remarked, the drain was essentially a deduction from the "potential surplus" of one country and an addition to that of another.(40) Since the savings or investment rate in colonial India was rather low, the share of the drain would be about one-third of the potential surplus; no society can develop with such a serious hemorrhage.

In subsequent nationalist writings, a greater stress was laid on the mechanics of colonialism, namely, the means through which the colony was kept underdeveloped. Marx had noted the systematic destruction of Indian crafts in his articles of the late 1850s.(41) R.C. Dutt, writing fifty years later, gave ample statistical evidence on deindustrialization in the early nineteenth century.(42) Without referring to Marx, Dutt also showed that Marx's hopes for the birth of modern industry in the wake of railway construction had not materialized. The colonial government stuck steadfastly to the doctrine of free trade until nationalist pressure forced it to concede the infant industry argument on a limited scale more than half a century after List had formulated it. A small number of industries (such as cotton, sugar, iron, and steel) sprang up; imports, however, as we have already noted, continued at high levels in many sectors.

Colonial rule had three other major features arresting the overall development of the country.(43) First, European (and particularly British) capital dominated many crucial sectors. Their monopoly position exercised through trade associations (i.e., the Indian Jute Mills Associations) or, more usually, through Managing Agencies (which controlled a large spectrum of firms for interconnected product lines), blocked the growth of indigenous capital. Second, the major financial institutions (such as organized banks) were racist in outlook, favoring European rather than local capital. Finally, in the field of government procurements, including railways, little encouragement was given to native capitalists; preference was always given to purchases from England or from British-owned enterprises in India.

Thus, colonial rule established a whole series of boundary conditions that left little scope for Indian capitalists. No wonder that the moneyed classes took to rack-renting on land trading, usury, and other unproductive activities.

During the course of World War II, India emerged as a net creditor to the United Kingdom and, with independence, several other changes followed. Over time, India began to receive massive amounts of foreign aid on concessional terms. A number of industries owned or controlled by foreigners passed into Indian hands. Racial discrimination disappeared in the field of finance and in government contracts. Protection of domestic industries was assured, leading to the creation of many industries. Indian capital had far more opportunities for expansion than previously. On the surface at least, the gains were quite impressive. Yet, if table 6.13 tells a true story, there must be a chasm between the surface and the underlying reality. Has there been a net transfer of resources to India from the rest of the world sinced 1947? Official statistics have almost consistently shown a negative balance of payments on current account, matched by a surplus on capital account. Of the capital flows, one can ignore relatively short-term commercial credits such as suppliers' credit which carry market rates of interest. Credit from the IMF may be discounted as repayments have to be made within a fairly short period of time. Of interest here are: (1) aid flows from foreign governments and international agencies such as the International Bank for Reconstruction and Development (IBRD), and the International Development Association (IDA) and (2) private capital in the form of equities. Corresponding to these inflows there are some annual outflows such as debt service charges on the non-grant part of the aid; and payment of dividends, royalties, and technical fees to the owners of foreign private capital.

There are a number of other factors which cannot be determined with precision, but which most analysts agree should be deducted from the net inflow figures. First, there is the excess cost associated with the nearly universal practice of tying aid. On the basis of my own earlier estimates regarding Western aid,(44) the pricing policy of the Soviets in their exports to the Third World,(45) and the lower limit of Myrdal's informed guess,(46) we would conservatively estimate the excess cost at 20 percent of the tied aid flows. Second, the practice of transfer pricing by transnationals is widely prevalent. The declared dividends distributed as a percentage of net worth or the stock of direct foreign investments has been improbably low; between 1964-65 and

Table 6.13. Net Transfer of Foreign Resources
to India, 1968-69 to 1975-76
(in millions of rupees)

	1968-69	1969-70	1970-71	1971-72	1972-73	1973-74	1974-75	1975-76
1. Foreign aid utilized	9,026	8,563	7,914	8,341	6,662	10,357	13,143	18,405
(a) of which tied aid	7,461	6,608	6,308	6,562	3,886	5,846	6,664	9,857
2. Inflow of private capital	253	219	334	431	284	487	(487)	(487)
(a) of which retained earnings	178	290	284	339	321	379	(379)	(379)
3. Debt servicing	3,750	4,125	4,500	4,793	5,074	5,958	6,260	6,869
4. Royalties, technical fees, etc.	161	183	(173)	(210)	(824)	(891)	950	(1,017)
5. Dividends on foreign capital	312	430	519	547				
6. Errors and omission in the balance of payments	1,137	145	787	652	316	2,075	2,961	2,420
7. Estimates of:								
(a) Aid-tying costs (20% on 1a)	1,492	1,320	1,262	1,312	772	1,169	1,333	1,971
(b) Smuggling	2,108	2,506	2,217	2,086	2,444	3,548	5,763	(2,881)
(c) Invoice manipulation	3,010	2,980	3,050	5,160	(5,676)	(6,244)	(6,868)	(7,555)
8. Net drain of foreign resources	2,869	3,197	4,544	6,327	8,481	9,420	10,884	4,200
	9,279	8,782	8,248	8,772	6,946	10,844	13,630	18,892
	12,148	11,979	12,792	15,099	15,427	20,264	24,514	28,092

Table 6.13. (Cont.)

Source: Rows 1, 1a, 3, and 6: Economic Survey, various issues.

Rows 2, 2a, and 5: RBI Bulletin, July 1975 and March 1978.

Row 4: RBI, Foreign Collaboration in Indian Industry, Bombay, 1974, for the period up to 1969-70 and an official statement in Parliament reported in the Economic Times, July 30, 1978.

Rows 7b and 7c: S. Nayak, "Illegal Transactions," and V. Pitre, "Illegal Transactions: A Comment."

Note: Figures in parentheses represent my estimates as explained in the text.

Note: Method for computing line 8: 1+2-(2a+3+4+5+6+7a+7b+7c)

1971-72, the latest year for which data are available, the percentage varied between 4.4 and 7.1.(47)

There are certain other outflows from the economy that cannot be attributed directly to foreign aid or investment. These are, rather, the results of the overall economic system of which foreign aid and investment are most important components. Specifically, these outflows arise due to the exchange control system. The "errors and omissions" item in the official statistics is quite substantial and consistently negative, though there are wide fluctuations from year to year. Between 1968-69 and 1974-75 the figure ranged from 0.3 to 3.0 billion rupees.(48)

Smuggling, manipulation of invoices for exports and imports, unauthorized expenses on foreign travel by Indians are widely acknowledged to be rampant. An official committee was appointed in November 1969 to assess the extent of leakages of foreign exchanges. Relying on informed guesses, it put the total at around 2.4 billion rupees consisting of smuggling (1.6 to 1.7), travel (0.35 to 0.40), and invoice manipulation (0.25 to 0.3), (the figures in parentheses being in billions of rupees).(49) Being official guesses, these are likely to have been grossly understated. S. Nayak,(50) in a recent study, obtained information on the value of smuggled goods seized, and assumed the seizure rate to be 10 percent, which was supported by some indirect evidence. For invoice manipulation, he compared Indian trade data with those of nine major partner countries in the West. Correcting for Nayak's computational errors as suggested by V. Pitre,(51) one finds that the volume of smuggling in 1970 and 1971 averaged 2.15 billion rupees and that of invoice manipulation, 5.16 billion rupees. There is no estimate for the leakage through travel abroad by Indians.

That is not the end of the story of invisible costs to the economy. For invoice manipulation, Mayak considered only partner country data;

unless the customs authorities abroad are well-equipped and motivated to prevent transfer pricing, the actual extent of the latter must be higher than what Nayak's figures reveal. Not only transnationals in India, but also Indian nationals and firms are widely known to be accumulating foreign exchange abroad; a good part of it is not illegal, but extra-legal. In the absence of some plausible estimates, these are left out of the data presented in table 6.13. For many items there are information gaps, especially for the recent years, which we have tried to fill in a rough and rather conservative manner. Private capital inflow figures are not available for the last two years so we have kept them pegged at the 1973-74 level. Data on dividends, royalties, etc. are not available for many years, but an official statement puts the total at an average of 950 million rupees for 1973-74 to 1975-76; the figures in parentheses in the table were obtained by intrapolation and extrapolation. Further, the smuggling estimates by Nayak end in 1974-75; in view of the drastic anti-smuggling measures as well as the declaration of Emergency in June 1975, we have arbitrarily reduced the 1975-76 figure to one-half the previous year's level. We might also point out that compared with 5.8 billion rupees in our table for 1974-75, in many newspaper reports the figure was put at 10.0 billion rupees. Finally, for invoice manipulation the latest estimate of Nayak pertained to 1971-72; we have assumed since then a modest annual growth of 10 percent or a total of 50 percent between 1971-72 and 1975-76, whereas India's overall trade turnover during the same period went up three times faster, or by 151 percent.

If one is to go by the net figures of table 6.6, it follows that since 1968-69, there has been a net drain of resources out of India varying between 1 and 1.5 percent of the GNP at current prices. We have not calculated the drain for the earlier years, but it may not be much less; while the extent of the smuggling and invoice manipulation were considerably smaller, the aid-tying costs were considerably higher owing to the excessive overcharging by the United States on PL 480 wheat aid, accounting for more than a quarter of all aid received by India up to 1967-68.

The net transfer of resource approach used here has been criticized because the "opportunity costs" are not properly spelled out. Hence, it is suggested by some that a cost-benefit analysis would be more appropriate. Let us examine one such interesting study on the private oil refineries in India.

R. Vedavalli's work is extremely well-researched, bringing out the mechanics of exploitation by the oil transnationals.(52) In the chapter on cost-benefit analysis, she considers three alternatives to foreign enterprise: continuing imports on refined products; the setting up of a public sector unit; and the formation of joint ventures. We shall concentrate on the first two.

In the first alternative, Vedavalli makes the following assumptions: 1) The quantities of import would be the same as the outputs of the foreign enterprises; 2) the import prices would be the same as those paid by the oil companies; and 3) costs incurred by the latter are taken at their actual values. It is found that foreign investment brought in a net gain of $625 million for India in 1955-69.

There is little to dispute on the cost side in (3) above, but not so for (1) and (2). The author has given precise estimates of overcharging by Burma Shell on imports of high speed diesel and other products between 1960 and 1964 as compared to the prices paid by the Indian Oil Corporation to the USSR; the rate of such overcharging varied between 10.1 and 18.1 percent for different years. After 1965, the foreign companies stopped such imports and the USSR, too, firmed up its prices.(53) Assuming the rate for 1959 was the same rate as for 1960, one can infer that India's import bill could have been reduced by $124 million. Further, if India were to import all its oil needs, it is more likely that it would focus on the development of neglected coal resources. If the import bill of $2,157 million assumed by Vedavalli were reduced by a third (which is not a very drastic assumption), and after allowing for the overcharging by oil companies, it can be easily seen that the net benefits for foreign investment fall to zero.

Turning to the more interesting second alternative, Vedavalli assumes that the public sector unit is financed by a foreign loan (from the USSR) bearing 2.5 percent interest and is fully amortized over the period; the output structure of the costs of crude oil, freight charges, and other expenses are the same for the Indian as far as the foreign companies; and the Indian company saves vis-a-vis the foreign companies on dividend outflows and lower operational expenses (e.g., head office expenses) in foreign exchange. The net costs of this alternative came to $80 million in 1955-69.

At least two points can be made within the cost-benefit framework. First, on crude oil, the foreign companies overcharged, as Vedavalli pointed out, to the tune of $73.4 million in 1959-69 on an f.o.b. basis. Regarding freight for 1962-66, the excess amounted to $14.2 million.(54) Combining these two and extrapolating for the whole period 1955-69, the cost of foreign investment went up by about another $100 million. Second, at the end of 1969 with regard to foreign companies, the Indian economy was saddled with an outstanding liability of $178 million. Deducting $133 million of capital actually brought in, India would have had to pay out of her own reserves the balance of $42 million if it were to nationalize the industry (as it actually did only a couple of years later). Hence, the cost of foreign investment should be reckoned at $225 million.

It can thus be seen that one can literally prove anything by suitable changes in the parameters of cost-benefit analysis, reflecting one's value judgments and/or prejudices. Besides, this kind of exercise is hardly feasible at a macro-economic level.(55) There is a lot to be said for the traditional net transfer approach which involves a smaller number of estimates. Of course, the basic axiom is there, namely, that nearly everything brought in through foreign aid or produced by a foreign company can be effectively procured abroad through a better husbanding of the country's own resources, or else a close enough substitute can be found through local production or foreign purchase.

The most misleading aspect of the usual cost-benefit analysis, derived from its neoclassical origins, is the virtual neglect of externalities. Fortunately, Vedavalli has taken some pains to point these out.(56) (1) Of the net value added by the foreign oil companies in India, the share of labor was only a fifth, the rest going to "capital and resources." Moreover, of the total, as much as a third was transferred abroad, only two-thirds remaining within the country. (2) The foreign companies made some efforts, according to Vedavalli, to substitute imports of rather minor items, e.g., storage drums and pressure vessels for LPG. Even here, it is likely that the companies were compelled to do so by the government. Vedavalli continues: "Only after 1966, when the public sector refinery at Koyali was commissioned, was a serious attempt made to procure 60 percent of plant and equipment from indigenous sources. This trend was accelerated during the construction of the Madras refinery in 1967 and 1968."(57) (3) In the field of design, the foreign companies had all the work done abroad; the same is true for the first plants in the public sector. From the Xoyali project on, the Indian share was already 40 percent, and this was further increased.

These externalities lie at the very heart of the development problem. There is hardly any instance anywhere in the Third World where a transnational has encouraged "backward links" to a greater extent than a comparable local enterprise; on "forward links," the former's contribution may be higher, but this may be of dubious social utility insofar as the transnational's product may have replaced a traditional labor-intensive intermediate good produced by local industry. In India, aluminum and stainless steel are used increasingly for making domestic utensils, but only by putting out of work hundreds of thousands of blacksmiths, potters, brass-workers, and others.

On the restrictive aspects of technology transfer through the transnationals there is now a good deal of evidence, most notably that presented in the two reports on foreign collaboration in Indian industry(58) and in Vaitsos' work on the Andean Pact countries.(59) Source-tying with respect to capital goods, intermediates, and raw materials and restrictions on horizontal transfer of technology within the host country (i.e., control over the selection of key personnel, discouragement of local R & D, limitations on exports) are some of the major ways in which the transnationals hamper the growth potentials of their subsidiaries, affiliates, or collaborators in the underdeveloped countries. In the discussion, however, more stress has been placed on foreign exchanges losses, actual or potential, than on the debilitating impact of such policies on the local economy.

The argument that transnationals also dominate a whole range of "sophisticated" product lines in individual Third World countries has again been studied extensively.(60) In the private corporate sector of the Indian economy, the transnationals carry a very large weight. An earlier study by this author showed that the TNCs' share in the aggregate sales of the private corporate sector went up from 26 percent in 1957-58 to 30 percent in 1972-73; the gross profit share rose from 36 to 50 percent over the same period. Statistical trend analysis revealed that there was a zero-trend for sales over the whole period, but a positive trend since 1965-66; for gross profits, the positive trend prevailed for the whole period.(61)

In the study just mentioned the author confined himself to companies which were owned or controlled by foreigners, as determined by the Reserve Bank of India. In practice, a number of the biggest Indian-controlled monopoly groups also maintain a complex pattern of association, financial ties, and other connections with transnationals, without necessarily being completely dominated by them. One of the ironies of the situation is that, while many Indian monopolies publicly clamored for a virtual expulsion of foreign capital in the colonial era,(62) today all the major chambers of commerce in India actively plead with the government on behalf of foreign capital. If one could equitably identify a "foreign-connected" sector(63) having more than "purely technical" collaboration arrangements with transnationals, it is likely that its share in the private corporate sector might turn out to be quite significant.

In view of the predominance of the foreign-connected as well as the foreign-owned sector, new entrants into many product lines are at times obliged to seek foreign collaboration or brand names.(64) All this helps to throttle indigenous R & D, delimit the spread effects (backward links) of new industries, and create a dependency syndrome among the elites. As a matter of fact, there is a whole range of industries (e.g., toothpastes, soaps and detergents, matches, radios, electronics, cigarettes, storage batteries, dry cell batteries, shoes, and cosmetics) where TNCs dominate the market, although high quality and reasonably priced local industry products are available.

Finally, we should point out that there is a close connection between aid flows from the West or Western-controlled international agencies and private capital inflows. For a variety of reasons, the ruling classes cannot dispense with either of these; the option of self-reliance, economic or technological, is much more arduous as well as perilous(65) compared to the ease and private affluence created by the present model of development.

THE POLITICS OF TECHNOLOGICAL CHOICE

How the activities of transnationals, with support from politically powerful elements within India and often the World Bank, have impeded the development of indigenous technology will be illustrated with three examples. All these are in the relatively "high" technology areas and in the public sector which could presumably look after national interests without being hamstrung by narrow profit considerations. It is also worth noting that, until very recently, most public sector enterprises set up with foreign collaboration, often on a turn-key basis, have been incurring huge losses running into hundreds of millions of rupees per annum.

The first example concerns Swaraj (a term meaning "self-rule" coined during the independence movement) tractors.(66) It is well-known that no basic innovations in the international tractor industry took place over the last 30 years and that a tractor is much simpler to manufacture than an automobile since it contains only 2,000 parts rather than the 15,000 in the latter. The Central Mechanical Engineering Research Institute, a government-financed R & D institution, assembled the first prototype in the 20-25 horsepower range in November 1967; and, by June 1971, after considerable efforts at improvement, the model tractor underwent rigorous tests at the Tractor Training and Testing Station in Budni. This was no mean feat since, of the eleven other tractors manufactured in India (all with foreign collaboration), only two others – Massey Ferguson and the Czech Zeteor – had passed this test. However, no public sector enterprise under the Central government took up the Swaraj tractor. Hindustan Machine Tools, looking for quick profits, started assembling the Zeteor rather than venture into Swaraj. Fortunately, a Punjab State government undertaking took up the project realizing not only the intrinsic worth of the tractor, but its very large employment potential since all the parts and components were to be locally manufactured. For other foreign brands, the indigenous component was much smaller, varying between 45 and 88 percent of the unit price. Last but no least, a World Bank team which visited the country did not evaluate the Swaraj tractor so that no farmer could use World Bank credit to purchase this tractor. The fact that the project went through despite such formidable odds was due to the unusual determination of a number of individuals and institutions, including the major development bank under the central government. Swaraj tractors still account for a very small fraction (just over 6 percent) of the total licensed capacity for the production of tractors in India.

Much better known is the case of the Indian fertilizer industry which, according to the 1956 Industrial Policy Resolution of the government, was reserved for the public sector.(67) Taking advantage of the food shortage in India in 1966, the World Bank and the International Monetary Fund imposed on the government a large devaluation of the rupees, the policy of import liberalization, and free entry of Indian and foreign private capital into the fertilizer industry.(68) While some private capital did enter the field, the bulk of production remains in the public sector. In the 1950s, a Planning and Development Division was created within the Fertilizer Corporation of India to create indigenous technology in this area. Although some technologies were, from the beginning, keen on developing coal-based fertilizers, the oil lobby successfully scuttled the idea for nearly 20 years until the oil crisis of 1973 erupted. Since then, efforts have been made to implement a large project with substantial indigenous know-how. In other areas, too, a lot of progress was made; among others, a number of catalysts were developed over the years. By the early 1970s, the Indian engineers had gradually mastered a wide range of technological problems and were in a position to set up plants on their own without any foreign collaboration. Yet, the politicians and bureaucrats had little faith in them. Thus, in 1972-73, contracts for five large plants went to the Japanese and Italians on the grounds that there was a tremendous shortage of technology in the country, that the foreigners had proven know-how, and that they promised to complete construction within record time – a promise that was not fulfilled. Then, in 1973-74, when World Bank credit was made available for modernization at Sindri and expansion at Nangal, the Bank insisted on giving the prime contract to a West German firm. Later, three more projects were negotiated with the Italians. Most recently, a 5 billion rupee project to utilize the Bombay High Gas seems to have been awarded to an American firm, while the Indian company will obtain a subcontract for a mere 50 million rupees. It has been reported that, whenever the company "tries to secure orders, it has to place them before the board for approval. But, it is alleged that the representatives of other public sector undertakings, on their return to their own organization, try to take away those orders from [the country] by fair means or foul."(69)

By far, the most sinister of all is the proposed collaboration agreement between Bharat Heavy Electricals Ltd. (BHEL) and Siemens, the West German TNC.(70) BHEL is a giant public sector company with an annual turnover of 5.5 billion rupees accounting for a significant part of heavy electrical output in the country. It has had a long series of technical collaboration agreements with both TNCs and the East European countries, including the USSR. Its own R & D sector has made notable progress over the years and has been moving toward increasing indigenization.

With regard to power generation equipment, the company has been producing up to the 200 MW (megawatt) capacity range. In 1973, it concluded that it should move on to the 500 MW units. In 1974, the Fuel Policy Committee of the government made recommendations along the same lines since it would be more economical in terms of fuel consumption; the Committee also recommended that "the design, development and manufacture of 500 MW generating unit should be entrusted to an Indian agency." (Emphasis in the original document.)(71) Indeed, an earlier government study had explored three alternatives in this connection: conventional license agreements whereby an Indian company would produce on license for a foreign manufacturer; initial purchase of finished units and manufacturing know-how as a package deal; and indigenous design and engineering effort with selective technical assistance and/or import of know-how.

Having assessed the available potential in India and the experience of past collaboration arrangements, the third alternative was preferred and a time-bound program adopted. However, in April 1974, an agreement with Siemens regarding high speed industrial turbines was made; production gathered momentum by 1977 but no design information was forthcoming as per the contract. Two more agreements were made in 1975 for power electronics and thyristor devices. At least in the latter one, it was revealed that, at the time of a contract for supply to Bokaro Steel, BHEL merely acted as a selling agent for Siemens.

Next, in September 1976, another 15-year agreement was signed with Kraft World Union (KWU), a Siemens subsidiary for power equipment in the range 200 to 1,000 MW.(72) Initially, 15 units of 200 MW will be imported at a cost of 120 million rupees each, while BHEL had been supplying similar units at only 64 million rupees under contract; thus, BHEL should incur a loss of several hundred million rupees – all in foreign exchange. Phased manufacturing of the KWU model will take a long time since the BHEL's factories are tuned to other models; investment for the changeover is estimated at 5,000 million rupees. Moreover, all the accumulated experience and R & D work within the company will come to nought.

The latest proposal is an umbrella-type agreement. For a wide range of products accounting for 40 to 70 percent of BHEL's turnover, according to various estimates, the TNC is to receive an annual lump sum fee of DM 5 million for the first ten years and 1.8 percent of BHEL's total turnover; the latter alone should amount to about 4 billion rupees over the next 15 years (the duration of the agreement), assuming a modest 10 percent rise per annum in the turnover. Additional payments have to be made also. Moreover, the agreement practically forbids BHEL from acquiring know-how in the designated areas from other sources without prior consultation with Siemens; and exports to some 84 countries are barred since Siemens is already established there. Further, the proposal also includes such software items as systems and applications engineering which may have a two-fold impact: first, it will discourage Indian efforts in this domain not only by the BHEL unit but also by other Indian firms in the public or private sectors; second, with the Siemens-BHEL tie-up in this field the market for products manufactured by Siemens' subsidiary in India (Siemens India Ltd.) will be greatly expanded at the cost of its rivals.

Indeed, all this is particularly ironical since BHEL made many significant advances on its own with respect to foundry forge plants, hydrogenerators, AC/DC motors, large motors, and 15 MW special turbines. While the proposed agreement is being discussed, the chairman of BHEL, Mr. Raghavan, organized large-scale discussions with the engineering and research personnel of the company who unanimously condemned it. But, then, the central government removed him from the post despite the written protest of all trade unionists belonging to different political parties. There are strong indications that the politicians and bureaucrats at the helm of affairs are determined to push through the agreement.(73)

THE ECONOMICS OF TECHNOLOGICAL CHOICE

One major obstacle to the adoption of labor-intensive technologies is the widespread belief in the efficiency of "modern" technology vis-à-vis the more "backward" one. Cost-benefit analysis, as generally practiced, provides a convenient rationale for this belief. In order to develop the counterargument, we shall refer to the famous debate on the relative merits of ambar charkha (an improved version of the hand-operated spinning wheel) versus the modern spinning mills conducted among the economists in India in the 1950s and early 1960s.

A government agency had proposed an ambar charkha program involving an outlay of 960 million rupees in fixed assets for employing three million hand-spinners. The yarn so produced would be costlier than mill-made yarn, so, to neutralize this difference, an annual subsidy of 510 million rupees would be required. Most economists (notably, A.K. Sen and C. Bettelheim) objected to this subsidy; they argued that if the initial sum of 960 million rupees plus the annual grants of 510 million rupees were invested in other projects yielding a net surplus, then, in the long run, more people would be employed than in the ambar charkha program (where the employment potential would remain frozen due to the absence of any surplus).(74) In fact, the government rejected the scheme.

The Sen-Bettelheim thesis is open to both theoretical and "practical" or, rather, politico-economic objections. Theoretically, it rests on the premise that, even in an economy with considerable unemployment, a rise in capital-intensity (the spinning mill vis-a-vis ambar charkha), real wages remaining constant, would create a higher surplus per unit of investment and, thereby, raise the growth rate of aggregate output and employment. Kalecki advanced two counterarguments.(75) First, if one allows for technical progress leading to an annual gain in labor productivity in both the old and the new plants, one may not be able to raise the growth rate of national income simply by raising the capital-intensity. Second, and this is more important, if the initial capital-intensity and investment rate are such that the unemployment rate is likely to remain unchanged, then a lowering of capital-intensity can enhance the growth rates of both national income and employment. Once full employment is attained, however, one has to opt for that capital-intensity which ensures the equilibrium growth rate in national income, i.e., the sum of the growth rates in labor productivity and in labor force.

Concretely, Sen and Bettelheim ignored the problem of the home market: (1) The standard Keynesian multiplier effect (in terms of additional production and employment in other industries) of employing three million spinners even at a low wage could not but be considerable. (2) The import-content of ambar charkhas has always been nil, whereas nearly 70 percent of textile machinery was being imported by India in the early 1960s.(76) There is little doubt that, apart from the foreign exchange drain, the multiplier effect within the country of producing the ambar charkhas would be much higher than that of the corresponding number of spinning mills.

In a mixed economy, such as of India, one cannot isolate the question of subsidy for a sector. Besides, one must also take into account the classes or groups which receive the subsidy and how it is likely to be utilized. Thus, while the ambar charkha program was denied a subsidy, a wide spectrum of big industries received the same, usually in the form of tariff protection. Bhagwati and Desai estimated, for a range of products, the excess of domestic wholesale prices over the landed costs of similar imports during the years 1961 to 1965; this excess as a percentage of the latter varied between 19 and 1,390 percent.(77) Susmita Rakshit made a detailed study of the cost of protection of sugar, automobile, and machine tools industries. For sugar, the Indian consumers incurred an excess expenditure ranging from 150 to 300 percent (the absolute amount being 1,410 million rupees in 1963-64 and 2,850 million rupees in 1970-71). The corresponding figure for autos in 1968 was 500 million rupees, while for machine tools, the amount was negligible.(78) Taking all such cases, the excess payment made by the Indian consumers (net of indirect taxes) for modern industrial products could easily run into several tens of billions of rupees.

Of course, we are not suggesting a dismantling of the tariff barrier, though this is what the World Bank and other proponents of free trade have been advocating. Our contention is that the primary objective in tariff policy in a Third World country with a high level of unemployment should be the creation of maximum employment; this is, moreover, an objective that has been systematically pursued by the industrialized countries for more than two centuries and continues to the present.(79) If, for the sake of maintaining the income and employment of sugarcane growers and sugar refinery workers in India, the consumers were forced by the government to pay a price higher than the international one, why could it not impose a 15 percent tax on mill-made yarn to create three million and more jobs?(80) Indeed, the same may be said of a whole range of products which can become competitive only if there is an element of subsidy in their favor.

The Draft Five Year Plan 1978-83 makes a case for preferring the traditional open pan sugar (khandsari) process to the modern vacuum pan crystal sugar process. While the latter's cost of production is 17 percent lower, the former's labor-intensity is 4.5 times higher, and fixed investments per unit of output are 50 percent lower than those of the former. It has been proposed that a differential excise tax be imposed on crystal sugar to make khandsari competitive.(81) The moot questions remain: Will this tax actually be implemented? Will it be extended to other products?

There is at least one area where a similar policy could create more than one million jobs. It is the manual dehusking of paddy rice which engaged over 600,000 persons in British India at the beginning of this century, but employs hardly anyone today on a full-time basis.(82) In the past, most workers on foot-operated pounders were women; the few that remain after rice mills and husking machines have eliminated most jobs are also women. It has recently been found that, on traditional pounders, the wage costs per unit of output are somewhat higher than the price charged by the owners of husking machines. On improved versions of the pounders fitted with ball bearings that double the labor productivity, unit wage costs are considerably lower than the full costs on machines.(83) A combination of physical control and/or indirect taxes on husking machines and rice mills could tilt the balance in favor of the traditional technology.(84) However, this scheme is unlikely to be viable if one allows the private entrepreneur to enter the scene with his usually large profit margin; some kind of workers' cooperative would be essential for the traditional technology to prevail.

THE COUNTERTHRUST OF SMALL INDUSTRIES

Whereas in the industrialized countries market forces have led to a continuous increase in the size of plants thereby indicating perhaps the historical validity of the economies of scale argument, there is no such unilinear trend in India. There are, indeed, many industries where the tendency is toward larger units, but there are also others where the opposite is true.

The most notable example here is that of cotton weaving.(85) Around the beginning of this century, handloom cloth accounted for 70 percent of total domestic production. By 1948-50 the mill sector had gained mastery with 80 percent of the market; in 1975-76, however, its contribution had fallen to less than half, the remainder being turned out by the handlooms and the small-scale powerlooms in the ratio of 4:3. According to the Draft Five-Year Plan 1978-83, future expansion will be concentrated in the last two sectors, creating an additional employment of 3.8 million persons.

An extremely interesting case is that of the match industry. The story has been narrated at length by Merkensten.(86) Until 1922, all matches were imported into India, mainly by the Swedish Match Co. which was then aspiring after a worldwide monopoly, and also from Japan. After a 100 percent import duty was levied in that year, production began in India and the Swedish company established its subsidiary, Western India Match Co. (WIMCO) in 1923. By 1928, WIMCO was controlling 40 percent of the Indian market and Indian nationalists clamored for some protective measures for Indian-owned units. A limited protection was, indeed, granted by the British Indian government. However, the Tariff Board, in its report of 1928, absolved WIMCO of the charge that it was deliberately trying to monopolize the market; the Board hoped that in the long run the company's market share would go down. In the 1930s, cutthroat competition began in this industry; in the end, 20 large Indian firms disappeared and there remained only one large Indian firm and many cottage industry units. Around 1947, WIMCO's market share stood at 80 percent and it continued at that level until the end of the 1950s. Meanwhile, the government of independent India formally decided to restrict WIMCO and promote the cottage units on employment grounds, the labor-intensity in the latter being about 17 times higher. However, there is little indication that the decision was implemented, since the licensed capacity as well production of the WIMCO continued to rise over the years. The small units derived the main benefit from the rebate on excise duty and steadily expanded their market share of the early 1960s; by 1969 they had captured nearly 60 percent, raising it to 70 percent in 1977. The success of the cottage industry, Markensten notes, was "probably less because of government support than because of its own increased competitiveness, both as concerned quality and marketing ability."(87) The Monopolies Inquiry Commission also came to the same conclusion.(88) More recently, Mr. George Fernandes, India's Minister of Industry, argued that WIMCO should be asked to leave the industry so that 200,000 more jobs could be created in the cottage sector.(89)

Mr. Fernandes also cited the soap and detergent industry where the Indian subsidiary of the giant TNC Unilever, has a market of 1000 million rupees per year. If the same products could be manufactured in cottage industry units (while maintaining low costs), employment could again go up by 0.3 million.(90) However, there was no government measure to back up the minister's public statements.

Footwear is another product whose market is dominated by a TNC, Bata, not by virtue of its low costs but, rather, through its financial power and marketing strategy. Although it has several highly mechanized factories, the greater part of its domestic sales are supplied by small scale producers. In the process, Bata earns a big trading profit. If production were concentrated in small units, and if the trading margin could be reduced through cooperatives, output and employment in the industry could expand substantially.(91)

Low capacity irrigation pumpset industry is one more line where production units of different sizes thrive side by side; the small sector accounted for over half of the average annual sales of 470,000 pumps between 1969 and 1974. A detailed study of such units in the Coimbatore district of Tamilnadu, a district that produced 40 to 50 percent of the national total, found that processing costs in small units were lower than in large units. To a large extent, this was due to lower wage rates. On the other hand, the small units rarely had their own marketing outlets and were obliged to sell at a big discount to the large units or to traders. Qualitywise, there were few complaints against the small producers.(92)

Bicycle manufacturing in India was started before independence. In the 1950s, an integrated plant was set up near Calcutta in collaboration with Raleigh, the well-known British company. Some other integrated plants were also established in other areas. In the 1960s, a number of concerns in Punjab entered the field, relying heavily on subcontracts given to small-scale units. Over the last few years, the large-scale integrated plants have been limping along with public assistance, while the Punjab producers are prospering and even winning foreign markets.(93)

The electrical ceiling fan industry is another instance where there may be no economies of scale at all. A recent study estimated the relative costs of production of a cottage and a big unit, employing 9 and 1,500 workers respectively. Out-of-factory costs per fan came to 208 rupees for the former and 205 rupees for the latter. If the small unit could purchase its raw materials at the same prices as the large unit, and if its wages were raised to the same level as those of the large unit, the out-of-factory cost of the small producer could come down to 193 rupees. It was also noted that the labor-content per fan was two to three times higher in the small than in the large sector.(94)

It would not be difficult to give many more examples. After all, small units do exist side by side with large units in a large number of industries. There are two fundamental factors that work against the small units: their lack of finance, and their inability to adopt an aggressive marketing strategy to stand up against the large sector. On the other hand, the employment potential is invariably much higher in the smaller than in the large industries. It should not be too difficult for the government to remedy the situation if there is a political commitment to reduce the rate of unemployment. It has moved in the right direction by raising from 180 to 504 the number of industries reserved exclusively for the small sector.(95) But the implementation is quite doubtful since many large units are well-entrenched in these areas.

ORGANIZATIONAL ALTERNATIVES

The potential for developing labor-intensive industries would be far greater if one could create productive organizations outside the capitalistic framework. The idea of director producers' cooperatives as a means of mitigating the harsh impact of market forces on the workers and peasants is pretty old and needs no further justification. What we shall try to establish is why certain activities are feasible only in such a framework, and not in another.

We may begin with the rural scene where the bulk of the country's poor and underemployed live. One has to conceive activities that do not involve investment beyond their means, and either fulfill some existing needs at a lower cash outlay or meet some new needs which they might feel are important.

Currently, the rural families belonging to the financial bottom 80 percent of the population buy, on an average, 30 meters of coarse cloth per year at a cost of about 100 rupees for a family of five persons. Instead of buying cloth, a cooperative of, say, 100 poor families in a village could buy the raw cotton, a small number of hand-operated cording machines, ambar charkhas and handlooms, and make the cloth much more cheaply (at 60 rupees per family). Here it is assumed that: (1) each family makes its own yarn for which no wages are paid; (2) the weavers, bleachers, and dryers, being specialists, are given market wages; and (3) a small charge to cover amortization charges on the fixed assets over 10 years and interest payments on the working capital needed to purchase raw cotton in bulk is levied by the cooperative on its members. The main advantages of this scheme lie in the reduction of trading margins at various points and the elimination of wage costs for spinning. Investment per family on fixed assets as well as working capital could be as low as 40 rupees, if the raw cotton stock is kept at a low level and the minimum number of fixed assets is purchased initially. For a more comfortable margin, a sum of 80 rupees per family would be adequate. It should not be too difficult for the cooperative to raise this amount from some financial institution. Further, the scheme should generate additional employment of 20 days per family on spinning and provide for two other full-time workers in weaving, dying, and other areas.

Another activity which can immediately be suggested for the cooperative is the manual pounding or grinding of paddy rice and other foodgrains mentioned already in the previous section. The viability of the scheme would increase if the women of each family undertook the task in terms of family consumption only. Under this scheme, there is no need to allow for wage payments; a negligible service charge for the use of the implement is all that each family would pay.

Cooperative endeavors in other areas such as cultivation (through joint ownership of draught animals and farm implements), blacksmithing (for the production of agricultural tools), housing, and sanitation by poor peasants can improve their conditions at least marginally; once some success is achieved, they can venture into new fields in accordance with their needs.

In the urban areas, too, a similar potential exists with regard to clothing at least. For most other products, it may not be feasible to produce mainly for self-consumption. The moment the producers' cooperatives start depending on sales through the market, the chances of success are likely to go down. Yet, if the producers' cooperatives can forge links with consumers' cooperatives promoted, for example, by trade unions, the vagaries of the market or, rather, the dominace of moneylenders-cum-tenders can be avoided. We have noted that small industries are already viable, and their position can be greatly strengthened if two-way cooperatives can be created.

At this point, a caveat is in order. The kind of alternative economic organizations just suggested would require a fairly high degree of cohesion and consciousness among the workers and the peasants. Moreover, attempts to form such organizations, especially in the villages, are likely to be opposed energetically by the exploiting classes. There is little doubt that, in most parts of India, the peasants and workers are not yet ready to undertake such programs on a wide front. Nevertheless, isolated voluntary agencies and influential sections within some political parties are thinking along these lines and small beginnings have already been made.(96)

ALTERNATIVE TECHNOLOGY

Throughout the Third World, there is an acute discontent at various levels about the quality and social relevance of scientific and technological work conducted at teaching and research institutions. While a handful of scientists working in India have made an impact on the international scene, their number as well as importance has gone down in comparison to the prewar years. On the other hand, many Indians working abroad have attracted attention in the recent past. It follows that the intellectual quality of Indian scientists is not at fault; rather, the malaise lies in the environment. They are divorced from the wider social and economic life in the country, as J.B.S. Haldane,(97) the eminent British geneticist, noted after he came to work in India in the late 1950s. A recent study on the research themes in chemistry in 30 Third World and 14 Western universities brings out in a telling manner the "tailism" of science and technology in our milieu.(98) As long as this trend continues, the results cannot but be disappointing. For, the success of Western science is largely due to one basic factor: the progress of Western societies vitally depends on the performance of their scientists who, in turn, are given the requisite facilities, e.g., adequate equipment and working conditions.

The same cannot be said of progress in India or most other Third World countries, which can ultimately be traced to the socio-economic-political characteristics of the dominant classes who have little faith in their own scientists. However, there are straws in the wind, and important political leaders in India, at least since the early 1970s, have been aware of the need for a change. Among scientists, too, an increasing number is now groping for an alternative path.

The Council for Scientific and Industrial Research (CSIR), the mammoth organization having several laboratories in different areas throughout India, took up the Karimnagar project,(99) envisaging a cooperative, interdisciplinary effort on the part of all the laboratories to scientifically study the development potentials of that district. At the Indian Institute of Science, one of the leading scientific establishments in the country, a special group entitled ASTRA (Application of Sciences and Technology to Rural Areas) has been functioning for the last few years. Similar steps have been taken by many other institutions.

The new slogan is appropriate technology (AT) which, as is often the case, means different things to different persons. I would argue that AT cannot exclude the "conventional" areas of research for capital-intensive industries. Certain industries developed in the West are equally necessary for India or other Third World countries. Railways, steel, and electricity belong in this category. Instead of slackening, the scientists ought to intensify efforts at indigenizing these technologies as soon as possible. As Homi Bhabha, the noted atomic scientist, aptly put it: "If technology is regarded as the engine of the development process, then foreign technology is acceptable only as the super-charger of a domestic engine and never as the engine itself."(100) In this field, however, the government has a decisive role. Nevertheless, the scientists as well as others can exercise some limited pressure on the government.

The distinctive examples of AT lie elsewhere.(101) There is, for instance, research on algae which can replace commercial fertilizers to a substantial extent, be used as a protein-rich food for both men and animals, and be grown very cheaply. Biogas is now being extensively discussed as a source of energy for cooking, for lighting, or for industrial purposes in the rural areas. According to some estimates, it is, on the whole, much cheaper as a source of power for the village than bringing in power from a huge generator situated several hundred kilometers away. The operational problems of large biogas plants are still to be mastered and the costs remain rather high for the village poor in India. Research on cheap solar cookers is also being conducted in various areas; the lowest cost reported so far is only 50 rupees, though its efficiency is yet to be ascertained. Similar experiments are being conducted with windmills in many centers.

In construction, many new ideas have been suggested by L. Baker, a British-born architect, who settled in Kerala in the 1940s. By systematically observing traditional Indian architecture, he has managed not only to reduce costs by about 40 percent vis-à-vis that of conventional houses, but also to increase the use of building materials that be manufactured locally in a highly labor-intensive manner. Thus, the utilization of cement, machine-made bricks, steel, and other high-cost materials is minimized. There are efforts elsewhere to develop soil-cement blocks, sun-dried mud-blocks, cement from a mixture of lime and paddy-husk ash, and so on.

Simultaneously, there are serious endeavors to raise the productivity of traditional crafts by rigorous study of work methods, but without using power-driven machinery. If successful, these would enhance the competitive strength of the crafts vis-à-vis factory industries, and consequently help expand employment. Some successes have been reported for mat-making, oil pressing, and other crafts.

Technologists at the Indian Space Research Organization (ISRO) in Thumba are engaged in extra-curricular research of some significance. In the cashew industry, a major source of industrial employment in Kerala, there exists a threat of unemployment owing to the use of sophisticated roasters. The ISRO scientists have devised a low-cost, small roasting oven with nearly as much engineering efficiency.(102) Near Bombay, a young engineer and an illiterate but highly skilled carpenter have together devised a screen printing machine which is as efficient as the more expensive and imported rotary screen printing machines; in view of its higher labor-intensity and the prospects of labor trouble in the event of retrenchment, many textile mills have opted for the latter.(103)

The potentials for AT would no doubt increase if the scientists could develop a stronger link with the prospective beneficiaries. If, for example, more time were spent in studying the concrete problems and obstacles facing the rural poor, and solutions were attempted through regular dialogues with the latter, the research would be more purposeful and the chances of acceptance would go up significantly. Here, again, many attempts are being throughout India.

When all is said, one must admit that cases of "proven" success, still less, a breakthrough, are very rare. But efforts have been very meager compared to the amount of time and resources (of, above all, talented scientists) spent on "conventional" research, the end-results of which have been no less disappointing. If even small advances are made on the employment front, if capital costs can be significantly reduced even in a few areas, if the underemployed poor peasants and the urban unemployed can raise their standards of living even by a small margin, then AT would amply justify itself. However, the objectives cannot remain fixed forever: once something like full employment is attained, the emphasis must be shifted from labor-intensity as such. But that need is unlikely to come about in the foreseeable future.

One must also point out that AT cannot be developed in the absence of support from political and other social forces, especially representatives of the toiling masses. For, without this support, the scientists on their own may not be able to forge the necessary links with the potential beneficiaries. In short, AT must be an integral part of a broader social and political movement.

CONCLUSIONS

In surveying the broad characteristics of the Indian economy since 1900, we have tried to underline both continuity and change. Per capita net material product and the sectoral distribution of workers in these major respects there is an overall stagnation; however, there were significant fluctuations, especially with respect to the former. Drain of resources from the country is continuing, but the modalities have altered radically. The most disturbing aspect of all is the growing rate of unemployment, camouflaged in official statistics by the rise in the proportion of nonworkers. On the other hand, some people may feel encouraged by the relatively faster expansion in output of the secondary vis-à-vis the primary sector, and that of the modern factories vis-à-vis the traditional household and small industries within the secondary sector as a whole. The latter trend, however, is being counteracted to a certain extent.

It is not the author's contention that the attainment of political independence in 1947 has brought no gains at all. Republican India has at least arrested the slow degeneration of the socio-economic fabric which continued for nearly two centuries under colonial rule. A number of sophisticated industries (some of which at least are socially beneficial) have been created, and the overall technological capabilities of the Indian workers, managers, and technologists have greatly expanded over the last three decades. But these advantages have not been utilized to usher in a self-reliant path of development.

To some extent, this failure can be traced to the hold that orthodox Western ideas on development (reinforced by a misreading of the Soviet growth pattern) have had on the Indian planners and policymakers. The roots of underdevelopment do not lie, as many theorists have argued, in India's low income as such or in the lack of savings or in the absence of the latest Western know-how, technological-cum-managerial, but, rather, in the internal class structure, and in the relationship of the dominant classes with the external world.

In the author's opinion, there are two preconditions of development. First, land relations must be altered so that actual tillers can acquire rights of effective possession over the land. Second, the dominance of foreign capital and technology must end. These two together constitute the main impediments to development. Without removing them, one cannot expand the home market nor establish the hegemony of indigenous technology, both of which are necessary to raise the per capita levels of output over the long haul. A small country here and there may escape the home market problem by relying on exports promoted by foreign capital. But a large country such as India or the Third World as a whole does not have this option, because the world market itself is fairly limited, esepcially with regard to items that developing countries can possibly specialize in.

In the sphere of international economic policy, as we noted at the outset, attempts should be continued to obtain better relative prices for Third World exports. On other points, the emphasis of the NIEO ought to be shifted somewhat. In view of the past experience with foreign aid, getting more and more of it cannot be a desideratum. Not that all aid is bad for the recipient, but most of it is. A notable exception is the form and content of Soviet aid to China. Despite shortcomings, there is little doubt that this aid greatly helped the Chinese technologists to prepare engineering blueprints on their own. It follows that Third World countries should be extremely selective in their acceptance of external assistance. In addition, the transnational corporations cannot be allowed to function as they do today. On the other hand, it is not feasible to shun all dealing with the TNCs. Once foreign ownership and control over assets in the Third World are done away with, there will be a greater scope for collaboration and cooperation with TNCs under the Japanese, Chinese, or Soviet models. Prior to acceptance, host countries must carefully analyze the appropriateness of the products or processes offered by the TNCs, including the potentials for their absorption and further development by domestic R & D personnel. Finally, cooperation among Third World countries should be intensified to minimize the market-dominance of transnationals' technologies. In particular, much greater stress than hitherto should be laid on cooperation in labor-intensive technologies which can effectively replace capital-intensive ones.

We have no illusion that these policy changes, domestic or international, can be implemented in the immediate future. Nevertheless, it is important to carry on the debate on the theoretical plane and expose the unscientific character of the dominant ideologies in the hope that a new constellation of political forces will emerge someday, to lead Third World countries toward economic emancipation.

NOTES

(1) V.K.R.V. Rao, "Changes in India's National Income - A Static Economy in Progress," Capital, Dec. 16, 1954. Rao's earlier work, National Income of British India, 1931-32 (London: 1941) is considered as most systematic and laid the basis for the official series compiled after independence.

(2) There are many studies in this area by a number of scholars, but Sivasubramonian's is perhaps the most thorough. (S. Sivasubramonian, "National Income of India, 1900-01 to 1946-47," Ph.D. dissertation, Delhi School of Economics, 1965.) In particular, I have made use of his information on agriculture which tallies with that of Blyn whose work has also gained wide acceptance. (G. Blyn, Agricultural Trends in India 1891-1947: Output, Availability, and Productivity, Philadelphia: 1966.)

(3) Directorate of Economics and Statistics, Ministry of Food and Agriculture, Agricultural Prices in India, 1951-52, New Delhi, 1954. The index covered 15 principal crops: rice, wheat, jowar, bajra, barley, maize, gram, linseed, sesamem, rope, mustard, groundnut, raw sugar, cotton juice, and tobacco.

(4) In neither case is the index fully satisfactory. For livestock, forestry, and fishing do not appear in the crop price index. Mining, gas, and water supply may be in the industrial raw materials of the miscellaneous group. But these deficiencies are unlikely to be serious.

(5) Also widely quoted are S.J. Patol's reconstruction of national income statistics. His estimates of the decennial average per capita net output from agricultural crops, factory industry, and mining at constant 1952-53 prices showed a decline from the peak of Rs. 164 in 1916-25 to Rs.136 in 1946-55. See his "Long-term Changes in Output and Income in India: 1896-1960" in Essays in Economic Transition, edited by S.J. Patel (Bombay: 1965).

(6) A.K. Bagchi, "An Estimate of the Gross Domestic Material Product of Bengal and Bihar in 1794 from Colebrooke's Data," Nineteenth Century Studies, No. 3, 1973. It is based on H.T. Colebrooke, Remarks on the Husbandry and Internal Commerce of Bengal (Calcutta: 1795), reprinted in the Census of India 1951, vol. VI, West Bengal, Sikkim and Chandernagore Part-Ic (Delhi: 1953). Note that Bagchi talks of the gross product, while Sivasubramonian's figures refer to the net product. This should not alter the situation much since there were no modern factories in 1794, which generally contribute to the depreciation fund in NMP estimates.

(7) R.C. Dutt, The Economic History of India Under Early British Rule, 1757-1837 (London: 1901, Indian edition, 1963), ch. 14.

(8) "Appendices" by B.R. Kalra in Census of India 1961, Vol. I India: Part II-B (iii), General Economic Tables (Delhi: 1965), pp. 6-20.

(9) The activity rates for "long-industrialized" Europe and North America reached the peaks of 48.8 and 39.0 percent respectively in 1920 and then fell steadily to 44.0 and 38.6 percent respectively in 1960. For Japan, the peak was in 1900 at 56.5 percent and the trough in

1950 at 43.6 percent; in 1960 the rate jumped to 47.1 percent, exceeding the 1930 level of 45.9 percent. For the underdeveloped countries taken together, the available figures from 1900 show a regular decline from 45.8 percent in that year to 59.8 in 1960. (F. Bairoch and J. Limbor, "Changes in the Industrial Distribution of the World Labour Force by Region, 1880-1960," International Labour Review, October 1968.)

(10) P. Sweezy and H. Magdoff, "Economic Stagnation and Stagnation of Economics," Monthly Review, April 1971.

(11) In the United States in 1975, a rather bad year, 8.5 percent of the civilian work force was unemployed as against 19.9 percent for those aged 16-19 years. In the 20+ age group, the male unemployment rate was 6.7 percent and that for females 8.0 percent. Relative magnitudes of this order also prevailed up to September 1977. Survey of Current Business Statistics, U.S. Dept. of Commerce, October 1977, p. S-13.

(12) We are largely echoing the arguments of R. Chatto-padhyay, "De-industrialization in India Reconsidered," Economic and Political Weekly, March 22, 1975. In his rejoinder, J. Krishnamurthy ("De-industrializa-tion Revisited," Economic and Political Weekly, June 26, 1976) rightly took Chattopadhyay to task, with copious quotations from different census reports, for denying that there were special problems in deter-mining women's status; in our own text we have taken care of this point. Krishnamurthy, however, advanced two further arguments. First, he noted the rise in real per capita incomes in 1900-09 and 1925-35 a la Sivasubramonian and other researchers. Yet the rise, as we have shown in table 6.1, was not of a sustained kind, and, in any case, was of a fairly small order of 10 to 20 percent. In most of the advanced capitalist countries, per capita real incomes increased by very much larger percentages on a sustained basis before the participation rates fell and provided a better justification to the opting-out hypothesis. Even this, as we saw in the text, was not all that convincing. Second, Krishnamurthy quotes from the Census of India 1931, Vol. I India Part, Report (Delhi, 1933, p. 274) that "there is a generally increasing tendency, as castes aspire to a higher social standing, to keep their women at home." This is a mere conjecture which has not been empirically tested. Hence, we find that the extraneous arguments advanced by Krishnamurthy to explain voluntary withdrawal from the labor force quite untenable. For the Thorners' view, see Alice Thorner, "Secular Trend of the Indian Economy: 1951-1961," Economic Weekly, Special Number, July 1962, and Daniel and Alice Thorner, Land and Labour in India (Bombay: 1962), ch. 7.

(13) National Sample Survey, Report No.255A for 1972-73, April 1976 (mimeographed), p. 11.

(14) J. Krishnamurthy, "Some Aspects of Unemployment in Urban India," Journal of Development Studies, Jan. 1975.

(15) S.K. Rao, "Measurement of Unemployment in Rural India," Economic and Political Weekly, Sept. 29, 1973.

(16) A.K. Sen, "Dimensions of Unemployment in India," Convocation Address, Indian Statistical Institute, Calcutta, 1973. Sen's calculations are based on the direct estimates of surplus labor in agriculture by S. Mehra, "Surplus Labour in Indian Agriculture," Indian Economic Review, April 1966.

(17) Monthly Abstract of Statistics, CSO, Delhi various issues.

(18) This conclusion was reached in a special survey on unemployment in the Delhi area, as reported by C.P. Malhotra, "Employment Implication for the Organized Sector in the Fifth Five Year Plan," Economic and Political Weekly, Jan. 25, 1975.

(19) All the data given in this paragraph are taken from R.J. Barnet and R.E. Muller, Global Reach: The Power of the Multinational Corporations (New York: 1974), pp. 166-67.

(20) Our approach, as we already noted, is close to that of Chattopadhyay, "De-Industrialization in India Reconsidered." In his critique of the latter, Krishnamurthy argues that if the entire working age population is used as a denominator, one may simultaneously witness "de-industrialization" and "de-agriculturization." (See his article cited in note 12.) Unfortunately, for Krishnamurthy, the same possibility remains as if one uses "total workers" as the denominator, or if one adopts his definition of "industrialization" as a rise in the share of industry in GNP, for this share may rise along with that of agriculture — both at the cost of the tertiary sector, or vice versa. The infatuation of orthodox economists with the output criterion of industrialization is, perhaps, a mirror image of the "commodity fetish" of the capitalist which Marx described so penetratingly over a century ago. By the output yardstock, the Persian Gulf Sheikhdoms would be the world's most industrialized regions — a patent absurdity. Fundamentally, industrialization is a social process which is much better reflected in the occupational than in the national income structure.

(21) Sivasubramonian, "National Income of India," p. 253. In Sivasubramonian's data, small-scale industries are lumped with household industries, whereas in the 1972 census the former are in the non-household sector.

(22) The preindependence figures refer to British India, while post-independence ones refer to the Indian Republic.

(23) According to the 1971 Census, there were 6.4 million workers in household industries and another 10.7 million in the non-household sector. Employment in manufacturing, electricity, gas, water, etc. was 5.2 million in 1971 in the "organized private and public sectors," i.e., in factories. For this last set of figures see the Economic Survey 1977-78, pp. 80-81.

(24) The standard works in this area are: D.R. Gadgil, The Industrial Evolution of India in Recent Times, 1860-1939, 5th ed. (Delhi: 1971); D.H. Buchanan, The Development of Capitalistic Enterprise in India, 1934 (reprinted in 1966); and A.K. Bagchi, Private Investment in India,1900-1939, Indian edition, 1975. The last one is particularly informative about the impact of government policy.

(25) Bagchi, Private Investment in India, p. 280.

(26) Ibid., pp. 226-27.

(27) Ibid.

(28) For another very interesting test of this hypothesis see V. Nagi Reddy, "Growth Rates," Economic and Political Weekly, May 13, 1978.

(29) See S.L. Shetty, "Structural Retrogression in the Indian Economy Since the Mid-Sixties," Economic and Political Weekly, Annual Number, February 1978.

(30) This problem is familiar to all students of Marxian economics. A number of theorists see underconsumption as one of the major causes of recurring crises in a capitalist economy. If real wages do not rise pari passu with the growth in output, the capitalists will, sooner or later, come up against the "realization" or sales problem.

(31) These include the total consumption of edible oil; sugar; salt; pan, tobacco, and intoxicants; clothing and footwear; and personal transport equipment. By rule of thumb, only a third of the expenditure on "medical care and health" is assumed to be on industrial goods, the rest being payments for services. Similarly, only half of "milk" and "other food" is taken on the assumption that this part enters industry in one form or another. Finally, one-half of "miscellaneous goods and services" is included.

(32) Suppose that there were originally two workers earning 100 and 350 rupees respectively and that, after one year, the earnings of both doubled. The average wages for "those under 400 rupees" would, in the first year, be 225 rupees and, in the second, 200 rupees. In fact, however, nobody's income fell, though the spurious average did.

(33) Report of the National Commission on Labour, New Delhi, 1969, pp. 224-25.

(34) "Trends in Employment Growth in the Factory Sector," Reserve Bank of India Bulletin, July 1971.

(35) R.G. Nambiar, "Import Substitution, Domestic Resource Coat, and Key Sectors in the Indian Economy," Economic and Political Weekly, June 11, 1977.

(36) D. Naoroji, Poverty and Un-British Rule in India (London: 1871).

(37) V. Anstey, The Economic Development of India, 4th ed. (London: 1952).

(38) "National Income of India," pp. 328 and 337. Among the best available studies on this subject are A.K. Banerji, India's Balance of Payments (Bombay: 1963); Y.S. Pandit, India's Balance of Indebtedness 1898-1913 (London: 1937); and D.N. Curtoo, India's Balance of Payments (1920-60) (Delhi: 1961).

(39) In making the drain equal to these outflows we are assuming: (1) The amounts raised in the London money market at commercial rates of interest as public loans by the government of India to finance its purchases of British goods could have been raised in India as well. (2) The overwhelming bulk of the outstanding foreign private capital in India toward the end of colonial rule was accumulated within the country. The initial capital came mainly from the savings of British bureaucrats, business executives, etc. in India and the rest from small inflows of equity capital. (3) These small inflows were no greater, and probably much smaller, than the excess costs of purchasing British goods financed through the above-mentioned public loans. For indirect supporting evidence on all three points see Bagchi, Private Investment in India, ch. 6. If our hypotheses are correct, it can be easily shown that there was no net gain for India on the capital account of her balance of payments; hence, there is no need to adjust downward the amount of overall drain revealed by the current account flows.

(40) P. Baran, The Political Economy of Growth (London: 1957).

(41) Karl Marx, "The British Rule in India" (1853), reprinted in K. Marx and F. Engels, The First Indian War of Independence 1857-1859 (Moscow: undated).

(42) Dutt, The Economic History of India.

(43) This paragraph is wholly based on Bagchi, Private Investment in India.

(44) N.K. Chandra, "Western Imperialism and India Today," Economic and Political Weekly, Annual Number, February 17, 1973.

(45) N.K. Chandra, "USSR and the Third World: Unequal Distribution of Gains," Economic and Political Weekly, Annual Number, 1977.

(46) G. Myrdal, The Challenge of World Poverty (London: 1970) suggests a range of 20 to 40 percent as aid-tying costs.

(47) "India's International Investment Position," Reserve Bank of India Bulletin, July 1975.

(48) Economic Survey, various issues.

(49) Report of the Study Team on Leakage of Foreign Exchange through Invoice Manipulation, Government of India, Ministry of Finance, 1971.

(50) S.S. Nayak, "Illegal Transactions in External Trade and Payments in India: An Empirical Study," Economic and Political Weekly, Dec. 10, 1977.

(51) V. Pitre, "Illegal Transactions in Trade and Payments: A Comment," Economic and Political Weekly, July 15, 1978.

(52) R. Vedavalli, Private Foreign Investment and Economic Development: A Case Study of Petroleum in India (Cambridge: 1976), Ch. 9.

(53) Ibid., pp. 78-80.

(54) Ibid., see tables on pp. 52 and 110.

(55) If one adds up the value of production of all import-substitution industries as was done in the annual reports of the Director General of Trade and Development, Ministry of Industry, one would get estimates of several billions of rupees. Under no circumstances could India be in a position to import such amounts. This point is further discussed in Chandra, "Western Imperialism and India Today."

(56) Vedavalli, Private Foreign Investment, ch. 10.

(57) Ibid., p. 178.

(58) Foreign Collaboration in Indian Industry. The first survey was published in 1968, and the second one in 1974, by the Reserve Bank of India.

(59) C.V. Vaitsos, Intercountry Income Distribution and Transnational Enterprises (Oxford: 1974).

(60) Ibid.; see also the data contained in the Report of the Monopolies Inquiries Commission, Delhi, 1965. These data have been most effectively analyzed to bring out the link between foreign capital and collaboration and high product concentration by K.K. Subrahmanian, Import of Capital and Technology: A Study of Foreign Collaboration in Indian Industry (New Delhi: 1972), pp. 211-18.

(61) N.K. Chandra, "Role of Foreign Capital in India," Social Scientist, no. 57, 1977.

(62) M. Kidron, Foreign Investments in India (London: 1965), pp. 19-26 and 65-73. Bagchi, Private Investment in India, p. 199, rightly points to the ambivalence of the Indian capitalists even before independence. Along with the rhetoric and practice of opposition, there was also a good deal of collaboration with foreign capital.

(63) The volume of "other equity," i.e., equity capital owned by foreigners in companies not controlled by them, rose, according to Reserve Bank estimates, from 392 million rupees in 1955 to 1,077 million rupees in March 1977. It is unlikely that the foreigners were merely silent partners in these concerns. In the author's study cited in note 61 he estimates the share of such "companies indirectly controlled by foreigners" in private corporate assets at 12 percent and in private corporate gross profits at 10 percent in 1972-73.

(64) Kidron, Foreign Investments in India.

(65) It is well-known that at least one Indian Minister in charge of the drug industry and his counterpart in Pakistan lost their jobs because of their determination to introduce, in a limited way, generic name drugs in lieu of the existing brand names.

(66) V.V. Bhatt, "Decision-Making in the Public Sector," Economic and Political Weekly, Review of Management, May 27, 1978.

(67) Reprinted in the Guidelines for Industries, 1975-76, New Delhi, 1976.

(68) Perhaps the best documentation on this episode is in M. Tanzer, The Political Economy of International Oil and Underdeveloped Countries (London: 1969).

(69) "FDPI - Victims of Discrimination?" Economic Times, Nov. 23, 1978.

(70) This account is based, unless otherwise stated, on P. Ramamurthy, Stop BHEL's Dangerous Truck with Siemens, CITU publication, New Delhi, 1978; and the editorial, "Prospects for BHEL," Economic Times Nov. 13, 1978.

(71) Report of the Fuel Policy Committee, New Delhi, 1974, p. 106.

(72) In a recent advertisement inserted in the leading newspapers, the BHEL management claimed that buyers prefer the KWU equipment to the earlier one manufactured by the company and that, since it is a commercial company, it is obliged to respect the consumers' wishes. This is an incredible argument for two reasons: Why should the consumers not have the freedom to buy other equipment, say, by GE, Brown Boveri, and so on? If consumer's preference were to be the main yardstick, then very little of manufacturing could develop in Third World countries. For the advertisement, see the Statesman, November 29, 1978.

(73) In the advertisement referred to in the previous note, the present BHEL management claimed that Mr. Raghavan had ordered the implementation of the proposed agreement. No evidence is furnished to show that Mr. Raghavan supported the move; nor is any reason given for Mr. Raghavan's removal from the post. Incidentally, the advertisement was in response to an unnamed book, most probably that of Ramamurthy.

(74) A.K. Sen, Choice of Techniques (Bombay: 1968), pp. 106-10; and C. Bettelheim, Studies in the Theory of Planning (Bombay: 1959), pp. 344-50. The rupee figures in the text are taken from the latter source.

(75) M. Kalecki, Selected Essays in the Economic Growth of the Socialist and the Mixed Economy (Cambridge: 1972), ch. 10. The rather long proofs of the propositions have been omitted in our text.

(76) Economic Survey 1976-77, New Delhi, 1977, p. 106.

(77) J. Bhagwati and P. Dessai, India: Planning for Industrialization (London: 1970), tables 16-4 and 16-5.

(78) S. Rakshit, "The Cost of Protection - A Study of Some Selected Manufacturing Industries," Ph.D. dissertation, Presidency College, Calcutta, 1975, tables IV.7, IV.9, IV.11, V.6, V.7, VI.1, and VI.10.

(79) The mercentilists were unequivocal in their espousal of protectionism as a means to better utilization of productive forces, especially labor. While the nineteenth century liberal tradition discredited this school, and only retained the infant industry argument later developed by List, Western governments have not cared much for the views of their own academics. Thus, in the post-World War II period, all the industrialized countries have been protecting their oldest industry, cotton textiles, in order to maintain adequate employment and a counter competition from the Third World. However, it must be admitted that none of these countries ever attempted to protect one (labor-intensive) domestic industry against another (capital-intensive)

domestic industry. The main reason has been the relatively high levels of employment maintained in these countries throughout the last couple of centuries. Expansion into new lines was generally vigorous enough to mop up the surplus labor from decaying ones; further, the productivity differential between an established and a new technology has, for the most part, been rather small so that the extent of job displacement at any one point of time has been rather small. For this last point see J.R. Hicks, A Theory of Economic History (London: 1969), ch. 9, especially pp. 148 ff. On the ideas of the mercantilists, in addition to the classic study of Eli F. Heckscher, Mercantilism (London: 1935), one may see the interesting remarks of J.A. Schumpeter, essentially a free trader in his economic analysis, in History of Economic Analysis ch. 7, particularly pp. 350-52.

(80) This has been calculated by the author by taking into account the total production of yarn in India in the early 1960s, and the differential costs of the two types of yarn. For the sake of equity, one could impose a higher tax, say of 50 percent, on finer yarn ultimately consumed by the more affluent sections.

(81) Draft Five Year Plan 1978-83, New Delhi, 1978, pp. 104-05.

(82) Including the factory and cottage industries, grain-parching and milling occupied 1.5 million persons on a full-time basis in British India in 1901, while the figure for India in 1971 was only 0.37 million. Foodgrain production, in the meanwhile, more than doubled from 52 to 108 million tons. The employment data are taken from Census of India 1901, vol. I-A: India Part II, Tables by H.H. Risley and E.A. Gait; and Census of India 1971, Series I-India, Part II special: All-India Census Tables (estimated from one percent sample data). Production figure for 1901-2 is taken from S. Sivasubramonian's article in V.K.R.V. Rao et al. (ed.), National Income and Allied Papers, Vol. II (Bombay: 1960); and for 1970-71, from Economic Survey 1976-77.

(83) No scientific study of the relative costs have been undertaken to the best of my knowledge. According to one estimate, the conversion charges per 60 kg. of paddyrice are 2.40 rupees for the husking machines; the wage costs on traditional pounders are 3.00 rupees while those on improved pounders are about 1.50 rupees. Capital charges for the pounders have been ignored since the fixed capital costs are negligible – 100 rupees for the traditional pounder and 230 rupees for the improved one.

(84) It would not be too unreasonable if one were to ask for limited subsidies. In fact, the Indian government has been paying an annual subsidy of nearly 5,000 million rupees to the rich farmers producing wheat in order to encourage them to grow more. For the political economy of high prices of selected agricultural commodities and food subsidies, see Ashok Mitra, Terms of Trade and Class Relations (London: 1977).

(85) The data for the earlier period are taken from M. Espen, "Emerging Trends in Cotton Textile Consumption," Social Scientist, Jan-Feb., 1977. The recent data for 1975-76 onward are taken from official publications.

(86) K. Markensten, Foreign Investment and Development: Swedish Companies in India (Lund: 1972), pp. 63-6 and 254-56.

(87) Ibid., p. 66.

(88) Report of the Monopolies Inquiry Commission, Delhi, 1965, p. 144.

(89) The minister's speech is reported in "Coimbatore Meeting - an Eye-opener for Janata," Statesman, March 28, 1978. See also the editorial in Economic Times, Nov. 24, 1978, on "Small Industries."

(90) Ibid.

(91) Some very useful information on the small-scale shoe industry in Agra and how it is exploited is given in "Footwear Workers of Agra Lead a Miserable Life," Economic Times, January 13, 1976; and in a letter to the editor by the General Secretary of Agra-Shoe Manufacturer's Association, "Footwear Prices," Economic Times, March 27, 1976. On the modus operandi of Bata, the author has collected some first-hand information from the small scale suppliers. Bata also controlled the overall output of its suppliers – a restrictive practice condemned by the Monopolies and Restrictive Trade Practices Commission. Details are given in N.K. Chandra, "Monopoly Legislation and Policy in India," Economic and Political Weekly, Special Number, Aug. 1977.

(92) M. Cartillier, "Role of Small Industries in Economic Development: Irrigation Pumpset Industry in Coimbatore," Economic and Political Weekly, Nov. 1, 1975.

(93) Based on personal interviews.

(94) S.K. Das, "Economies of Scale and Implications for Policy: A Study of Electrical Ceiling Fan Industry," Economic and Political Weekly, May 27, 1978.

(95) The Statement on Industry before the Indian Parliament on December 23, 1977.

(96) These issues are discussed at greater length in the present author's "Industrialization and the Left Movement: On Several Questions of Strategy in West Bengal," Social Scientist, Numbers 73-76, 1978.

(97) J.B.S. Maldane, Science and Indian Culture (Calcutta: 1965).

(98) G. Lake, "The Structure of Science and its Implication for Science in Developing Countries," M.Sc. thesis, Manchester University, 1971; and also E. Turkean, "The Limits of Science Policy in a Developing Country: The Turkish Case," Science Policy, (2). Both are quoted in C. Cooper, "Science Policy and Technological Change in Underdeveloped Countries," World Development, March 1974.

(99) See the initial report, "Karimnagar: District Development - A Summary," CSIR, New Delhi, 1973 (mimeographed).

(100) Quoted in An Approach to the Science and Technology Plan, National Committee on Science and Technology, New Delhi, Jan. 1973.

(101) The information on various experiments, unless otherwise speci-fied, are taken from A.K.N. Reddy and K.K. Prasad, "Technological Alternatives and the Indian Energy Crisis," Economic and Political Weekly, Special Number, Aug. 1977; A. Makhijani, "Energy Policy for Rural India," Ibid.; B.G. Verghese, "Algal Promise: Time to Set up Backyard Sindris," Statesman, Oct. 5, 1977; and Annual Report 1975-76, ASTRA, Indian Institute of Science, Bangadore, 1977.

(102) S. Shetty and K.P. Kannan, "Small Roasting Ovens and Large Roasting Ovens for Processing of Raw Cashew Nuts: Some Tech-nological and Economic Issues – A Preliminary Note," paper presented at the Seminar on Alternative Technologies held in August 1977 at the Centre for Development Studies, Trivan drum.

(103) "Achievement: Tale of Two Men and a Machine," Economic Times, Nov. 22, 1978.

7 Food, Natural Resources, and the New International Economic Order: The Case of India

M.T.R. Sarma

INTRODUCTION

The problems of food and natural resources figure prominently in discussions on the New International Economic Order. To bring about the improved competitiveness of natural resources, the Programme of Action on the Establishment of the NIEO called for:

- discouragement of new investment for the expansion of the capacity to produce synthetic materials in cases where natural materials can satisfy the requirements of the market;
- measures to expand the markets for natural products in relation to synthetics; and
- fuller utilization of the ecological advantages of natural resources.

It is also recognized that the solution to the economic problems faced by developing countries, such as India, that are traditionally dependent on natural resources to provide the basis for economic development, requires appropriate action to diversify the end-uses of natural products facing competition from synthetics and substitutes so that they can obtain the competitive advantage in international trade.

Problems of food and natural resources were accorded special attention in the context of the NIEO at both the Sixth and Seventh Special Sessions of the General Assembly of the United Nations, and a

*The views expressed in this paper are those of the author. The author is grateful to Professor Prakash Tandon, Director General; and H.I. Bhatty, Deputy Director General of the National Center on Applied Economic Research (NCAER) for their kind permission to produce this paper.

World Food Program has been proposed to improve agricultural production and the storage and distribution of agricultural inputs and outputs. Issues related to this problem are food aid, policies to improve market competitiveness by eliminating tariffs on food and other agricultural products from developing countries, and the building up of a World Foodgrain Security System. The problems and policies of the Indian government in the areas of food and agriculture are well documented.(1) In order to make the tasks manageable, only a broad synoptic review of some policies on food and on ways to avoid the waste of some natural resources is attempted in the next section. The problems of competitiveness of natural products vis-à-vis synthetics in the case of the rubber, jute, and cotton products of India are discussed in the third section of this chapter.

FOOD AND NATURAL RESOURCES

For the establishment of a just and equitable NIEO, national policies and strategies of development in the fields of food and natural resources should be consistent with the overall objects of the NIEO, and should promote harmony and cooperation between the developing and the developed countries. The imbalance between world food demand and supply, as well as the rise in oil prices in recent years, have pointed out the growing importance of such an interdependence in the process of economic development of all countries. The primary commodities produced and exported by developing countries to the industrialized countries face not only the obstacles of tariffs and of nontariff barriers, but also the problem of price instability, which affects both consumers and exporters. This is especially true for such products as rubber, jute, sisal, and cotton which can be replaced by synthetic substitutes and, therefore, might experience a long-term decline in demand.

Policies for food and natural resources, particularly in a developing country like India, should be facilitated by removing any obstacles for the establishment of a prosperous egalitarian rural society. As the Report of the National Commission on Agriculture (NCA) put it, the policy and strategy of development should lead to an adequate supply of goods and services to sustain a rising standard of living, and sufficient employment and income opportunities for the masses to generate effective demand for these goods and services.

It is now generally agreed that the main thrust of policy should be to secure demand-supply balance in various agricultural commodities as well as distributive justice over a period of time, and that investment policies should seek to allocate resources within agriculture to secure both efficiency in production and the generation of maximum employment opportunities.

It may also be relevant to note that any obstacle or constraints that may exist in the achievement of a dynamic and diversified agricultural economy should be removed so that efforts can be directed toward an integrated program of crop production, livestock, and poultry, fisheries, and forestry. For this process, the NCA recommended that: "A re-ordering of the agrarian structure should receive a very high priority in the development strategy to lay a sound foundation." Keeping in view the main goals of policy, the land policy should ensure intensive utilization of land, create widespread productive employment, and reduce disparity. It should induce changes in property relations and social structure in rural India with a view to enabling wider involvement and participation in development. The undue concentration of ownership and use of land should be avoided through a rigorous implementation of ceilings on both ownership and operational holdings. However, the current ceiling limits should be deemed to have been laid down on a long-term basis and should not be altered for a sufficiently long period to encourage investment in land and production. Also, there should be a minimum time gap between legislative enactments and their imple-mentation to avoid aberration and promote sufficient stability to foster investment. The emphasis should be on personal cultivation to ensure adequate attention to land and increased productivity and production. The agrarian structure should be based on peasant proprietorship, strengthened and supplemented by cooperative and joint farm enter-prises, and backed by the necessary supplies and services for optimum utilization of land. State assistance should be given, on a preferential basis, to the small cultivators who get together for joint farming. Leasing out should, however, be allowed by small owners within the size class of marginal farmers, and in the case of exempted persons due to their special circumstances. With respect to other forms of tenancy and sharecropping, these should be abolished and the tenants and share-croppers vested with proprietary rights on a date to be specified by the state government. Efforts should be made to identify all surplus land for distribution to the landless and marginal farmers, priority being given to the landless (particularly Harijan), tribal, and backward com-munities. In this process, caution is needed to prevent distribution of village common lands as part of the land distribution program. Such lands should be preserved and utilized for the general good of the village community, particularly for the benefit of the weaker section. Housing sites should be provided for the landess who cannot be given land, and they should be assisted in the building of houses as well as with the practice of subsidiary occupations at home.

Recommendations of the National Commission on Agriculture

In the context of establishing a NIEO with reference to food and natural resources in India, the following policies and programs are relevant for the promotion of agricultural growth with social justice.(2)

The consolidation of fragments of land holdings into compact areas should be an important aspect of land policy for both operation economy and production benefits.

For diversifying production, increasing return from land, employment, and income, and ensuring a balanced supply of food and fodder, the farmer should be encouraged to take to mixed farming, supplementing cultivation with subsidiary occupations (e.g., raising livestock, poultry, fish, and silk worms, and bee-keeping). This would ensure a year-round use of resources and labor potential of the farm family and livestock.

The animal husbandry development policy should be based on the application of science and technology to animal production. Its objective should be diversification of the agricultural production base, improvement of human nutrition, provision of supplementary income to the weaker sections of the rural community, and increasing the employment potential. The essential elements of this strategy should be to improve the productive potential of livestock and poultry, including draft power of cattle, and to arrange for production of feeds and fodders only for the production stock and to weed out inferior, uneconomic, and surplus animals. Improved husbandry practices and better health care should form important components of this strategy.

For improving the productivity of cattle and buffalo, the policy should be to adopt scientific methods of breeding, to provide adequate feeds, fodders, and animal health care, and to improve management practices. A close tie between intensive cattle and buffalo development programs and dairy plants will be necessary for providing a ready market for the milk producers and ensuring remunerative prices. With a view toward effecting progressive improvement in the milk yield, a considerable proportion of the existing population of low-yielding cows and buffalo should be replaced with cross-bred cows and improved species of indigenous cows and buffalo. In such a milk-production-enhancement program, the approach should be to identify suitable areas and to undertake integrated cattle and buffalo development along with milk marketing projects.

The best policy for the development of dairying, appropriate to Indian conditions, would be to produce milk in the rural areas for supply to the urban consuming centers. Small and marginal farmers and landless laborers should be associated with the milk production programs. Collection, processing, and distribution of milk and the manufacture of milk products should be organized, as much as possible, through cooperatives of the milk producers themselves. The development of dairying should be effectively interwoven with the economy of the villages. A national milk grid with conservation facilities should be developed to even out seasonal and regional imbalances and to reduce rural urban inequalities in milk consumption. The new policy should aim at self-sufficiency in milk and milk products, thereby increasing the export quantity of finished and sophisticated products.

The sheep population should be increased at a faster rate. Large-scale crossbreeding programs using exotic breeds of sheep should be undertaken for a rapid increase in wool and mutton production. A greater part of the arid regions should be utilized for range land and pasture development. The natural pastures in the northern temperate regions should be improved. Leguminous fodders should be included in the cropping pattern in irrigated areas, and large blocks of government range lands should be developed, mainly as grass reserves.

Marketing of wool and live animals in major sheep rearing tracts should be organized through sheep farmers' cooperatives and wool boards, which should take up the responsibility of sheep shearing, wool grading, and storage. Marketing yards should be set up for sale of live animals. A policy for realizing a higher trade balance in wool or woolens should be followed. Its main features should be:

1. progressive restrictions on the export of raw wool;
2. encouragement of exports of manufactured woolen goods;
3. close linkage between wool production and manufacture of woolen goods; and a linking of carpets with the scheme of handicrafts boards/khadi boards functioning in the area; and
4. simplification of the procedure for payment of drawback claims on duties on woolen goods for export.

Since goats cause considerable damage to natural vegetation, their number should be reduced to a manageable limit and stabilized. It is necessary to devise suitable management systems to exercise greater control over their movement and feeding habits. Goats should be kept out of areas where soil conservation practices are being introduced. Lopping of trees for the feeding of goats should be avoided and the stall-feeding of milk goats should be encouraged. The approach should be oriented toward raising meat production, increasing breeding among taller and medium-sized breeds, and cross-breeding exotic dairy types with select meaty-type bucks. The crossbreeding of indigenous with exotic dairy breeds of goats should be undertaken to increase milk production. Milk capabilities of better indigenous dairy breeds should be improved through selective breeding.

The genetic make up of the indigenous pigs should be gradually changed by introducing exotic breeds of boars. For organizing production, producers' cooperatives should be formed and the supply of quality pigs and balanced feed, as well as adequate health care and marketing facilities should be ensured. Intensive pig breeding areas should be developed around the bacon factories and pork processing plants. The bacon factories should adopt a pricing policy for pork and pork products favorable to the producers in order to give encouragement to pig production.

Poultry development should aim at self-sufficiency in the production of quality chicks and increased production of eggs and poultry meat. This could be achieved through an adequate supply of poultry feed at a reasonable price, quality control, proper marketing of poultry products, and the adoption of appropriate breeding strategy. In areas where a high standard of poultry husbandry exists, high producing straincross or incross hybrid chicks should be made available. For poultry farms in the intermediate stage of development, crossbred birds would be preferable. In the rural areas, where backyard poultry rearing practices are predominant, the most practical breeding program would be to upgrade the local stock with improved exotic varieties. The crossbred males should be reared under a semi-intensive or free-range system so that they are not at a disadvantage when distributed in the village. All indigenous cocks and cockerels should be replaced by crossbred males. Early action should be taken for licensing all commercial hatcheries to avoid disease. Producers' cooperatives should be organized for providing necessary inputs for the poultry farmers.

An effective veterinary service should be developed to keep livestock free from disease to ensure optimum production. For achieving this, the funds of the Veterinary Departments will have to be supplemented. A phased program of levying a charge for the treatment of livestock, including prophylactic vaccinations, should be introduced immediately. Private veterinary practice should be encouraged by providing suitable incentives to veterinarians in protecting the health of livestock. Biological production centers should be converted into corporations with a certain degree of autonomy so that these could function with some freedom from the usual restrictions of government rules and regulations.

Modernization of slaughterhouses should be regarded as a development activity and not as a commercial venture. There is considerable scope for building up an export market for buffalo meat, especially to the countries in the Middle East. To achieve this objective, the quality of the buffalo meat should be improved. The export of meat and meat products should be brought under the control of some organized agency and quality control ensured. An organized marketing service for meat animals should be established in the cooperative sector.

The overall policy should be to encourage dispersed development, each area specializing in the development of the livestock and poultry which suits the environment. Each area must have a program for increasing feed and fodder resources. Wherever necessary, controlled and rotational grazing should be adopted to allow for adequate regeneration of the grasses.

Development of inland fisheries should be undertaken as a priority industry to increase the availability of low-cost animal protein. As Indian carps remain the mainstay of fresh water culture, their seed stocks have to be increased several fold for undertaking increased stocking densities to obtain optimum yield from all culturable waters. A major aim should be the optimum use of water resources, i.e., ponds and tanks, for fish production. For encouraging the development of fisheries, greater attention should be paid to the requirements of small fishermen. Since waterbodies are indivisible, small fishermen should be encouraged to form cooperatives for fishery development. Rights in culturable fisheries should be granted an as outright lease on reasonable terms to enable utilization of long-term credit. Similar procedures should be adopted for water under government control. Since a large number of tanks and ponds are not utilized because of private ownership rights, the state governments should take control of such water areas and utilize them for pisciculture. With regard to reservoirs in irrigation projects, the interests of fisheries should be kep in view starting with the planning stage.

Marine fishing policy should be altered with a view toward an exclusive fishing zone adjoining the coast. The emphasis on distant water fishing fleets should be replaced by more concentrated efforts for the exploitation of the seas within 320 kms. of the Indian coast with emphasis on small and medium-sized trawlers. The inshore fishing areas and coastal creeks should be developed for higher yields through the cultivation of prawns, mollusks, and other suitable coastal fish. In marine fisheries also, the small fishermen should be given preferential facilities in terms of fishing boats, gear, and landing facilities. It will be essential to take necessary measures which delimit fishing zones through legislation in order to avoid conflicts among the nonmechanized crafts and mechanized boats and larger fishing vessels, and to avoid friction among fishermen of adjoining states. Up-to-date information on marine fish stocks should be built up through comprehensive research. Oceanographic research will have to be intensified so as to develop fully the strategy to utilize the extended resources of pelagic fisheries beyond the traditional zone of exploitation of coastal regions, particularly in the West.

Fishery development should invariably be accompanied by arrangements for storage so that the fishermen are not required to dispose of their catch at throw-away prices. Infrastructural facilities, i.e., fishery harbors, should be developed to support marine fishery development. In order to utilize fully the resources of the deep waters, infrstructural facilities should be provided in the public sector, which could then give the lead to the industry as a whole. A policy for developing specialization in the construction of trawlers should also be fostered.

Special attention should be paid to crustacean fisheries, which have great export potential, by way of a comprehensive survey of resources; a regular monitoring of the status of the fisheries; and diversification of production and processing centers, export products, and export markets. In this sector, small entrepreneurs as well as large businesses need to be encouraged, as scope exists for both.

In view of the increasing demand for forest-based products, there is need for an increase in the productivity of forest and their scientific management along modern lines. The national forest policy should rest on two pivotal points. First, it should meet the requirements of raw materials for the forest-based industry and provide small timber, fuelwood, and fodder for the rural community. Second, it should satisfy the present and future needs for protection and regeneration of the forests. All the requirements must be met in full and self-sufficiency achieved as early as possible. There should not only be a dynamic forestry production but also an extensive social forestry program. Forests must have an adequate share of land, and no deforestation should be permitted without the approval of the state legislatures. Since interdependence between forestry and forest industries sectors is vital, integrated planning for raw material production and forest-based industry would have to be a major aim of future policy. The required institutional changes should be made and infrastructure built up for the purpose. The price of the forest produce for the industries should be so fixed as to pay for the cost of plantations, and the maintenance of production forests, yet leave a profit. Possibilities should be explored for cultivating plantation crops, such as rubber, coffee, and cashews, in suitable locations on forestland to the extend that they do not interfere with the production of industrial wood.

The domestic needs of the people living near forest areas, for small timber, fuelwood, and fodder, are to be met primarily through widespread adoption of social forestry programs, which would lessen the burden of production forestry. Since free supply of forest produce to the rural population and their rights and privileges have brought destruction to the forests, prices should be attached to forest produce for the rural population but these prices should be kept at a reasonable level.

Forestry programs should encourage wildlife development and environment balance. Some ideas, carefully selected and distributed to embrace varied natural conditions and ecosystems, should be devoted to the principal use of Nature and Wildlife Conservation.

Reducing crop losses should be an important objective of development. A policy of integrated pest control must be adopted. This will include evolution of pest and disease resistant varieties, treatment of seed before sowing, prophylactic and curative spraying during the crop season, biological control, and control of pests through agronomic practices. For optimum results, the adoption of pest control operations on an area basis is essential and should be made compulsory with provisions to recover proportionate costs from the beneficiaries. In the choice of chemicals, those with greater risk of pollution should be discouraged. An important aspect will be the education of farmers regarding proper use of pesticides.

In the labor-abundant situation in India, the basic approach should be to meet farm power needs by utilizing, as the first priority, the available manpower and draft animals. Implements should be improved and used to gain better efficiency in man and animal power and to enable precise farming. Agricultural machinery should be used on a highly selective basis, but may be allowed to reduce the power gap in areas which exhibit a marked shortage of both man and animal power. In areas of surplus labor, suitable control must be exercised to see that mechanization is not used to avoid labor-management problems, and that it does not depress wage levels. In the course of agricultural development, the use of machinery should be so regulated as to facilitate continuous progress toward full employment. In some land development work, mechanical support will be justified for undertaking heavy work and expediting developing which will result in larger and sustained employment. Similarly, mechanical and electrical support is also justified in irrigation.

Electricity should be made available for energizing pumpsets and for rural industries in practically all the villages by 1990. The supply of electricity for agricultural operations should be given top priority and an uninterrupted and unflutuating supply ensured. Special consideration should be given to the extension of electricity to fishing colonies along the sea coast.

Means of Implementing NCA Recommendations

Considering the overall constraint on credit, adequate weight must be given to the small and marginal farmers, agricultural laborers, and rural artisans with respect to the amount of credits and the level of interest rates. An important aspect of credit policy should be to help the farmers to reach a self-sustaining stage through the principle of gradation which would encourage them to plow back their surpluses into agriculture. In providing credit to medium and large farmers, the capacity to provide their own funds should be kept in view.

For upgrading and modernizing agriculture and for an efficient utilization of credits by the weaker sectors, an integrated and supervised credit structure will have to be built. This structure would consist of farmers' service societies (FSS) at the grass roots level, controlled by the small and marginal farmers and agricultural laborers, which would be linked to a commercial bank or a cooperative central bank for the necessary financial and managerial support. The FSSs should also encourage and finance viable units of suppliers of inputs, customs service, storage and transportation, and marketing in their respective areas. All types of credit should flow through this single agency to ensure appropriate control and use. Increasing use of institutional sources should be made to provide access to resources for large-scale area development programs such as common area development.

To ensure reasonable returns to the producer and to ensure the availability of goods at reasonal costs to the consumer, an efficient marketing structure has to be developed. In general, the farmers should have marketing facilities within a radius of five kilometers of the place of production. The existing weekly markets should be developed into assembling or submarkets. New markets should be organized in areas brought under irrigation and areas of intensive production. The bigger markets should be given priority, and the necessary amenities provided therein. All the agricultural commodities which enter the market should be graded, and those designated for export should be inspected as well. To ensure the high quality of the processed products, improved processing facilities should be established near the centers of prodution. These processing and marketing activities should be organized as much as possible on a cooperative basis, the primary cooperative marketing societies being linked with the commodity operations such as those for food, cotton, and jute.

Public distribution of essential commodities will have to be a permanent or a semipermanent feature of economic management in the country, given existing shortages. In such a situation, the procurement prices of cereals have to be below the prevailing market prices in order to meet the needs of the public distribution system. Since the issue price has to be related to the purchasing power of low-income consumers, the procurement prices, although higher than the minimum support prices, cannot be much above the issue prices minus the cost of distribution, plus, at best, a small element of subsidy. With respect to commercial crops, the prices at which the commodity cooperatives and other agencies are to buy the crops should be determined after taking into account their impact on the domestic industry, the economy, and exports. The principle of price support should be extended to livestock, poultry, fishery, and forest products.

There are several aspects of agricultural development which induce regulation in the interest of the common good. For example, consolidation of holdings, soil conservation, land development, drainage, and plant production programs have to be organized on an area basis. If a majority of the beneficiaries agree, there should be provision made for the obligatory participation of others.

Further, with regard to fertilizers and pesticides, quality control is important. Improved seeds need certification guaranteeing purity and germination. Food products need to be certified as uncontaminated. For this, also, appropriate legislation will be necessary. While, in general, regulation of crop acreage through legislation may not be feasible under Indian conditions, in some cases, establishing certain areas for growing certain varieties of the crop (as in the case of cotton), and for prohibiting the cultivation of certain crops (i.e., tobacco in certain potato areas that are prone to diseases) may become necessary in the interest of agricultural production. Land reform, minimum wages, and restriction on movement are other spheres in which legislation is necessary. In all these cases, it is desirable to have a certain amount of uniformity subject to local adaptation and modifications.

The NCAER has to take upon itself the responsibility of ensuring national priorities for the lowest level of rural households and the small and marginal farmers. In order to create adequate opportunities for employment and to ensure a minimum income for this sector of the rural population, a national strategy of expediting growth not only in crop production but also in livestock and poultry production, fisheries, and forestry is needed. Considering their importance, these programs are of national significance and thus the NCAER should assume a large measure of responsibility for the formulation of appropriate policies. In addition, it must guide the states in executing the programs.

Given proper training in the appreciation and adoption of modern technology in agriculture and related activities (including rural crafts and small-scale industries), rural labor could increase its productivity and earnings. Providing technical training to youths in backward areas is essential to the promotion of growth of agro-industries in large numbers and to the securing of employment among the rural unemployed and underemployed. Rural employment policy should, therefore, have the objective of providing intensive training for the rural work force in all the productive activities in which they are participating, including the imparting of new skills in traditional occupations. In the rural areas, women have traditionally had a recognized role in earning a livelihood for the family through their participation not only in the production but also in the marketing of agricultural produce and a variety of products of village industries. Female labor performs a wide range of duties on and off the field such as dibbling, transplanting, weeding, harvesting, rearing livestock and poultry, kitchen gardening, sericulture, compositing, application of manures and fertilizers, grain storage, and seed preservation. Their contribution to the family income is, therefore, considerable. With the increasing emphasis now being placed on the adoption of improved agricultural methods, the sustained and more effective participation of rural women in productive activities can only be achieved through orientation and training in the various functions which rural women will continue to fulfill both in and outside the farm. Illiteracy is no doubt a major impediment to the spread of knowledge among women.   In training programs emphasis should, therefore, be placed on promoting functional literacy among rural women, so that the vast rural female labor force can be efficiently harnessed for improving rural life in general.

Preventing Waste of Natural Resources

Agriculture in India — besides providing food, forage, and raw material for industry — generates enormous quantities of by-products which either go to waste or are utilized uneconomically. As Bhagwan Dass recently reported, Punjab Agricultural University is actively engaged in research to develop methods for the complete use and recycling of different types of waste of natural resources.(3)

The University's Department of Processing and Agricultural Structures has demonstrated that paddy straw can be used profitably to manufacture substitutes for jute bags. Bags designed and fabricated from paddy straw can be used to handle and transport potatoes. About 100 bags can be made from a quintal of paddy straw and each bag, of 25 kg. capacity, costs about 3 rupees. Another use for paddy and wheat straw has been developed by the Soils Department; they can be used as mulch. Applied at four to six tons per hectare after sowing hybrid maize, the mulch increased the yield of grain about 18 percent (36.8 to 43.5 quints/hectare). The favorable effect of mulch is attributed to a reduction in soil temperature.

For better use of rice husk as a cheap source of energy, the Department of Processing and Agricultural Structures has developed a cyclone-type furnace which is intended to replace the less efficient grate type presently used in rice mills. Particles of rice husk are floated in the combustion chamber, where each particle gets enough oxygen for complete combustion. The furnace is very efficient and capable of burning 50 kgs. of husk an hour. It can be used to heat air or water or to dry crops.

Corncobs have been used by the Department of Biochemistry to produce citric acid for use in preserving fruits. A method has been developed to prepare a suitable hydrolysate from cobs for the growth of Aspergillus niger, which synthesizes citric acid.

The leaves of certain vegetables – cauliflower, radishes, turnips, and carrots – which generally go to waste, contain valuable proteins. Protein concentrates prepared by biochemists from some of these vegetables have been evaluated for their growth promoting ability. There are indications that they can serve as a good supplement for whole wheat flour.

The Department of Processing and Agricultural Structures has found that pine needles going to waste in hilly areas can be used as insulation material for cold storage. They have a thermal capacity comparable to other commonly used insulants in addition to being resistant to fungi, termites, and other insects.   With the use of this material for insulation, a saving of about 30 percent can be effected in constructing a cold storage facility.

The soil microbiologist at the University has developed a biogas which uses wastes such as straw, leaves, and kitchen leavings instead of cattle dung (gobar) in its formation. As this waste material is light and floats, a stirring mechanism has been provided to submerge the material. About 20 kgs. of straw waste fed to the plant daily produces about six cubic meters of biogas. The residue may be used as manure. The composition and properties of biogas and manure thus produced are similar to those from gobar gas plants.

A large number of chemicals may be derived from agricultural wastes.   Among them polymers appear economically promising. A process to produce polymers and to convert them into plastic foam is being developed by the Department of Mechanical Engineering. Reinforced foam will be evaluated as a material to make roofs and panels.

The Department of Processing and Agricultural Structures is working out the details to establish a paper recycling plant at the University. This will use paper cuttings, rags, and crop wastes, e.g., wheat and paddy straw to make paper suitable for file covers and other products.

One of the most important animal wastes is cattle dung. It can yield two valuable products – gobar gas (biogas) and fertilizer. But there are many problems, such as high cost and low production in winter, which stand in the way of popularizing these uses. The Department of Civil Engineering has developed a new gobar gas plant in which the most expensive component, the gas holder, has been eliminated and gas is stored in the pit itself which is closed at the top. The other costly material, the bricks, has been replaced by stabilized soil. These innovations are expected to reduce the cost of a plant considerably. Moreover, eliminating the gas holder will make the plant less vulnerable to corrosion because the holder is damaged through contact with the acid produced in the digestion process. It has been observed that if the gas plant is covered in the cold season with jute cloth and dried grass, which act as insulation, the production of gas could be increased about 48 percent. This will help solve the problem of less gas production because of the low temperature in winter months. The Department of Zoology is exploring the possibility of using cattle dung to breed fish. For that purpose, a fish seed farm comprising a series of tanks has been established at the University.

The Department of Animal Sciences has also done commendable work on the use of cheap agro-industrial by-products to develop economic and efficient poultry rations. Their experiments have shown that defatted rice bran can replace half the bran in poultry mashes and silkworm pupae meal can replace half the fishmeal.

DISPARATE DEVELOPMENT AND THE NIEO

In India, to overcome the obstacles to the establishment of a NIEO, measures will also have to be devised and implemented effectively which tackle the problem of disparate development not only among different classes of rural populations but also among the regions with varying endowments.

For the establishment of a new economic order at the national or international level, agricultural development based on social justice is essential. Although most of the necessary initiative has to come from within the individual developing countries, international action and support are needed in addition to the program of a World Food Security system. The latter is needed to support the development effort of Third World countries like India, and to benefit small and marginal farmers and landless laborers by creating diversified employment and income earning opportunities. Specifically, the author would like to endorse the following suggestions of Professor V.K.R.V. Rao(4) for international action.

Continuing and extended support should be provided for national and international research on seeds, not only from the point of view of high yield and fertilizer response but also genetic resistance to pests and diseases, increase of protein content, and adaptability to different agro-climatic and other ecological conditions. This research has to be continuous as the rate of obsolescence in new varieties is quite high, and national, regional, and world banks with genetical resources that include all varieties of seed – wild, traditional, and new – should be maintained and added to with time. Research on seeds needs to be extended to pulses and oil seeds and to crops providing industrial raw materials. Research also needs to be extended to dry land farming, flood inundation and upland farming, diversification of agriculture, rotation of crops, and livestock and fishing industries. Above all, international action should give priority to research that will be guided by social and ethical considerations of what can be done to confer special benefits to the small farmers and weaker sectors of the agricultural community.

Technical and, if necessary, financial assistance should be extended to the developing countries in Asia to improve the utilization of their existing irrigation systems with special emphasis on drainage, water control, and the availability of water to all the cultivated acreage included under their command areas.

Continuing assistance should be supplied for new irrigation projects with special emphasis on ground water exploitation and minor irrigation (which is more amenable to water control), as well as emphasis on drainage and a complete process of storing – from the reservoir to the time it reaches the farmers' field in the case of major and medium-sized irrigation works.

Internationally owned and operated factories should be established on a nonprofit-no-loss basis, for the manufacture of chemical fertilizers and other chemical inputs which would include the participation of natural gas and oil producing countries and countries with advanced technical know-how and operating skills in the field. The output of these factories should be earmarked for the small and marginal/sub-sistence farmers in the developing countries, with adequate safeguards for controlled distribution and actual utilization by the cultivators for whom it is intended.

Assistance should be given to developing countries to set up a wide network of storage depots for agricultural outputs and inputs. These would not only provide the marketing facilities needed for the success-ful operation of new technology but also would help in the building up of buffer stocks for national use and contribute to the basic food stocks required for ensuring World Food Security in accordance with the proposals of the Director General of the Food and Agricultural Orga-nization of the United Nations (FAO).

Action must be taken by the developed countries to eliminate or substantially reduce their tariffs and other barriers to the import of foodgrains and other agricultural goods from the developing countries.

Foreign exchange support for credit programs undertaken by the national agricultural banks in the developing countries, based on the criteria the World Bank is using in giving support to industrial banks in these countries (as illustrated by the Industrial and Credit Investment Corporation of India [ICICI]) must be initiated.

Assistance should be provided for training programs for extension workers, especially in water control and agronomic practices so essen-tial for the success of new technology. These training programs should utilize personnel drawn largely from the developing countries.

Periodic reports should be made by all the developing countries on the progress of new technology, its effects on production, distribution, and savings; and, more importantly, its effect on the participation of small and subsistence farmers in the new technology and the gains accruing therefrom.

Support for national and international research on the social, economic, cultural, and political aspects of agricultural development and the new technology should be forthcoming, as well as their effects on the developing countries. These studies should be primarily inter-disciplinary in character and aim at presenting an integrated picture of the results of development projects.(5)

Other Natural Resources of India

In the case of the nonrenewable critical natural resources of India, the following conservation perspective has been provided by the Planning

Commission of India, for 1978-83, which may be relevant to note in the context of the establishment of the New International Economic Order.

Nonrenewability of critical resources requires that the depletion of mineral resources be judiciously planned. The present knowledge of mineral reserves is admittedly inadequate because survey and exploration work has not yet been carried out in all parts of the country. In fact, only 46 percent of the total geographical area had been mapped by 1975. The available estimates of reserves are not only based on incomplete mapping but, where mapping has been completed, the investigations have been "preliminary" in the case of many materials. Reserve estimates based on preliminary surveys are denoted as "indicated" or "inferred" as distinguished from "measured" estimates based on detailed investigations. In the case of kyanite, chromite, copper, limestone, asbestos, and bauxite, 80 to 90 percent of the estimates are merely "indicated" or "inferred."

The ratio of "inferred" to "measured" reserves is also low: 64 percent of iron ore, 84 percent of kyanite, and the whole supply of barytes, mica, chromite, and magnesite. Although for many metals considerable recycling possibilities exist, recycling remains underdeveloped in India, except in the case of certain types of metallic scrap.

The magnitude of the presently known, recoverable reserves, and their balance life in 1987-88, calculated on the assumption of depletion rates of 1977-78 continuing are given in table 7.1. It will be seen that the balance life is strikingly short for manganese ore and chromite, copper and zinc, rock phosphate, and coking coal. Therefore, in planning production and trade in sectors absorbing these intermediates, it will be necessary in the future to establish acceptable depletion rates. In addition, the following policy measures need early attention:

- Integrated geological mapping of the whole country, on a suitable scale, should be given very high priority. Exploration to shift reserves from the "inferred" to "measured" categories should be expedited.
- Trade, pricing, and royalty policies should be adjusted to induce socially optimal rates of depletion.
- Depending upon foreign exchange availability, imports of scarce materials, such as copper, lead, zinc, rock phosphate, coking coal, crude oil, and asbestos should be maintained at significant levels in relation to requirements, so that the depletion of domestic reserves is slowed down.
- Leasehold patterns should be modified to facilitate better reserve measurements and optimal depletion.
- Research and development efforts to develop technologies for the exploitation of low-grade and complex ores should be intensified, particularly in the case of nonferrous metals.
- Research efforts, and the monitoring and adaptation of foreign technological development should also be intensified in order to develop renewable or less scarce substitutes for nonrenewable materials and sources of energy.

Table 7.1. Magnitude of Recoverable Reserves
(In million tons)

Minerals	Estimated Recoverable Reserves*	Depletion 1977-78	Balance life at 1987-88 production levels (in years)
A. Where production is suggested to correspond to demand plus export:			
a) Non-coking coal	32,000	1,290	191
b) Iron ore-Hematite	9,400	650	126
c) Iron ore-Magnesite	860	60	106
d) Bauxite	1,970	33	352
B. Where production is suggested to correspond to demand only:			
a) Manganese ore	74.79	17	30
b) Chromite	13.10	1.6	52
C. Where production plus import is suggested to correspond to demand:			
a) Copper	3.68	0.52	53
b) Zinc	3.42	0.54	31
c) Lead	1.50	0.19	52
d) Rock Phosphate	30	10.20	20
e) Crude oil		200	
f) Coking Coal	3,100	345	66

*For iron ore (hematite), iron ore (magnesite), bauxite, manganese, copper, zinc, and lead, recent estimates (January 1, 1977) of reserves have been adopted for estimating recoverable reserves. For other minerals, recoverable reserves have been computed on the basis of reserves on January 1, 1975.

*For iron ore (hematite), iron ore (magnesite), bauxite, manganese, copper, zinc, and lead, recent estimates (January 1, 1977) of reserves have been adopted for estimating recoverable reserves. For other minerals, recoverable reserves have been computed on the basis of reserves on January 1, 1975.

Source: Government of India, Draft Five Year Plan 1978-83, Vol. II, Planning Commission, New Delhi, pg. 31-33.

PROBLEMS OF COMPETITIVENESS OF NATURAL PRODUCTS VIS-A-VIS SUBSTITUTES

One of the objectives of the NIEO is to improve the competitiveness of natural materials facing competition from synthetic substitutes by removing obstacles through appropriate national and international policies and programs of action. In this context, the problems of three important natural products of India – rubber, jute, and cotton – will be analyzed.

Rubber

India now has a relatively well-developed rubber plantation industry. Domestic production of natural rubber rose from 15,880 tons in 1950-51 to 150,000 tons in 1977-78. The average yield per hectare increased from 280 kgs. to 800 kgs. during this period. Most of the production of natural rubber – 95 percent of the total output – is in Kerala State. Under the International Rubber Regulation Agreement of 1934, natural rubber exports from the producing countries were severely restricted in order to arrest sharply declining international prices of this commodity. As a producing country, India was also a party to this agreement. As a result of these restrictions, domestic availability improved and gave an incentive to establish rubber manufacturing units in India. However, real growth and development of the rubber manufacturing industry in India took place only after Independence in 1947. The Rubber Act was passed by the government of India in 1947 and the Rubber Board was established under the Act, making it possible for the development of natural rubber plantations along sound economic lines.

At present, there are 86 large and medium-sized units and about 2,500 small-scale units engaged in the manufacture of a wide range of rubber products.

The entire requirement of the rubber industry in terms of natural rubber, SBR synthetic rubber, reclaimed rubber, and rayon tire cord is being met from indigenous production. Requirements of carbon black, nylon tire yarn, and rubber chemicals are also being met up to 90 to 95 percent from domestic production (see table 7.2).

Table 7.2. Production and Consumption
Levels for Natural and Synthetic Rubber

Type of rubber	Production (In metric tons)		Consumption (In metric tons)	
	1948	1977	1948	1977
Natural	15,400	161,610	19,000	142,763
Synthetic	Nil	27,000	--	34,543

Source: Government of India, Draft Five Year Plan 1978-83, Vol. II, Planning Commission, New Delhi.

The first synthetic rubber factory in India started in 1963 with the commissioning of the plan of Synthetics and Chemicals Limited at Bareilly, with the production capacity of 30,000 tons per annum. In addition to producing SBR (Styrene-Butadiene Rubber), this unit has started production of nitrile rubber. Indian Petro-Chemicals Corporation Limited (IPCL) at Baroda set up a plan to produce polybutadiene rubber with a total installed capacity of 20,000 tons per annum. There are, at present, two major chemical manufacturing units — Bayer (India) Limited in Bombay, and the Alcali and Chemicals Corporation of India Limited in Calcutta — producing a wide range of accelerators, antioxidents, retarders, and stabilizers with a licensed capacity of a little over 12,000 tons. A third unit, Mindia Chemicals Limited in Bombay, has already started trial production.

The rate of growth of rubber consumption in the country has been 8 to 10 percent per year for the past decade. At this rate of growth, the current level of production of natural rubber may not meet the entire rubber requirements of the country in the future. On the international scene, too, according to the Controller of the Malaysian Rubber Research Unit, natural rubber supplies will be inadequate to meet consumer needs from the early 1980s unless output and productivity are increased in the natural rubber industry throughout the world.

Consumption of SBR, polybutadiene rubber, and nitrile rubber is expected to increase in India. According to projections made by the National Organic Chemical Industries Limited (NOCIL) total consumption of synthetic rubber will increase from 167,000 tons in 1977 to 417,000 tons in 1988, requiring production levels of 34,000 tons styrene, 126,000 tons of butadiene, and 2,000 tons of acrylonitrile.

The main problems faced by the manufacturers of rubber products in India relate to cost, quality, and availability of raw materials. Except for special purpose synthethic rubbers and sulphur, India is almost self-sufficient for most of the raw materials required by the rubber industry. In order to reduce waste of this natural resource, India has several plants manufacturing "reclaimed rubber" from scrap tires and tubes.

With regard to domestic pricing policy for natural rubber, the government of India asked the Tariff Commission to analyze the cost structure of the plantation industry and recommend a price that could help it to undertake development plans for the future. Natural rubber has been under price control since 1942, except for a few short interruptions. The minimum price for natural rubber has been increasing; it stood at 6.55 rupees per kg. in 1977, which does not take into account the increase in productivity (the average yield of natural rubber rose from 300 kgs. per hectare in 1950 to 800 kgs. per hectare in 1977) and which is also not consistent with the cost of production. However, the government of India has taken into account the need to increase the minimum prices for natural rubber because of the pressures from the plantation industry and the Rubber Board.(6)

There is need to create enough buffer stocks of natural rubber in India to meet at least four months' average domestic consumption

requirements. International agreements should be designated to stabilize the prevailing prices in order to facilitate imports and exports.

The Rubber Research Institute at Kottayam (Kerala), established by
the Rubber Board, has developed high yielding types and also effected
improvements in budding techniques and in balanced application of
fertilizers. The NCA felt that there was further need to breed varieties
of rubber resistant to abnormal leaf-fall and the powdery mildew
disease. It is also necessary to breed special varieties for the proposed
new areas in the States of Maharashtra, Andhra Pradesh, and Orissa,
which have conditions less humid than those of Kerals and Assam. The
Rubber Board's scheme of assistance to rubber plantations should be
modified to benefit the small growers. The handicaps of the small
holders could be overcome by organizing them into effective cooperatives. Financial aid and international technical assistance to
stimulate the expansion of rubber plantations to other states is desirable in the context of the NIEO.

Jute and Jute Products

Bast fibers (i.e., jute, mesta, ramine, sunhemp, flax, and agave) are put
to a variety of uses such as packing, flooring, furnishing and backing
materials, woolenized fabrics, fishing nets and lines, marine and industrial ropes, twines, cardages, and cables. Jute and meste face severe
competition from synthetics. Even so, they have the advantages of low
cost, strength, and stability. The advantage of the comparatively low
prices of jute and related goods has to be maintained by paying
continued attention to improved productivity. Diversification of the
end-uses of jute and related fibers, such as textiles, flooring and
construction materials, and woolenized goods, should receive constant
attention by India as well as other countries in the context of
establishing the NIEO.

As the NCA Report points out, there is adequate information
through research work, the results of which should be utilized in
effecting yield improvements. The real obstacle is, however, the slow
pace of development and extension activities. International aid and
action in this field might strengthen domestic efforts. The Committee
on Public Undertakings (1977-78) of the Sixth Lok Sabha (Parliament of
India) in its Third Report of Jute Corporation, published in April 1978,
observed that India has an important role in the world jute market by
accounting for 30 percent of global output and 40 percent of global
export. However, the falling, or at best stationary, trends in the
production of raw jute have now posed a danger to India's export
performance of jute manufactures in terms of quantity, as will be seen
from the figures in table 7.3 pertaining to the last ten years.

The main policy problem with regard to improving the productivity
of jute in India is to ensure remunerative prices to the jute growers and
to eliminate exploitation by middlemen in jute trade between growers
and manufacturers. Beginning with the 1961-62 season, concerted

action toward achieving the objective of price stability in jute was initiated by the government of India. The Jute (Licensing and Control) Order 1961, was promulgated under the Essential Commodities Act, and measures were taken, inter alia, to regulate the purchase and stock of jute with jute mills. Subsequently, the Jute Corporation of India Limited was established in 1971, and entrusted with the task of marketing raw jute, including its import and export. The Jute Corporation of India will have to play a more effective role in ensuring more remunerative prices to jute growers; in addition, the existing credit institutions should help jute growers in the rural sector by providing credit on more liberal terms.

Table 7.3. Exports of Jute Manufactures

Year	Quantity (thousand tons)	Value (millions of Rupees)
1965-66	900	2,880
1969-70	571	2,067
1971-72	671	2,653
1972-73	581	2,500
1973-74	563	2,275
1974-75	589	2,968
1975-76	516	2,483

Source: Economic Survey, 1976-77, Ministry of Finance, Government of India, New Delhi, 1977, p. 104.

Cotton and Cotton Textiles

Of the 7.6 million hectares presently under cotton cultivation in India, Gujarat and Maharashtra States account for 57 percent. Madhya Pradesh and Karnataka rank next with 22 percent of the country's cotton area. Except in Gujarat, the yields in the other cotton regions are low, being 45 to 65 percent of the national average.

Cotton production in India has varied widely in the past. In the last decade, production fluctuated between a peak of 7,782 million bales (of 175 kgs. each) in 1971-72 to about 5.9 million bales in 1965-66, as may be seen from table 7.4. Stabilization of cotton production and improvement in the yields of cotton obtained in India will have to be tackled through appropriate domestic policies of research on cotton and those relating to agronomic and plant protection schedules, as well as through pricing and marketing policies. In the case of cotton, the competition from synthetics is not a serious problem in India. However, it is relevant to note that India is in a favorable position with regard to coarse cotton, which is not produced by other countries, and the production of coarse cloth, in which competition is negligible. The competitive export market is in favor of long-staple and superior

Table 7.4. Cotton: Production, Import, Export, and Apparent Consumption

Quantity: Lakh bales of 175 kgs. each
Value: Rupees in crores

Year ending 31 August	Production* (Quantity)	Import		Export		Apparent consumption (Quantity) (Cols (2&3) -5)
		Quantity	Value	Quantity	Value	
1	2	3	4	5	6	7
1960-61	59.59	11.65	69.02	3.07	13.70	68.17
1965-66**	59.37	5.57	40.07	1.93	8.61	63.02
1970-71	59.82	9.10	109.85	2.00	16.78	66.92
1971-72	77.82	7.90	101.74	2.47	21.67	83.25
1972-73	69.56	4.68	64.90	1.84	18.39	72.40
1973-74	67.24	1.88	37.30	3.66	39.97	65.46
1974-75	73.59	1.15	24.98	0.97	12.60	73.77
1975-76	69.70	1.66	26.15	4.27	58.23	67.09

*Based on Trade Estimates

**Value figures from 1966 onward are in terms of devalued rupee and hence not comparable with figures for the predevaluation period.

Source: Handbook of Statistics on Cotton Textiles Industry (10th Edition) Indian Cotton Mills Federation, Bombay.

medium-staple cotton. Even for the domestic market, there is scope for the use of synthetic man-made fiber substitutes without seriously affecting the interests of the cotton producers in India. However, the export of cotton textiles and ready-made garments from India to the industrially advanced countries presents problems that need to be tackled in the context of the establishment of the NIEO.

CONCLUSION

The case study of India in the fields of food and selected natural resources attempted in this chapter demonstrates that the obstacles for the establishment of the NIEO could be removed by appropriate domestic policies and programs that require national action, as well as policies and programs that require international action. Most of the action for growth with social justice in the fields will have to be taken within each developing country, as India has been trying to do with a shift to an integrated rural development that will generate additional employment and income earning opportunities for the poor and economically weaker sectors of the society. International action should be such that it will provide the necessary financial and other resources to facilitate a process of economic development that will reduce poverty and improve the levels of living in India. Concerted action is required at both the national and subnational levels to improve productivity and reduce the waste of food and natural resources. This process should be facilitated by financial aid as well as trade policies of the developed countries.

Developed countries should stop labor-intensive industries such as cotton textile and ready-made garments within their own countries and, instead, import the products of such industries from developing countries like India. In the area of food, in addition to the creation of the World Food Security System under the aegis of the FAO, the developed countries should encourage the use of appropriate technology and modern scientific knowledge to improve productivity and promote a sustainable growth of output and employment.

In the process of overcoming the obstacles to achieve the objectives of the NIEO, the development strategy of developing countries should be designed to attack the problems of poverty, unemployment, inequality, and structural backwardness more directly and efficiently. The government of India and the Planning Commission have recognized this imperative need and the approach of the Draft Five Year Plan for 1978-83, prepared in 1978, spells out programs of development aimed at solving these problems in that country.(7) The major task is to utilize the available human, material, and financial resources for a new pattern of growth in pursuit of the goals of full employment and distributive justice.

The policies and strategies for development of the agricultural sector in India suggested by the NCA and presented in this chapter provide the basis for planning of an integrated rural development in India.

If appropriate and timely international action is taken to promote such a plan of development, it will certainly enable a developing country like India to overcome many obstacles, and the prospects for the establishment of a just and equitable national and world economic order will be bright.

NOTES

(1) See, in particular, the Report of the National Commission on Agriculture, 1976, Government of India, Ministry of Agriculture and Irrigation, Department of Agriculture, New Delhi, 1977.

(2) Ibid.

(3) Bhagwan Dass, "Farm Waste is No Waste," Indian Express, New Delhi, November 29, 1978, p. 9.

(4) V.K.R.V. Rao, Growth with Justice in Asian Agriculture - An Exercise in Policy Formulation, United Nations Research Institute for Social Development (UNRISD), Geneva, 1974, pp. 80-82.

(5) Ibid.

(6) See for example, Rubber News (Bombay) 18 (2) (November 1978).

(7) See the three volumes of Draft Five Year Plan, 1978-83, Planning Commission, Government of India, New Delhi, 1978.

8 Natural Resources and Raw Materials in Southeast Asia
Vitchitrong na Pombhejara

INTRODUCTION

Natural resources is a term with different connotations. In its narrow sense, it is confined to nonrenewable resources (mineral deposits) and the physical environment of specific geographical areas (land, soil fertility, climatic conditions, rivers, mountains, natural harbors). But in a broader sense, natural resources also connotes the renewable resources forming the basis of primary industries, namely, agriculture, forestry, livestock raising, and fisheries products. In other words, in this connotation the term covers practically every commodity produced from natural products as distinguished from manufactured products. In this context, rice, rubber, timber, kenaf, tapioca, sugar, copra, cattle, and fish are as much natural resources as tin, oil, bauxite, coal, and iron ore. In this chapter, the broader connotation will be adopted.

With regard to raw materials, the working definition employed here covers all natural resources which serve as material imputs for processing and producing certain products. Many of the raw materials have gone through one or more steps of primary processing such as selection, sorting, and grading before being placed on the market. In some cases, they are smelted or purified. The raw materials which have been processed or semiprocessed are usually referred to in the market as commodities.

Southeast Asia is a traditional producer and exporter of raw materials and of natural resources as defined here. Favored by climatic and soil conditions, the region is rich in agricultural resources including forests. In addition, deposits of various economic minerals are also to be found. These natural resources are the economic base on which the Southeast Asian economies' potential development depends so much. These valuable resources tempted European powers in the nineteenth century and Japan in the early part of the present century to colonize Southeast Asia. It is not a historical misinterpretation to state that the

164

great Pacific War of 1942-1945 was, in part, an armed struggle over the natural resources of Southeast Asia.

While the economic development of Southeast Asia has been viewed as a desirable objective and strenuous efforts have been constantly made by both the individual countries and international bodies to achieve it, there appear to be obstacles blocking the road to progress. One of the obvious barriers to Southeast Asia's resource-based development is the limit imposed on the market expansion of some of the region's natural resources by competition from synthetic substitutes. As a result of scientific research and technological progress in the industrially developed countries, synthetic products have been developed to replace natural products in their role of industrial raw materials. In other cases, substitutes have been purposely developed for various end-uses previously served solely by natural commodities. While it is futile to blame technological development and economic innovation for Southeast Asian economic problems, the fact is that, in many cases, natural resources have already lost their technical battle against the synthetic substitutes. Moreover, they are losing the economic struggle as reflected by the gradual shrinkage in their share of the world market. The effects of competition from substitutes on sectoral as well as national economic development in Southeast Asian countries have been far-reaching. Not only has their development process been retarded, the employment opportunities of an already large idle labor force further restricted, and the necessary foreign exchange earnings reduced, but the unfavorable impact of competition from synthetic substitutes is also felt in the long-term investment decisions, creating a feeling of uncertainty with regard to the future of these economies. In the final analysis, the threat from synthetics has a tendency to widen the gap between rich and poor nations as well as to aggravate socio-economic injustice in the world economy. Undoubtedly, this constitutes one of the main obstacles to the establishment of the New International Economic Order.

The main economic problem of many primary commodities and mineral resources has been large price fluctuations that have adversely affected both the producing and consuming countries. While producers have been handicapped by marketing uncertainties and have been discouraged from maintaining their regular supplies, consumers have been unwilling to take risks on both prices and supplies of their raw materials, and thus have been forced to look for substitutes in synthetics or other products.

To resolve the problem of price fluctuations, proposals have been made within and outside U.N. channels for the creation of international buffer stocks for individual agricultural and mineral commodities. This technique for achieving price stability has also been endorsed by UNCTAD with a view to applying it to a large group of commodities with the financial support of the Common Fund. The idea behind this ambitious technique is the belief that price stability will necessarily secure markets for natural resources threatened by synthetics and other substitutes.

Whether the achievement of price stability will necessarily secure the market for natural commodities in the long run is still not clear. The problem becomes more difficult when considering the many implications involved in establishing and administering international buffer stocks. There are great difficulties, for example, in the area of financing. We cannot realistically expect the financing to come from consuming countries, at least not in sufficient amounts to make such international buffer stocks effective. Besides, there are other problems in various aspects of buffer stocks' administration: storage, transportation, floor and ceiling prices, as well as the permissible flucuations in price. Again, there is the question whether price stability is really the answer to the problem.

It should be realized that the battle of natural resources against their synthetic substitutes is largely an economic one. Whether the objective is to drive the synthetics and substitutes out of the market, or to check their further encroachment, there is only one solution: natural resources must be competitive in price, quality, and deliveries. There is no other way to improve the competitiveness of the natural resources vis-à-vis synthetic substitutes. In other words, prices must be lower, quality equal, and deliveries prompt. Focusing on price stability alone is not a sufficient means to hold the world market.

In this chapter the question of how to improve the competitiveness of natural resources vis-à-vis synthetic substitutes in the world market will be approached from an economic point of view and within the context of the Southeast Asia region. The delineation of the problem involved is neither thorough or exhaustive, since the purpose of the chapter is simply to offer some thoughts on the matter with the view to exploring alternatives.

THE PROBLEM OF SYNTHETIC COMPETITION

The existence of substitutes is nothing new in the realm of economics, either in theory or in practice. In economic theory, subsititutes play an important role in demand determination. When the substitutes' prices go up, there will be a greater demand for the natural product and vice versa, provided that the price of the product itself remains unchanged. How strongly the influence of the substitutes' price movements are felt in the demand for and the price of the product will depend on the degree of substitutability. Perfect substitution is, of course, a rare phenomenon because each product has a certain combination of unique elements and thus maintains some differentiation among the various products. Product differentiation is conditioned by a wide range of factors, from individual taste to buyer' goodwill, and from location of supply to delivery services.

In the real world, it is almost impossible to find any single product which has no substitute. Oil has gas and coal as substitutes for fuel sources. Aluminum and plastic are substitutes for tin in packaging. Butter has as a substitute margarine, which is made of vegetable and palm oils. Corn, wheat, and barley are substitutes for rice in the starch component of human diets. In fact, searching for substitutes is an essential part in the struggle of mankind for survival and it has played a crucial role in scientific and technological progress. The existence as well as the emergence of substitutes are facts of life, past, present, and future.

From the strictly economic point of view, the existence of substitutes is considered a blessing. They not only offer wider scope for competition, a prerequisite for efficient allocation of productive resources, but their close connection with technological progress is one of the necessary conditions for economic expansion. Each discovery of a substitute indicates that one or more productive uses has been found for products whose economic values are now greater than before. We must realize that most, if not all, of the main products in great demand today first appeared on the market as substitutes. This is true of copper, steel, tin, rubber, kenaf, or sugar-cane. It is also evident that each technological and scientific breakthrough brings with it a number of substitute discoveries.

Technically, synthetic products have been developed from petrochemical technology; and, economically, their effects have been most strongly felt by natural rubber, natural fibers, and other materials utilized for containing and packaging. During the past thirty years, industries and businesses as well as households have witnessed the emergence of synthetic rubber, synthetic fibers, and plastic products of a wide range to take the place of natural raw materials in industry, trading commodities, office equipment, and household utensils. In fact, there are only a few areas left where synthetic substances have not made inroads into consumer usage. Scientific research and technological development have rendered synthetic substitutes highly competitive with natural products in terms of technical properties, commercial attractiveness, and cost to the consumer. In many cases, the synthetics have proven to be technically superior to the natural materials. In other cases, they are tailored to suit specific technical or commercial requirements such as strength, impermeability, non-fragility, and coloring. However, it is in the area of price competitiveness that the synthetic products have won their decisive battle against natural materials.

The recent history of synthetic rubber is significant in this regard. In the 1950s, faced with rapid losses in both market share and prices, Southeast Asian producers were forced to launch a vigorous replanting program with high-yielding clones initially in Malaysia, the world's largest natural rubber producer.

The remarkable increases in yields and quality have been attributed to improved cultural practices, better tapping techniques, and the use of yield stimulants. Through the efforts of the Rubber Research Institute in Malaysia, natural rubber has been increasingly exported in technically standardized form in 70 to 75 pound bales compared with the traditional 250 pound bales of smoked rubber sheets graded and specified by visual inspection. This vast improvement in standardi zation of natural rubber has substantially increased the product's marketability in competition with synthetic substitutes.

While counterresearch and development may have been to a large extent responsible for the natural rubber's success in maintaining its present one-third share of the world's rubber market, there remains a deep concern over its long-term prospect in the future. To be competitive in terms of production costs, there is the need for fundamental organizational changes, perhaps for an overall switch from small holdings to large entities where more efficient management and greater capital intensiveness could be put into effect. There are also many disadvantages of natural rubber. For instance, a rubber estate takes a minimum of six to seven years to come into production, whereas a synthetic plant can be put to work within a much shorter period of time. There is also an enormous discrepancy of labor productivity between natural and synthetic rubber production processors. Whereas a one-man year of labor would produce, at best, two tons of natural rubber, it could generate up to 1,000 tons or more in a synthetic rubber plant. As labor costs are expected to increase, the relative competitiveness of natural rubber is indeed at stake in the long run.

On the other hand, in recent years there has been an optimistic outlook for natural rubber. The sharp increases in oil prices tend to adversely affect the cost of synthetic production. As the prices of synthetic rubber have moved upwards, some gains have been made by natural rubber in the share of the world market. Nevertheless, it should be carefully noted that the effects of the increase of the oil prices are not likely to be confined to any particular industry. Such effects will be spread all over over the economy, pushing up costs of production indiscriminately. In other words, it is not expected that natural rubber could continue to count on the increase in oil prices to its advantage in the competition with the its synthetic competitors.

The situation in the kenaf industry is not very different. One of the largest producers and exporters of kenaf in the world, Thailand is also facing competition from synthetic fibres. Botanically, kenaf or "Thai jute" is different from jute. Although the soft fiber contained in the best of the stalks has properties very similar to jute fiber and could be used as a jute substitute, jute fiber is inherently finer than that of kenaf and can be used to make finer yarns. Because of this inferior natural quality, kenaf is much cheaper than jute in the market.

In recent years, largely as the result of high prices for tapioca which have diverted farmers' efforts to that commodity, kenaf production in Thailand has declined to an average of 200,000 to 300,000 metric tons per annum. Not unlike rubber and other primary commodities in the world market, kenaf has been subject to extreme price fluctuations which, in turn, are mainly responsible for wide fluctuations in the fiber's output. In the international market, kenaf has to compete with jute. In many cases, jute and kenaf fiber are mixed or blended, the proportion varying with end usage and local practice. There are cases where kenaf fiber of uniform quality can be almost completely substituted for jute of lower grades.

Competition with jute is, however, only a part of the story. In reality, both jute and kenaf, as well as some other natural coarse fibers, have been competing with synthetic products. For kenaf, the competition from synthetics can be either direct or indirect; but, either way, unless the synthetic threat is checked, the prospect of kenaf in the long run is, indeed, very gloomy.

Direct competition from synthetics is clearly seen in the international market of gunny sacks. Until recently, most if not all containers for agricultural products were made of natural fibers. Raw sugar, rice, wheat, corn, barley, and wool were packed in gunny sacks mainly made of kenaf fiber. Even fertilizers were packaged in gunny bags. With the successful introduction of plastic materials, practically all wool is now packed in plastic containers. In many countries, plastic bags are also being used for rice. The sharp decline in demand for gunny sacks has not been caused by technical reasons, but rather by price competition from their synthetic substitutes. Nowadays, gunny sack producing countries, Thailand included, have been exporting at prices which are below their costs in order to maintain their market share.

THE INTERNATIONAL BUFFER-STOCK STRATEGY

Technical improvement in natural materials' competitiveness vis-à-vis synthetic substitutes, though meriting serious attention, is not likely to achieve its goal within a reasonable period of time. Most of the producers of natural materials are developing countries lacking both financial resources and research capacity. In addition to that, a scientific experiment performed with natural commodities usually takes a relatively long time to produce results. For instance, it takes six or seven years for the rubber tree to be ready for its initial tapping. The question of technical improvement, therefore, though important, will have to be secondary to economic considerations.

Appropriate attention will have to be directed toward relevant economic measures. There is certainly room for improvement in the economic properties of the natural commodities in order to increase competitiveness in the world market. Thus, removal of marketing disadvantages is the crux of the problem.

There exists a number of obvious marketing disadvantages responsible for noncompetitiveness on the part of natural commodities: irregularity of supply, lack of standardization, price fluctuations, and, most crucially, noncompetitiveness in pricing. It is recognized that some strategy is needed to cope with all these disadvantages as a whole. Obviously, such a strategy requires a cooperation between producer and consumer.

For more than twenty years, an international arrangement on one natural commodity has served as the prototype of producer-consumer cooperation. It is the International Tin Agreement which has continuously been in effect on a renewable five-year basis since 1956. The objectives of such agreements are manifold and emphasize the problems of maintaining a balance between world production and consumption, preventing excessive price fluctuation, promoting export earnings, and ensuring an adequate supply at prices that are fair to consumers and remunerative to producers. Membership is open to all producing and consuming countries, and each group has an equal voting power in the International Tin Council. The Council, whose functions are the administration and supervision of the agreement, holds regular meetings in order to assess demand and supply conditions, and to decide on the activities of its buffer stock, the appropriate price range, and export controls.

The International Tin Council has three main instruments to achieve its objectives. The general instrument is a price-supporting buffer stock of up to 20,000 metric tons, provided solely by the producers either in cash or in metal as determined by the Council. Agreements between the consuming and producing countries are based on the floor price at which the buffer stock must be bought, and also on the ceiling price at which it must be sold. These floor and ceiling prices are adjustable depending on market conditions. The effectiveness of the buffer-stock operation depends mainly on its size, but also on the level of management skill involved. The two other main instruments are export controls and the setting and changing of the price ranges. These instruments are to be resorted to only when the buffer stock proves ineffective in countering price weaknesses.

Perhaps some degree of success in the experience of the international buffer-stock under the Tin Agreements has led many natural resources-producing countries, with the endorsement of UNCTAD, to believe that an international buffer-stock arrangement is the answer to the marketing problems of natural commodities in general. In the first place, they are attracted by the idea of bringing consumers and producers together to agree on prices and demand and supply conditions. Secondly, it seems to be generally believed that if a sizeable internal buffer stock could be established, prices of natural commodities could be sustained at an appropriate level regardless of competition from synthetics and other substitutes. In some cases, advocates of the international buffer-stock strategy see such an arrangement as a convenient and effective way in which the financial responsibility for carrying stocks is shared by importing and consuming countries. In extreme cases, they even wish to see practically the whole international stock financed by the consumers.

Formed in 1967, the Association of Natural Rubber Producing Countries (ANRPC) has advocated the establishment of a price stabilization scheme including an international buffer stock of rubber. The producing countries of jute and kenaf, particularly India and Bangladesh, have also expressed their interest in an internationally financed international buffer-stock.

While the effort to bring together producers and consumers to participate jointly in a cooperative scheme which would benefit both sides is unquestionably the ideal, it must be remembered that the international buffer stock is not necessarily the best technique for establishing such an international cooperative arrangement. Pragmatism is often overlooked when minds are clouded with sentiments.

When we speak about a buffer stock, we must think of the problems of product standardization, physical storage, management skills and practices, price ranges, and, above all, financing. These problems are real, burdensome, and gigantic. They are not easily solved and, yet, even the slightest degree of success in the scheme depends on the complete and unequivocal solution of all these related issues.

Let us briefly consider some of the elements in the creation of an international buffer stock. First, one must consider product standardization and specification. For the commodities whose products are technically specified and standardized, there will be few problems involved. There are, however, some commodities whose product gradings vary from time to time and also from one locality to another, and grade mixtures are not uncommon. In addition, visual inspection is, so far, the only method for specification. For these commodities, the problem concerning specification and standardization alone renders an international buffer stock impractical. Storage is another problem involving difficulties. Some commodities cannot be stored over a long period of time as their technical properties are subject to rapid deterioration. Apart from that, the storage costs can be enormous as they require proper facilities and handling techniques. There is also a question of where the commodities should be stored, as well as who shall pay the costs.

The question of desirable price ranges is common to all commodities. The terms "remunerative," "fair," "appropriate," and so on are not difficult to conceive on paper. But when it comes to reality, each term is likely to mean different things to different interest groups. We can determine "monopolistic," "equilibrium," and "subsidized" prices, but it is not easy to fix a price which is "fair" to everyone. Again, if a relatively wide range is allowed for price movement, there is no point in creating an international buffer-stock. But, if the objective is to achieve a narrow price range, there is a need for a sizeable international buffer stock, which is beyond the financial capacity of many countries. There are a number of studies on the relationship between the width of the price band and the required size of the international buffer-stock on various commodities. None of this appears to be encouraging from a practical point of view under the present global political circumstances.

Finally, let us suppose that an international buffer-stock is really established, and the objective of price stability has been somehow achieved. The question still remains whether the encroachment of synthetics on the natural commodities market is checked. Looking at ITC, what has its relative success in price stabilization brought to the tin industry? Sounder development? Higher growth of tin consumption? Neither of these. There are those who believe that the ITC pricing policy has hampered the development of the tin industry, and, at the same time, enabled substitutes such as synthetics to capture a larger share of the packaging business.

An alternative is to be found in other schemes guided by pragmatism. The improvement in the competitiveness of natural commodities depends on two essential conditions, namely, cooperation between consumer and producer and competitive prices. Regarding cooperation, agreements must be reached between consuming and producing countries on long-term transactions of the commodity in question. The consuming countries must commit themselves to long-term purchases of the commodity at specified minimum prices. The producing countries, on the other hand, must be committed to supply the commodity at the prices agreed upon. These agreements will ensure a minimum market share of the natural commodity.

As for the prices, agreements should be concluded at least one year in advance of the time for delivery, and they should be based on the current market prices at the time of the agreements. There is no better way of determining a competitive price than accepting the current market price as a guideline. Any attempt to deviate from it would not help the producer in maintaining the market share. In other words, if the alternative suggested is that between price stability and the stability of the market share, the choice should be the latter. Nevertheless, should stability in the return to the grass-root producers in the country be deemed necessary, there are domestic means of stabilization at the government's disposal. There is no reason why farmers or miners have to be directly affected by price fluctuations in the world market.

Thus, an alternative proposal is essentially that of a shift from price stability to stability in the volume of transactions determined in advance for a long period, leaving to governments in both groups the responsibility of seeing that the agreed targets of supply and demand are fulfilled. In discharging this obligatory responsibility, governments in both consuming and producing countries may find it necessary to exercise various policy measures at their own discretion.

It is conceivable that cooperation between consuming and producing countries may take the form of an international agreement under a council, like ITC, to supervise the fulfillment of the obligations. As an additional means of international cooperation, consuming and producing countries may create research bodies aimed at improved efficiency in the production of the products, both technical and economic. To improve or even to maintain its competitiveness, research is an absolute necessity. It should not be forgotten that it was research that brought synthetic substances into the market. In any case, financing is more likely to be available for research than for the establishment of an international buffer-stock.

BIBLIOGRAPHY

Ahmad, Nafis. Economic Resources of the Union of Burma. U.S. Army Natick Laboratories, Boston, Massachusetts, 1971.

Avsenev, M.M. The Democratic Republic of Vietnam - Economy and Foreign Trade, Leningrad, 1960, CCM Information Corporation, New York.

Bank of Thailand. Monthly Economic Bulletin, 1977.

Beers, Howard W. Indonesia - Resources and Their Technological Development. The University of Kentucky Press, Lexington, 1970.

Connelly, Philip and Perlman, Robert. The Politics of Scarcity. The Royal Institute of International Affairs, Oxford University Press, 1975.

Economic Data for Investors in Indonesia. The Central Bank of Indonesia, Djakarta, 1968.

The Economy of the Union of Burma. International Bank for Reconstruction and Development and the International Development Agency, Washington, D.C., 1972.

Financial Times and British Airways. Southeast Asia's Natural Resources and the World Economy, Kuala Lumpur, September 17-20, 1974.

Frederick, L.J. (Ed.). The New International Economic Order and UNCTAD: The Implications for Malaysia. Malaysian Economic Association and Malaysian Centre for Development Studies, Kuala Lumpur, 1975.

Kebschull, D. and Schoop, H.G. "The Importance of Raw Materials in Economic Development," in Natural Resources and Development. Vol. 2, Institute for Scientific Cooperation, Tubingen, 1975.

Leong, Goh Cheng, and Morgan, Gillian C. Human and Economic Geography. Oxford in Asia College Texts, Oxford University Press, 1973.

MacBean, Alastair I. and Balasubramanyam, V.N. Meeting the Third World Challenge. St. Martin's Press, New York, 1976.

Malaysia - A Basic Guidebook for Potential Investors. Federal Industrial Development Authority, Kuala Lumpur, 1977.

McHale, T.R. Rubber and the Malaysian Economy. MPR Publications, Singapore, 1967.

Mikdashi, Zuhayr. The International Politics of Natural Resources. Cornell University Press, Ithaca and London, 1976.

National Economic and Development Authority. Philippine Year Book, Manila, 1977.

Pombhejara Vitchitrong na. "Review of Some Basic Problems of the Kenaf Fibre Industry in Thailand," in Obstacles to Trade in the Pacific Area. School of International Affairs, Carleton University, Ottawa, 1971.

Thoburn, John T. Primary Commodity Exports and Economic Development. John Wiley & Sons, London-New York-Sydney-Toronto, 1977.

Twenty-Five Years of Economic and Financial Statistics in the Philippines, Vol. V. Central Bank of the Philippines, Manila, 1974.

Tyabij, Amina. "Agricultural Commodities, Mineral Commodities," in Highlights of the ASEAN Economy, Singapore Airlines Ltd., Singapore, 1977.

United Nations. Statistical Year Book for Asia and the Pacific, 1976.

Wanigatunge, R.C. "Exploitation of Natural Resources in ASEAN Countries," in Economic Problems and Prospects in ASEAN Countries, edited by Saw Swee-Hock and Lee Soo Ann, Singapore University Press, 1977.

9 The Economic Development of the Members of the Association of Southeast Asian Nations (ASEAN)

Lim Chong-Yah

The discussion in this chapter refers mainly to the five Asian states, namely, Indonesia, Malaysia, Philippines, Singapore, and Thailand, belonging to the Association of Southeast Asian Nations (ASEAN). With a total population of 250 million and a land area of 3,050,000 square kilometers, they form nearly three-fourths of the Southeast Asian population and occupy slightly more than two-thirds of the region's land area. All the five countries have important trading, investment, financial, shipping, communication, aviation, and educational ties with the advanced industrial nations. As can be seen from table 9.1, they trade mainly with industrial countries. Their economies are basically oriented toward those of the United States, Japan, and the European Economic Community.

The five ASEAN countries experienced a rapid rate of economic growth in the 1960s and 1970s (see table 9.2), generally exceeding the growth targets set up by the United Nations for the First Development Decade (5 percent of GNP) and for the Second Development Decade (6 percent of GNP). Between 1960 and 1976, their real per capita income grew from an average of 2.4 percent yearly for the Philippines to 7.5 percent for Singapore, contrasting with the corresponding 0.7 percent growth rate for Burma and 0.9 percent for the average of the 34 nations defined by the World Bank as "Low Income Countries."

Singapore, Malaysia, the Philippines, and Thailand are classified by the World Bank as belonging to the developing Middle Income Countries; while Indonesia, in terms of per capita income, is shown among the most affluent of the Low Income Countries. Burma and the three Indochina nations are all placed on the Low Income Countries list, with Kampuchea and Laos almost right at the bottom of the list.

Table 9.1. Destination of Merchandise Exports of Southeast Asia
(Percentage of Total)

From	Developed Countries		Developing Countries		Centrally Planned Economies	
	1960	1966	1960	1966	1960	1966
Kampuchea	61	..	28	..	11	..
Laos	0	32	100	68	0	0
Burma	23	28	71	71	6	1
Vietnam	..	..	..	..	..	..
Indonesia	54	78	38	21	8	1
Thailand	47	60	51	38	2	2
Philippines	94	83	5	12	1	5
Malaysia	59	62	35	34	6	4
Singapore	39	49	54	49	7	2
Low Income Countries	71	65	25	30	1	1
Middle Income Countries	81	72	15	24	1	1
Industrialized Countries	73	71	19	21	4	5
Capital Surplus Oil Exporters	75	72	25	28	0	(.)
Centrally Planned Economies	18	..	7	..	72	..

Source: Adapted and derived from statistics in World Development Report 1978 (World Bank, Washington, D.C., 1979).

Table 9.2. Growth Rates of Southeast Asian Countries
(Average Annual Percentages)

(1)	(2)	(3) Actual GDP		(4) Industry		(5) Merchandise Exports		(6) Merchandise Imports		(7) Inflation rate		(8) Population Growth rate	
Country	Actual GNP Per Capita 1960-76	1960-70	1970-76	1960-70	1970-76	1960-70	1970-76	1960-70	1970-76	1960-70	1970-76	1960-70	1970-76
Kampuchea	..	3.8	..	8.4	..	-3.3	-2.8	-3.0	-1.5	3.8	98.6	2.7	2.8
Laos	1.8	..	3.3	..	..	..	..	..	..	5.6	22.3	2.4	2.5
Burma	0.7	2.6	..	2.8	2.8	-11.1	-3.5	-5.6	-20.0	2.7	16.1	2.2	2.2
Vietnam	..	..	..	..	..	..	..	..	..	..	..	2.8	2.6
Indonesia	3.4	3.5	8.3	4.7	12.4	2.0	8.2	2.0	20.6	180.0	22.7	2.2	2.4
Thailand	4.5	8.2	6.5	11.7	8.2	5.2	9.5	11.3	3.5	1.9	10.3	3.1	2.9
Philippines	2.4	5.1	6.3	6.0	8.7	2.9	3.4	7.2	4.6	5.8	15.1	3.0	2.8
Malaysia	3.9	6.5	7.8	6.4	9.6	8.9	4.3	5.6	6.5	-0.2	7.0	2.9	2.7
Singapore	7.5	8.8	8.9	12.6	9.1	4.2	14.1	5.9	13.9	1.1	8.1	2.3	1.7
Low Income Countries	0.9	3.6	2.9	6.7	4.5	3.6	-0.4	4.6	-1.4	3.1	9.8	2.4	2.4
Middle Income Countries	2.8	5.7	6.0	7.6	7.2	5.2	3.8	6.6	6.3	3.2	12.5	2.7	2.7
Industrialized Countries	3.4	4.7	3.2	5.7	3.2	7.6	7.3	8.6	9.5	4.2	9.3	1.0	0.8
Capital Surplus Oil Exporters	7.0	..	..	..	..	7.6	-9.1	11.1	28.3	1.0	33.3	4.0	4.2
Centrally Planned Economies	3.5	4.3	3.9	..	..	..	10.4	..	10.5	..	..	1.2	0.9

Source: Adapted from <u>World Development Report 1978</u> (World Bank, Washington, D.C., 1979).

PROBLEMS OF PRIMARY EXPORTS

Nearly all Southeast Asian countries, in varying degrees of importance, are exporters of primary products.(1) Primary products constitute 77 percent of the total merchandise exports of Thailand, 82 percent for Malaysia, 83 percent for the Philippines, and 99 percent for Indonesia (see table 9.3). These countries maintain that the terms of trade of these products have moved against them vis-à-vis their industrial imports from developed industrial nations. Using 1970 as the base year, the commodity terms of trade dropped to 87 for Malaysia in 1976, 82 for Thailand, and 69 for the Philippines (see table 9.4). In part, the drop must be attributed to the rise in the price of oil since those countries depend heavily on imports. Moreover, they are also concerned about the instability in the prices of their primary exports.

Since many of their most important exports (such as natural rubber, tin, palm oil, and tropical timber) are also the exports of other countries outside Southeast Asia, they seek to join forces with these other exporters to achieve greater price stability and particularly higher prices for these primary exports. The success of OPEC in raising petroleum prices gives them a definite boost in this search. Their support for the proposed Common Fund must be viewed as an attempt along this line.

In the short-run, there is no substitute for petroleum in a wide range of uses. However, this cannot be said of, say, natural rubber, which is, by far, the most important commodity export from Southeast Asia; natural rubber has to face serious direct competition from synthetic rubber. About 67 percent of the world consumption of rubber takes the form of synthetic rubber. Table 9.5 gives statistics on world synthetic and natural rubber production by country. Before World War II, there was no synthetic rubber, and there were attempts through international commodity agreements to stabilize and raise the price of natural rubber.(2)

If natural rubber prices were raised through, say, an international price scheme or an international cartel, consumers would immediately turn more and more to synthetic rubber. Additional synthetic rubber plants would be established, even in those countries that still do not have them. Moreover, as experience in the past has shown, other nonagreement countries that can grow natural rubber would take advantage of the situation to produce more of it; so that in the long run, there would be more natural rubber and more synthetic rubber supplies pressuring the downward movement of rubber prices. Thus, the natural rubber producing countries would be unintentionally encouraging the emergence of more competitors. If the commodity agreement were to cover synthetic rubber as well, that would be a different proposition altogether. However, thus far, the discussion in and outside UNCTAD is confined to natural rubber.

In other words, not all commodities can benefit from operations like the one so successfully carried out by OPEC. There is much more scope for such an operation on irreplaceable natural resources, like petro

Table 9.3. Structure of Merchandise Trade of Southeast Asia

Country and Region	Percentage Share of Merchandise Exports				Percentage Share of Merchandise Imports					
	Primary Commodities		Manufactures		Food		Fuel		Other	
	1960	1975	1960	1975	1960	1975	1960	1975	1960	1975
Kampuchea	100	..	0	..	10	..	7	..	83	..
Laos	..	..	..	..	..	..	..	..	..	..
Burma	98	97	2	3	14	..	4	..	82	..
Vietnam										
Indonesia	100	99	0	1	23	13	5	5	72	82
Thailand	98	77	2	23	10	4	11	22	79	74
Philippines	93	83	7	17	15	11	10	22	75	67
Malaysia	94	82	6	18	..	18	..	12	..	70
Singapore	74	57	26	43	21	11	15	25	64	64
Low Income Countries	99	94	1	8	17	21	7	10	76	68
Middle Income Countries	95	82	5	17	16	14	8	14	77	71
Industrialized Countries	48	24	52	76	17	11	10	17	73	73
Capital Surplus Oil Exporters	..	99	..	1	..	..	..	..	..	..
Centrally Planned Economies	65	47	35	53	11	..	10	..	80	..

Source: World Development Report 1978 (World Bank, Washington, D.C., 1979).

leum. That is why tin is still under an international commodity agreement (the fifth post-World War II international tin agreement). As can be seen from table 9.6, 61 percent of the world's supply of tin comes from three Southeast Asian countries – Malaysia, Indonesia, and Thailand. Indeed, tin has the longest commodity agreement history.(3)

Table 9.4. Foreign Trade Elasticities and Terms of
Trade of Southeast Asia

Country	Terms of Trade 1970 = 100		Foreign Trade Elasticities*
	1960	1976	1970-76
Kampuchea	102	178	..
Laos	..	..	..
Burma	104	81	-1.1
Vietnam	..	..	..
Indonesia	120	238	1.0
Thailand	97	82	1.5
Philippines	108	69	0.5
Malaysia	115	87	0.6
Singapore	..	102	1.6
Low Income Countries	..	..	-0.1
Middle Income Countries	..	..	0.6
Industrialized Countries	..	..	2.4
Capital Surplus Oil Exporters	..	..	..
Centrally Planned Economies	..	..	2.6

*Quotients of export growth rate over GDP growth rate.

Source: World Development Report 1978 (World Bank, Washington, D.C., 1979).

An international commodity agreement on bananas, for example, is bound to fail. Not only can bananas be easily grown in other nonagreement countries but they can rot, and this makes a buffer-stock scheme impossible. And, yet, bananas are listed as one of the 18 key commodities that should be supported by the proposed Common Fund as a way to achieve the New International Economic Order. Other selected key commodities include natural rubber, tin, sugar, tea, and coffee.

For commodities that cannot profitably come under international control, the best solution would be to reduce the costs of production and increase the scope of uses. There is also a strong case for continued pressure directed at the removal of tariff and nontariff barriers in

Table 9.5. World Production of Natural and Synthetic Rubber, 1975

Ten Most Important Producers	Natural Rubber (thousand tons)	%	Ten Most Important Producers	Synthetic Rubber (thousand tons)	%	Ten Most Important Producers	Synthetic or Natural Rubber (thousand tons)	%
Malaysia	1,478	45	United States	1,941	29	United States	1,941	19
Indonesia	825	25	Japan	789	12	Malaysia	1,478	15
Thailand	349	10	France	350	5	Indonesia	825	8
Sri Lanka	149	4	Germany, F.R.	278	4	Japan	789	8
India	136	4	United Kingdom	253	4	France	350	3
Siberia	83	3	Netherlands	216	3	Thailand	349	3
Nigeria	45	1	Italy	200	3	Germany, F.R.	278	3
Philippines	35	1	Canada	173	2	United Kingdom	253	3
Zaire	25	1	Germany, D.R.	144	2	Netherlands	216	2
Vietnam	20	1	Brazil	129	2	Italy	200	2
(Total)	(3,145)	(95)	(Total)	(4,473)	(66)	(Total)	(6,679)	(66)
Others	153	5	Others	2,302	34	Others	3,394	34
WORLD	3,298	100	WORLD	6,775	100	WORLD	10,073	100

Source: Derived from International Rubber Study Group, Rubber Statistical Bulletin, September 1976.

Table 9.6. World Production of Tin-in-Concentrates and Consumption of Primary Tin Metal
1976

Main Producers	Production Tin-In-Concentrates		Main Consumers	Consumption Primary Tin Metal	
	thousand tons	percent		thousand tons	percent
Malaysia	63.4	36	U.S.A.	53.9	28
Bolivia	28.1	16	Japan	34.7	18
Indonesia	23.4	13	Germany, Fed. Rep.	14.8	7
Thailand	20.5	12	United Kingdom	13.1	7
Australia	10.4	6	France	10.5	5
Brazil*	5.9	3	Italy*	7.4	4
Zaire	4.0	2	Poland	5.1	3
Nigeria	3.7	2	Canada	4.7	2
United Kingdom	3.3	2	Sweden*	4.6	2
(Total)	(162.7)	(92)	(Total)	(148.8)	(76)
Others	15.3	18	Others	46.6	24
WORLD	178.0	100	WORLD	195.4	100

*not members of the International Tin Agreement.

Source: Derived from International Tin Council, Tin Statistics, 1966–1976.

industrial countries for primary products, particularly semiprocessed primary products, which often are discriminated against under the common practice of "tariff escalation."

Not all international commodity agreements and price fixing, with or without buffer-stock support, will work, particularly in the long run, to the advantage of the producing countries, including those of Southeast Asia. The specific conditions of demand and supply of each product, particularly their elasticities, should be taken into account before specific commodity agreements are advocated. What OPEC can do with petroleum, other countries would not necessarily be able to do with many other commodities, particularly those having ready substitutes. This, however, cannot be said of other depletable resources such as copper, phosphate, bauxite, iron ore, and manganese, also listed among the 18 commodities under the Integrated Programme for Commodities (IPC) to be used for the proposed Common Fund.

BARRIERS AGAINST INDUSTRIAL EXPORTS

All the five ASEAN countries have achieved, with the help of foreign investments and in varying degrees of success, a notable amount of industrialization. Many of them, particularly the Philippines, Indonesia, and Thailand, have obtained this through the support of an inward-looking, import-substitution policy.(4) Nevertheless, recently they are moving more and more toward an outward-looking, export-oriented strategy. As can be seen from table 9.2, their industrial exports have shown an impressive growth. Whereas in 1960, for example, manufactures constituted only 2 percent of Thailand's merchandise exports, in 1975, the amount went up to 23 percent. The corresponding figures for Malaysia were 6 to 18 percent and for the Philippines, 7 to 17 percent. However, in the case of Indonesia, even by 1975, only 1 percent of the merchandise exports took the form of manufactures. In the pursuit of an outward-looking, export-oriented policy, the Southeast Asian nations are all faced with tariff and nontariff barriers in advanced industrial nations although, despite such barriers, most of them have been able to show impressive achievements.

The high rates of unemployment and high inflation rates in many of the economically advanced industrial nations certainly have helped to make matters worse. They have made their countries more protectionistic. However, many industrialized countries have instituted a generalized system of preferences (GSPs) in favor of developing economies. Through UNCTAD, ASEAN countries have received some benefits from this system.

The crux of the problem still lies in the inability of the industrial nations to bring about a structural change in their own economies so that, in the interest of a more rational international division of labor, labor-intensive and low-technology manufacturing activities can be phased out to low-wage developing economies, including those of Southeast Asia. Unless the industrial nations are prepared to accept this structural change, there is little the developing countries can do about it, even as a group. The developing countries can, however, continue to press for freer trade and the removal of tariff and nontariff barriers for exports from the Third World.(5) But even if there were no trade barriers, that would not imply automatic industrial development in the Third World. All it would mean is the removal of some of the more serious obstacles to industrialization.

The monoloplistic position of shipping lines dominated by industrial nations is also of concern to Southeast Asian countries. All ASEAN countries have responded by improving their own nationally owned and managed shipping lines, as an addition to shipping services available in the region.

The protectionist policy of countries like Australia is well-known. It extends to civil aviation and tourism, trying to discourage passengers, through a surcharge, from stopping over in Southeast Asia enroute from Australia to London and back. Currently, ASEAN countries are putting up a joint stand against such policies. It is on these issues related to protectionism that UNCTAD should continue to take up the challenge, as a better and more promising way to arrive at a NIEO, instead of concentrating its efforts on the achievement of international commodity agreements for items such as natural rubber, bananas, pineapples, palm oil, or coconuts.

One collective attempt would be to try to have an across-the-board tariff cut for all the productions of the Third World, including manufactured goods, semimanufactured goods, and primary commodities. This would mean a preferential tariff arrangement for Third World products only, falling into the realm of collective self-reliance, without involving negotiation or pleas for help from the industrial nations.

FOREIGN EXCHANGE INSTABILITY

Since the floating of the British pound in 1972, major currencies, including the U.S. dollar, have joined in the floating international exchange rate system. The weakness of the U.S. dollar, which is still the main currency used for settling international indebtedness and as a foreign exchange reserve, has contributed greatly to the exchange rate instability all over the world, including Southeast Asia. Southeast Asian countries can do very little, if anything, to stabilize the U.S. dollar. The local response has been to untie their foreign exchange rates from the U.S. dollar and to allow their exchange rates to float with some intervention. They have also responded by using a basket of currencies as reserves and as an aid in deciding on the exchange rates. The ASEAN nations have also instituted a kind of collective lender of last resort arrangement, though thus far no member nation has made use of the facility.

Whatever the demerits, the international exchange instability did not prevent Singapore from growing into an important financial center for Asian dollars. Nor has it prevented others, including Malaysia and

Thailand, from having relatively strong and stable currencies. Similarly, tourism, foreign trade, and foreign investment have grown remarkably in all ASEAN countries, despite the global exchange instability. Indeed, regardless of the oil crisis, the region appears to have performed better economically in the late 1970s than in the 1960s. However, the Indonesian economy could not be included in this statement, if it had not been for OPEC, of which it is a member.

ATTEMPTS AT INTRA-ASEAN COOPERATION

In May 1975, the collapse of the American-backed anticommunist governments in Indochina ushered in a new area in Southeast Asia. The first ASEAN summit was held in Bali, Indonesia, in February 1976. This meeting gave the regional organization a fresh and important momentum.

In the economic field, the main areas of intra-ASEAN cooperation have turned out to be what is known as ASEAN PTA (Preferential Tariff Arrangements) and the so-called package deal industrial projects. Under ASEAN PTA, through regular commodity by commodity quinpartite negotiation, tariff cuts are given to agreed commodities for "made in ASEAN" products within the region. The number of items that come under this preferential system grows from time to time, though the amount of the intra-ASEAN tariff cut is still generally small, mostly 10 percent. There has been no agreement on the period during which these intra-ASEAN tariff preferences are to be available. It is still too early to assess the impact of the ASEAN PTA on the hitherto small intra-ASEAN trade or on regional development, but the number of items under the PTA has grown rapidly, currently standing at 1,326 items.

The package deal approach refers to the allocation of one industrial project to each country – urea for Indonesia and Malaysia, diesel-engines for Singapore, soda-ash for Thailand, and super-phosphate for the Philippines. At the Second ASEAN Summit held in Kuala Lumpur in August 1977, the Japanese Prime Minister promised a soft loan of US $1 billion to help finance these five projects. Nevertheless, this approach has been criticized by this writer and others as a poor and inefficient way of promoting economic development through regional cooperation.(6)

Other than intraregional cooperation, ASEAN has put up a commendable joint front in negotiating with other countries. Industrial nations in such a dialogue include Japan, Australia, the United States, and the European Economic Community. The Association must be viewed as a serious and extremely commendable attempt at regional self-help, but no nation can really be helped unless it is prepared to help itself. The experience of ASEAN has shown that, for the Third World (in addition to global efforts at self-help), regional groupings too, if realistically conceived and administered, can have a useful role in the economic and social development of the countries concerned. It is through ASEAN that the Japanese government has agreed to limit its production of synthetic rubber. It is also through the Association that the European Economic Community has accepted a widening of the scope and range of GSP, and the cumulative rule of origin for ASEAN countries.

DOMESTIC POLICY ISSUES

True, international and regional environments can be strategic factors in promoting economic development in middlesized and small countries, such as those in Southeast Asia; but it would be erroneous to relegate domestic issues to less important codeterminants.

Nearly all countries in Southeast Asia are suffering from population explosion (see table 9.7); partly concomitant with this are urban growth, unemployment, and underemployment. Population decisions are within the realm of domestic policy. Unless this issue is effectively tackled, the developing countries will be trying to create a NIEO with a crippling handicap, especially for countries that are already over-populated.

There is also a problem associated with the revolution of risking expectations without the ability to meet the needs of the explosive demands. There is a serious shortage of capital, entreprenurial skills, organizational and managerial ability, and technical know-how. The economic and social intrastructure in nearly all Southeast Asian countries is still very poor. The bureaucracy in most of them is inept and inefficient, and often corrupt. A New International Economic Order cannot come from the economic disorder of member nations. Thus, it is crucial to pursue domestic order as a concomitant quest.

The role of multinational corporations is a controversial one in some countries, but they are welcomed by ASEAN.(7) This is particularly so in Singapore. The MNCs may be likened to a fire. They can serve a good purpose, but they can also burn the house down. In Singapore, there are three factors that in combination reduce the ills, alleged or real, of the MNCs. One such factor is a stable, united, able, and uncorrupt political leadership. The other factor is a stable, competent, and also uncorrupt civil service. Indeed, where the bureaucracy is corrupt, distortions, inefficiencies, and injustices of all sorts will emerge, with or without MNCs. The third factor is the existence of a strong, responsible, well-organized, and nationally oriented local trade union movement. This is particularly important as a partner, not a countervailing force, in economic development. The value MNCs bring to Singapore is not just capital, as this can be raised locally, but management know-how and technology. But, most important of all, access is provided to worldwide marketing networks, even if they do not include the home country of the MNC, as is often the case.

Technology transfer must be based on a conducive environment. To ensure that the mechanism functions, there is need for an able civil service and an able political leadership to activate and supervise its smooth functioning. Most unfortunately, many developing countries

Table 9.7. General Economic Statistics on Southeast Asia

(1) Country	(2) Population (millions) Mid-1976	(3) Area (thousand square kilometers)	(4) GNP per Capita (US$) 1976	(5) Total GNP (millions) (US$) 1976	(6) Merchandise Trade (millions US $) (a) Exports 1976	(6) (b) Imports 1976	(7) Distribution of GDP(%) (a) Agriculture 1960	(a) 1976	(b) Industry 1960	(b) 1976	(c) Services 1960	(c) 1976	(8) Percentage of labor force in agriculture 1970	(9) External Public Debt millions US$ 1976	(9) as percentage of GNP 1976	(10) Gross International Reserves millions US$ 1976	(10) In months of import coverage 1976
Kampuchea	8.1	181	90*	729*	30	100	5	..	17	..	32	..	78	..	..	..	..
Laos	3.3	237	90	297	6	46	33	..	12	..	55	..	79	..	..	..	..
Burma	30.8	677	120	3,696	187	117	33	47	12	11	55	42	67	321	9.7	126	6.1
Vietnam	40.7	333	160*	6,512	..	..	..	..	..	..	..	..	76	240	3.7*	..	..
Indonesia	135.2	1,904	240	32,448	8,547	5,673	45	29	17	34	38	37	66	10,141	29.1	1,499	0.9
Thailand	43.0	514	380	16,340	2,980	3,572	40	30	19	25	41	45	80	822	5.2	1,893	5.5
Philippines	43.3	300	410	17,753	2,433	3,950	26	29	28	34	46	37	53	2,126	12.3	1,640	4.1
Malaysia	12.7	330	860	10,922	5,707	4,245	40	29	18	30	42	41	50	1,619	12.1	2,472	6.8
Singapore	2.3	1	2,700	6,210	6,585	9,070	4	2	18	35	78	63	3	687	11.8	3,364	4.1
Low Income Countries	1,214.6	21,354	150	193,654	21,098	20,668	52	45	12	19	35	39	85	..	20.9	..	2.4
Middle Income Countries	894.8	38,764	750	900,752	171,671	183,793	26	21	23	32	46	45	51	111,467	17.0	74,532	2.6
Industrialized Countries	683.8	31,650	6,200	4,719,977	621,695	659,956	9	6	41	41	47	52	11	..	..	138,749	1.6
Capital Surplus Oil Exporters	12.2	3,928	6,310	71,331	54,400	18,850	..	..	..	..	..	..	32	..	..	32,160	..
Centrally Planned Economies	1,207.7	34,582	2,280	1,340,347	77,624	84,126	..	..	..	..	..	..	39	..	..	..	..

*estimated by Lim Chong-Yah.

Source: Adapted and derived from statistics in World Bank's World Development Report 1978 (World Bank: Washington, D.C., 1979).

lack an effective and efficient civil service system. The trickling down effect of foreign investment can be reinforced by a built-in system of efficient fiscal policy. But this implies the existence of a mechanism to carry out equitable and suitable policies, so that the benefits of wealth creation reach the vast majority of the population. In many developing countries, such a mechanism is grossly defective and greatly inadequate.

CONCLUSIONS

Given the present international economic order, ASEAN nations, despite serious handicaps of one form or another, have been able to grow faster economically than many industrial nations. This does not imply that, with a better international environment, the same countries would not be able to show a still better performance. Most probably, they would. In varying degrees, they subscribe to the general aims of a NIEO and support its general modus operandi.

A NIEO can be achieved at three levels simultaneously: the domestic level, the regional level, and the global level. In a global forum, it is to be expected that attention would be centered on global issues and relations. But this should not blind us to the fact that the global economic order is made up of regional economic orders which, in turn, are closely linked to national economic orders. For most developing countries, the author's own emphasis and priority would be to put the domestic house in order as a concomitant to the pursuit of a NIEO.

At the regional level, there must also be regional self-help, regional self-reliance, and this can be brought about through organizations and pressure groups.

On a global scale, the author has advocated, as a collective self-help measure, looking into the question of an intra-Third World across-the-board tariff cut for Third World products. This is to supplement global common efforts, such as seeking ways and means of lowering and removing tariff and nontariff barriers in industrial nations for imports from developing regions. International commodity agreements should be carried out on much more discriminatory and selective bases.

Finally, it is well said that heaven will help those who help themselves. Unless the Third World countries are prepared to help themselves – at national, regional, and international levels – they will be left further behind in economic and social development, and the NIEO will fail.

NOTES

(1) For a general explanation of how this situation has come about, see Arthur Lewis, The Evolution of the International Economic Order (Princeton, N.J.:   Princeton University Press, 1977). See also his Tropical Development, 1880-1913 (Boston: Allen and Unwin, 1970). For

the case study of one developing country, see Lim Chong-Yah, Economic Development of Modern Malaysia (Oxford: Oxford University Press, 1965).

(2) For details of such attempts, see Lim Chong-Yah, Economic Development of Modern Malaysia, Chaps. 3 and 4; and Thomas R. McHale, "Commodity Control Schemes for Rubber: Retrospective and Prospective," Kajian Ekonomi Malaysia 1 (2), (December 1964): 19-29.

(3) For a brief history of tin control, see Lim Chong-Yah, Economic Development of Modern Malaysia, Chap. 2; Yip Yat-Hoong, "Post-War Tin Control — With Special Reference to Malaysia," Kajian Ekonomi Malaysia 1 (2), (December 1964): 15-87; and Lim Chong-Yah, "A Reappraisal of the 1953 Tin Agreement," Malaysian Economic Review 5 (1), (April 1960): 13-24.

(4) For a good study on this subject, see Kunio Yoshihara, Japanese Investment in Southeast Asia (Honolulu: University of Hawaii Press, 1978).

(5) "Reducing protection in the industrial countries would further help the economic growth in the developing countries and, with these countries spending their foreign exchange earnings to a large extent on the importation of machinery and equipment, it would ultimately benefit the industrial countries." Bela Balassa, "Reducing Policy Conflicts for Rapid Growth in the World Economy," Banca Najionale del Lavoro Quarterly Review, September 1978, p. 28.

(6) See Lim Chong-Yah, "A Dissenting View of ASEAN Industrial Projects," ASEAN Business Quarterly, 3rd. Quarter 1978; and also by the same writer, "ASEAN Economic Cooperation and Economic Reality," United Malaysian Banking Corporation Economic Review, 14 (1), (1978); and "ASEAN Industrial Projects: Significance and Feasibility," Asia Pacific Community, no. 2, Fall 1978.

(7) For the pros and cons of having MNCs, see United Nations, Multinational Corporations In World Development, (New York: United Nations, 1973).

10 Indonesia and the New International Economic Order

Heinz W. Arndt

INTRODUCTION

As a prominent member of the Group of 77, Indonesia has lent strong and loyal support to the demands for a New International Economic Order. The views of its government have been set out in a variety of official statements and documents. This chapter is a purely personal assessment, by a foreign economist, of the relevance to Indonesia of some of the more important NIEO propositions and of obstacles to their realization in the Indonesian context.

Among developing as among developed countries, there are notable differences of emphasis and style on the North-South problem in general and on particular NIEO issues. Thus, while Indonesia's spokesmen have consistently concurred in the proposition that a New International Economic Order is necessary because the existing international economic order basically serves the interests of the industrialized countries and thereby contributes to the ever widening gap between the wealthy and poor nations, they have been emphatic that reform of the existing order requires, in the words of Professor Widjojo Nitisastro, the leader of the Indonesian delegation to UNCTAD IV at Nairobi, "a new harmony of political will" between developed and developing countries. "Therefore, let us not talk about economic warfare, however strong our respective economies might be. No one country will ever survive such economic warfare, and all countries will undoubtedly be losers."

Indonesian spokesmen have also warned against expecting too much from changes in the international economic system. For the less developed countries, the essential problem is how to achieve full participation in the growth of the world economy. The achievement of full participation will require more than mere improvements in the order of the world economy. It is only by an appropriate combination of national policies pursued by governments of developing nations toward and within their own respective societies and an international frame-work which is conducive to the consistent implementation of such national policies that it is meaningful to speak of a new order of any kind.

> In this context, I unequivocally stress the prime responsibility of national governments within their own respective societies and towards their own people. . . . It is obvious, however, that developing nations need an international framework which is conducive to . . .policies of that nature. . . . Past and contemporary experience bears ample evidence that national policies aimed at creating conditions of social stability through growth with equity are persistently impeded by external disturbances.

In order to see the relevance of NIEO issues to Indonesia in perspective, it is necessary to understand the difficulties created by the international system through external disturbances in the wider context of the enormous problems that Indonesia has faced since independence, and in some degree still faces, in the task of economic development. Before turning to specific NIEO issues, therefore, the dimensions of these problems need to be briefly outlined.

INDONESIA'S DEVELOPMENT PROBLEMS

Indonesia, with a population of 130 million and a per capita income (according to the latest edition of the World Bank Atlas) of $220 in 1975, is one of the poorest large countries in the world. In the first 15 years after independence, political and social objectives were given priority over economic development.   After 1965, priorities were reversed. But despite the notable achievements of the development policies of the past decade, and despite Indonesia's considerable natural resources (including oil), formidable problems of underdevelopment, of poverty, malnutrition, and underemployment, remain, especially in Java. To appreciate the dimensions of the task confronting Indonesia as a nation and its government, one has to remind oneself of the contraints which have hampered the development effort.(1)

Consequences of Colonial Rule

Three hundred years of Dutch colonial rule gave Indonesia a dualistic economy, with a highly efficient plantation section and an infra-structure of transport, irrigation, banking, and administration, and the small beginnings of modern manufacturing industry (mainly cotton weaving). It supported public health services which, by steadily reducing the death rate, accelerated population growth; an education system which did little if anything to provide professional or vocational training for Indonesians who were also almost entirely excluded from higher positions in which they might have gained administrative, professional, or business experience; and a legacy of fierce nationalist resentment against the Dutch in particular and (white) foreigners in general.

Old and New National Elites

Most of the wealth and power of the old fedual elites of Java and the other islands that had survived Dutch rule disappeared in the post-1945 revolutionary turmoil. But many, from the Sultan of Yogyakarta down, retained their social status and influence among the new national elite that emerged in the Republic. This consisted at first of leaders of the nationalist movement, intellectuals, and politicians, and of those who rose to positions of command in the armed forces during the struggle for independence.

The higher ranks of the bureaucracy were filled party by promotion from below, party by numbers of graduates educated at Dutch and other foreign – and during the 1950s increasingly also at local – universities. What had been a slow process during the preceding decade became a sudden transformation with the expulsion of the Dutch in 1957, the nationalization of all Dutch-owned enterprises, and the subsequent takeovers of foreign-owned firms. Thousands of positions – in senior ranks of the bureaucracy and in the top echelons of nationalized estates, banks, public utilities, and other enterprises – became suddenly available, with the duties, salaries, houses, offices, and social status of the former Dutch or other foreign incumbent, but little of their professional qualifications or practical experience. Many of the new administrators, under the challenge of new responsibilities, did wonderfully well. But the overall effect was a drastic decline in the efficiency of administration and management which, as was increasingly reflected in declining output and accelerating inflation, eroded the salaries of the new ruling class and tempted many into corruption.

Sukarno's policies helped to promote a very great expansion of the armed forces, each with its own new officer corps. Another consequence of the expulsion of the Dutch was a vacuum in the business sector which, in the absence of any significant class of indigenous entrepreneurs, was quickly filled by expansion in the number and scale of operation of overseas Chinese who, under the Dutch, had played a much more subordinate role as small-scale middlemen.

Ideologies

The intellectuals and politicians of the independence movement in Indonesia grew up imbued with an eclectic anticapitalist ideology which, for all Sukarno's efforts to devise a "socialisme à la Indonesia," was little different from that of Nehru, Nkrumah, Nasser, and other Afro-Asian leaders of the time. It condemned capitalism and imperialism; it distrusted market forces which needed to be corrected or replaced by national planning and direct government controls; it preferred state to private ownership of business enterprises; and it professed egalitarian concern for the welfare of the masses. As in other countries with massive underemployment, ideological preference for government ownership and control was strongly backed by the interests of all those anxious to obtain or retain government jobs. Under Sukarno, anticolonialist nationalism, initially and ostensibly a means to national unity and identity, assumed frenzied dimensions which diverted national energies and economic resources into aggressive militarism (and, incidentally, sided with Moslem conservatism to delay by twenty years the adoption of family planning as a national policy).

Heritage of Underdevelopment

Beneath the new ideologies, imported or Indonesianized, a cultural heritage persisted which, in some respects, compounded the problem. One element in it was the Javanese emphasis on <u>musyawara</u> (talking things over) and consensus, the desire to avoid "confrontation" in personal relations. Like the other Javanese tradition, mutual support in "shared poverty," it no doubt made it easier for people to live in harmony with one another, but it did not make for economic efficiency. Reinforced by a half-baked "welfarism" which demanded the Western welfare state without Western productivity, these traditional attitudes were (and remain) primarily responsible for the symptoms in Indonesia of what Myrdal has called "the Soft State." Another element was the traditional value system of the educated elite who looked down on manual work, especially farming, and often even on trade and other business. The consequent scarcity of people trained in practical skills, such as used to be imparted in the West by apprenticeship and later in technical colleges, was (and remains) a major source of industrial inefficiency.

Economic Decline

From 1930 until 1950, the Indonesian economy was buffeted by world depression, scorched-earth policies, Japanese occupation, and revolutionary and civil wars. From 1950 until 1958, successive governments struggled to promote economic development in conditions of chronic inflation, balance-of-payments difficulties, and increasing political instability. From 1958 until 1965, under Guided Democracy, orderly processes of government gradually disintegrated and inflation turned into hyperinflation, ever-changing and multiplying regulations superimposed new direct controls on unenforceable older ones, output of nationalized estates and industrial plants declined, and smuggling further dissipated the country's dwindling foreign exchange earnings. As Sukarno's diminishing capacity to raise further foreign credits prompted him to tell the world to "go to hell" with its foreign aid, economic activity continued despite, rather than because of, the government.

Development Policies 1966-78

The new government, led by General Suharto, took over the reins of power in Indonesia in 1965-66. It was decided that, at least for a decade, economic objectives (first stabilization and rehabilitation and then development) focusing on increasing the country's productive capacity had to be given priority over other objectives.

It was not until mid-1966 that the gradual transfer of political power from Sukarno to Suharto enabled the new team of economic advisers under Professor Widjojo, with some help from an IMF mission, to work out a short-term program of economic stabilization and rehabilitation. This succeeded in two years, by quite orthodox fiscal-monetary measures, in bringing the raging hyperinflation under control; and, meanwhile, restored some semblance of order to the public finances. Some of the worst disincentives to productive effort were removed through direct controls and distortion of relative prices; the balance-of-payments situation was patched up through a moratorium on foreign debt service, new emergency credits, and decontrol of foreign trade and payments; and the task of rehabilitating the run-down infrastructure of ports, roads, irrigation, and other public works was begun. In 1968, the emphasis shifted toward a resumption of economic development. From April 1, 1969 (within the framework of the first Five Year Plan), primary emphasis was placed on food (especially rice) production, improvement of infrastructure assisted by foreign (bilateral and multilateral) project aid and technical assistance, and expansion of productive capacity with the help of foreign direct investment, especially in mineral and manufacturing industries.

In their primary objectives, these policies were remarkably successful. Inflation was brought under effective control by 1969, though there have been temporary setbacks since, due in part to international influences – the commodity boom of 1972-73 and the OPEC oil price increase of 1973-74. During the periods of the first (1969-74) and second (1974-79) Five Year Plans, Indonesia enjoyed a period of sustained economic growth, at an estimated average annual rate of 7 percent, based on a major and successful effort to increase rice production through application of new technology (though partly offset by lagging production of other staple food crops), development of mineral and other natural resources (especially oil and timber), and rapid development (from a small base) of a modern manufacturing sector.

As in other rapidly developing countries in the Third World, the benefits of economic growth have been unequally distributed. Hard evidence is sparse, but it is clear that inequality in the distribution of income has increased greatly in the cities, though it may have diminished somewhat in rural areas. The majority of the Indonesian people have almost certainly benefited, in terms of material living standards, from the economic growth of the past decade. But it is possible, even likely, that some of the poorest – in the areas of greatest Malthusian pressure in rural Java and in the kampung slums of the big cities – are worse off in terms of per capita real income and food consumption. Unquestionably, the poverty of the many has become psychologically more intolerable because of the increasingly evident display of the comforts of the well-to-do and the luxuries of the rich.

Economic recovery since 1966 and boom conditions in some sectors of the economy have undoubtedly provided greatly enhanced business opportunities of which the ethnic-Chinese business community has been in the best position to take advantage; some share has gone to foreign companies doing business in Indonesia and some to officials – civil and military – with useful signatures to sell or influence to wield. Whether there has been more corruption under Suharto than under Sukarno is a moot point, but there has certainly been much more money available to be corrupt with.

Obviously, personal corruption tends to attract more attention than what may have been much larger and economically more serious distortions in resource allocation by power holders for their own benefit. The resplendent modern office buildings erected in recent years (not only in Jakarta but in many other cities) for Pertamina and other state enterprises, for Bank Indonesia and other state banks, for government departments, for all branches of the armed forces, even for local government authorities, have probably diverted far more resources from more worthwhile social or economic purposes than all the financial gains from corruption put together. Similarly, much has been made by critics of the large expenditure of scarce foreign exchange on imports of luxury cars; but for every luxury car imported on private account or for personal use, numerous others have been imported for "legitimate" official purposes. The peculiar difficulty about this kind of diversion of resources is that it is so easily rationalized as being in the "national" or "public" interest. Of course, this is true in developed countries as well.

Under pressure of increasing public criticism of these features of the regime, policy emphasis has shifted significantly in recent years from economic to social objectives. Beginning with the second Five Year Plan, higher priority has been given to measures to widen employment opportunities, to give wider access to education and other social welfare services, and to suppress corruption. How effective this shift of emphasis has been in practice is a matter for debate, but there is now wider recognition in Indonesia of the need, to quote again from Professor Sumitro, for "a drastic reorientation in development strategies and objectives, where the social phenomena of poverty and unemployment and their eradication are regarded as economic priorities of the first order."

DEVELOPMENT ASSISTANCE

Aid and Investment

The history of independent Indonesia includes two contrasting experiences of foreign aid. During the first period, 1950-65, Indonesia received little aid until ideological rivalry motivated a large flow of credits for military and civil projects which, in the increasingly chaotic state of the Indonesian economy in the last years of the Sukarno regime, left behind few real assets of value but substantial foreign debts. During the second period, since 1966, the consortium of Western creditor countries (and Japan) first organized a moratorium ("rescheduling") of the outstanding foreign debts: and, then, assisted by the IMF, World Bank, and the Asian Development Bank (ADB), provided aid in increasing volume. Initially, this consisted largely of program aid (balance-of-payments support and food aid) but in recent years, especially since the dramatic improvement in the balance-of-payments situation that resulted from the OPEC increase in the price of oil, almost entirely in the form of project aid. Thanks to the very large rise in Indonesia's export earnings since 1973, the debt ratio has remained low, though a temporary rise for the next two or three years, due to repayment obligations on debts originally contracted by the state oil enterprise, Pertamina, causes some concern.

There is a school of thought, among Indonesians as well as among foreign observers, which questions the wisdom of Indonesia's heavy reliance in the past ten years on external resources, official development assistance, and private capital inflow. There are those who preach self-reliance on moral and psychological grounds, who believe that a country does better to stand on its own feet and that acceptance of foreign aid is undignified and demoralizing. There are others who maintain that foreign assistance undermines domestic effort by reducing the sense of urgency among policymakers and the public at large, whether about mobilization of domestic saving or food production or development of independent technological capability. Still others are particularly critical of the policy of relying for development assistance on a consortium of First World countries and for capital and for knowhow on transnational corporations and other private investors for these same countries in the belief that this enmeshes Indonesia in dependence on Western imperialism.

Indonesia's policymakers recognize that there are many disadvantages in the aid and investment relationship. However, they have no doubt that, subject to certain safeguards which they believe have been and can be adequately maintained, the trade-off favors continuance of the policy of the past decade. Indonesia's official spokesmen have, therefore, insisted in international discussion on the need for the industrialized countries – especially the United States, West Germany, and Japan – to show in a tangible way their unqualified commitment to development aid targets. They have also called on the oil rich countries to increase their contribution of funds for recycling. Similarly, the

Indonesian government continues to be anxious to attract private investment for the development of natural resources and industrial development, though on terms and conditions which safeguard Indonesia's national interests. Since the OPEC oil price increase of 1973-74 which for some years greatly increased Indonesia's export earnings, the emphasis in Indonesian official thinking has shifted somewhat from access to capital to access to technology. More will be said about this in a later section of this chapter. Suffice it to note here that this shift of emphasis has in no way diminished Indonesia's concern to attract direct foreign investment or development assistance. For it is precisely the importance of transnational corporations as sources of modern technology and business knowhow that makes their contribution to Indonesian economic development seem indispensable for some time yet, and it is partly because foreign industrial technology is so expensive that development assistance in the form of aid or loans is thought necessary.

Debt Relief

Indonesia's official participants in North-South debates have concurred in the NIEO demand for a comprehensive attack on the debt problem of developing countries. But Indonesia's own experience and interests have led them to emphasize the possibility, or even necessity, of a differentiated implementation at the individual country level. In particular, it has been suggested that the case-by-case approach may be appropriate within a general frame of reference, entailing a set of commonly agreed principles for rescheduling of debts, or even, where necessary, the conversion of official loans into official grants for the poorest countries.

It seems reasonable to conclude that Indonesia has little interest in any general scheme of debt relief. Its own experience of a case-by-case approach is favorable, while its continuing interest in access to the international capital market must make it wary of any changes that might reduce the confidence of international lenders. But it is ready to press with other Third World countries for help in the form of debt relief to the poorest countries.

The Link

A theme that continues to be prominent in statements on NIEO issues by Indonesian official spokesmen is the idea of a "link" between SDR creation and development assistance to Third World countries. They rightly point out that, if the needs of the world economy for international liquidity require the creation of international money, there is a strong case in equity for channeling the resulting seigniorage to poor rather than to rich countries. For the time being, with the worldwide move toward flexible exchange rates, the rise in the price of gold, and the slowdown in the rate of growth of world trade, SDR creation and thus the Link have become dead issues, but their significance may well revive at some future time.

Exchange Rates

To a greater extent than most other Third World countries, including its ASEAN partners, Indonesia has in recent years maintained a fixed exchange rate between the rupiah and the U.S. dollar, and its spokesmen have generally expressed a belief in the importance of stable exchange rates for world trade.   But opinion among professional economists in Indonesia, official and unofficial, is divided on the question of whether Indonesia is wise to adhere to the link with the U.S. dollar or whether, in the longer run, it has more to gain from a more flexible exchange rate policy. The issues are complex and not well understood outside the economic profession.

TRADE IN PRIMARY PRODUCTS AND MANUFACTURES

As an exporter of primary products, Indonesia has a natural interest in many aspects of the Integrated Programme for Commodities. But it has reasons, in its own experience, for the caution which its official spokesmen have shown in supporting particular proposals.

Even before the OPEC oil price increase, half of Indonesia's export earnings was accounted for by crude oil. The price increase raised this share to nearly three-quarters. Clearly, Indonesia must be doubtful about any schemes which, whether through indexing or through other forms of price stabilization, would have deprived it of this windfall. While, as a passive OPEC member, Indonesia was a happy beneficiary of the OPEC cartel action of 1973-74, it has been wary of attempts at a similar approach to other commodities, such as copper (CIPEC), where production quotas to keep up the price seem an unpromising approach to the longer-run maintenance of export earnings. Its own experience with rubber restriction schemes during the interwar period reinforces this skepticism.

Integrated Programme for Commodities (IPC)

The leader of the Indonesian delegation at UNCTAD IV unambiguously declared international commodity trade to be the issue on which the overall success or failure of the conference would be judged. Like many others from the Third World, Indonesian official spokesmen have frequently given support to the Prebisch thesis about a secular decline in the terms of trade for primary products, relying largely on evidence from Indonesia's experience for the years 1950 to 1970.(2) But Indonesia's official stance on relevant aspects of the IPC has been cautious.

While on the alert for opportunities to extend the exercise of market power from oil to other basic materials, Indonesian opinion is not hopeful that cartel action of the OPEC type will prove practicable in relation to other commodities of which it is a major producer. Its spokesmen have emphasized that Indonesia is interested not in raising prices or in maintaining them at a high level by restricting supply but in stable earnings in real terms. Even for this purpose, there is little enthusiasm for formal indexation of commodity prices since, as Dr. Daoed Joesoef has pointed out, "Indexation tends to freeze raw material prices for unlimited periods, including the prices of commodities for which real demand has in fact decreased during the price-freezing period."

By contrast, Indonesia has been a very active proponent of commodity price stabilization through buffer stocks and a supporter of the concept of a Common Fund. Indeed, Indonesians like to claim Indonesian intellectual parentage for the idea of international buffer stocks. Here, too, the Indonesian approach, based on past experience (especially in the case of rubber), is a moderate one which stresses the importance of trying to reconcile the interests of producers and consumers. Indonesia has actively participated in planning regional buffer stock schemes for rubber, copra, and other tropical products. Without excessive optimism about the contribution that a Common Fund can make to financing such schemes, it has an obvious interest in the realization of the Common Fund proposal.

As in some other primary exporting countries, there is in Indonesia a surprising tendency to place more confidence in price stabilization schemes than in schemes for the stabilization of export earnings of the Stabex type. Contrary to the opinion of most professional economists who regard stabilization of the earnings of producers as the most important objective and point out that stabilization of prices is liable in some circumstances to destabilize earnings, the tendency in Indonesia is to dismiss compensatory financing and Stabex as no more than palliatives which do not touch the crux of the problem. That is not to say, however, that Indonesia does not welcome generous compensatory financing such as that provided by the liberalized IMF facility. In the same spirit, Indonesian spokesmen urge extension of the EEC Stabex scheme to all Third World countries through "globalization of the Lomé Conference."

Synthetics Competition

Indonesia has suffered from synthetics competition with some of her natural products, especially rubber. But, in this particular case, the rise in production costs of the synthetic product that followed the OPEC increase in the oil price has improved the relative competitive position of natural rubber. In the Indonesian view, natural products can, in most cases, hold their own if they are produced with the best available technology and efficient farm or estate management, as Malaysian (and some Sumatran) rubber estates and Indonesia's own rapidly growing palm oil industry have demonstrated.

Exports of Manufactures

The past ten years have been a period of unprecedentedly rapid industrial development in Indonesia, but it has been almost wholly of the import-substitution type. Modern sector growth, moreover, has been fairly capital-intensive and, in part, at the expense of traditional small-scale industry, so that direct employment generation has been disappointing. Wages are lower in Indonesia than in any other country in East Asia. Indonesia might, therefore, be expected to have a comparative advantage in labor-intensive manufacturing, and to be able to compete increasingly effectively in world markets for such products, as real wages rise rapidly elsewhere in East Asia. In practice, however, the advantage of low wages is generally offset, and often outweighed, by deficiencies of business management, government controls, and other factors which keep down labor productivity and raise unit labor costs. As a result, Indonesia has so far been unable to penetrate export markets for products of labor-intensive industries (other than a small volume of batik and other handicraft products and elementary processing of timber and other raw materials). On the other hand, some of its highly capital-intensive, resource-based modern sector plants, established with external capital and technical assistance (such as oil refineries, and fertilizer and cement factories) are quite efficient. They have begun to export and have fair prospects of doing so in increasing volume.

Unlike most other countries of East Asia, therefore, Indonesia has at this stage little to gain from improved market access to OECD countries for Third World labor-intensive manufactures, and this applies as much to the GSP as to the MNT approach. Indeed, Indonesia has probably suffered more from preferential schemes (such as the EEC's Stabex arrangements under the Lomé Convention) which have discriminated against it than it has benefited from schemes (such as those of the United States, Japan or Australia) in which it has been included. Similarly, while Indonesia has played a prominent part in the formation and development of ASEAN as a regional organization, it has been reluctant to agree to any far-reaching intra-ASEAN trade liberalization which, in its view, would expose its own vulnerable manufacturing industries to excessive competition from more efficient industries in the partner countries.

For all these reasons, it is not surprising that, while giving general support to Third World demands for improved access to markets of the developed countries for LDC exports of manufactures and condemning developed country protectionism, Indonesia has put particular emphasis on two demands which are most relevant to its present stage of industrialization: assistance in processing of raw materials for export, and transfer of technology. These problems are interconnected in

Indonesian eyes because Third World countries are compelled to sell their produce "to the world market in its rawest forms due in general to the low level of technology they possess."

TRANSFER OF TECHNOLOGY AND TRANSNATIONAL CORPORATIONS

Thoughtful Indonesians are acutely conscious of Indonesia's weakness in modern know-how and in business management as much as in technology. There is probably no aspect of the NIEO that has provoked as much professional interest and discussion as the problem of transfer of technology. But Indonesian official spokesmen have also shown themselves to be well aware of the dilemmas inherent in the problem.

On the one hand, as the example of Japan suggests, it is in the last resort not only inequality in natural resource endowment but also, and perhaps chiefly, inequality in technical and organizational skills that accounts for the gap in living standards and economic power between the First and Third Worlds. "It is upon the degree to which the less developed countries master technology and employ it to bring economy into a parallel state with those of the advanced countries that currently dominate international trade, that their future as equal participants in the world economy depends."

On the other hand, it is all too easy to speak glibly of transfer of technology. As Professor Sumitro has pointed out, what can be bought or borrowed or transferred is, at best, the blueprint, design, or equipment, the artifacts or results of the dynamic process of scientific discovery and technological development, not the process itself. Even where transferred technology is appropriate, in principle, to the conditions of a Third World country, its adaptation and effective use demand an indigenous infrastructure of trained and experienced scientists, engineers, production managers, mechanics, and process workers. Transfer of technology, he argues, can at best serve as a "bridging phase" in the course of a program to develop one's own capabilities, a program the time dimension of which he puts, perhaps optimistically, at 10 to 25 years.

There has been much discussion in recent years about the dangers to a country such as Indonesia of importing Western technology which, it is said, is inappropriate to the factor proportions of a labor-abundant and capital-scarce country. Critics of the policies of the past decade claim that reliance on Western technology, whether through direct invesment by transnational corporations or through technical assistance, has accentuated the dualistic structure of the Indonesian economy and aggravated the problem of underemployment. Indonesian economists are ambivalent on this issue. While admitting that the type of technology appropriate for many less developed countries should, perhaps, be more labor-intensive and job-creating, in both the industrial and agricultural sectors, than is the case in the industrialized states, they do not think Indonesia can afford to be without some advanced technology sectors, partly because, in many industries, choice of technique is limited — the so-called "technological gap" between traditional and modern techniques is often a vacuum — partly because relatively advanced technology is essential to the quality of industrial products demanded in export markets, but, above all, because of a belief that no country can aspire to a significant role in the modern world that falls entirely behind in the technological race.

As has already been mentioned, it is primarily because they see transnational corporations as "powerful engines of growth" with vast, accumulated technological and marketing know-how, that Indonesian policymakers continue to regard them as indispensable agents in Indonesia's industrial development in its present phase. The problem is to reconcile the interests of the TNCs in terms of return on investment and security of investment with an adequate share in resource rents and adequate safeguards of the economic independence and development objectives of the host country. It is in this spirit that the Indonesian government has sought in various ways to tighten up the administration of its foreign investment law while continuing to give TNCs adequate incentives to direct investment, preferably in the form of joint ventures. In this spirit, also, Indonesia supports the Third World case for international agreement on a code of conduct for transnational corporations.

Another facet of transfer of technology of special interest and relevance to Indonesia is new technology in agriculture. In the past decade, Indonesia has benefited greatly from the modern agricultural technology based on high-yielding varieties which has been made freely available from organizations such as the International Rice Research Institute, and continues to receive much bilateral and multilateral technical assistance in upgrading technology and management in its rural industries. The new rice technology, however, has, in recent years, run into problems which, again, illustrate the wider dilemma of the appropriateness of transferred technology. Even when foreign technology is made available free and gratis, there remain the problems of adapting it and using it effectively in local conditions.

FOOD AND NATURAL RESOURCES

Despite the high priority accorded to food production, and notable successes achieved in its first two five-year development plans, Indonesia remains dependent on food imports, and this dependence has increased in the last few years as domestic demand has expanded rapidly with rising population and per capita income. Indonesia, therefore, has a very direct interest in the proposed International Food Programme, especially in food aid and international food reserve stocks.

NOTES

(1) This section is largely taken from Heinz W. Arndt, "Development and Equality: The Indonesian Case," World Development, February-March 1975.

(2) Everything here depends on the period chosen. Indonesia's terms of trade declined between 1950 (the peak of the Korean War commodity boom) and 1970 (the year preceding the commodity boom of the early 1970s); but they rose between 1939 and 1959 (and between 1968 and 1978) and they were higher in 1978 than 40 years earlier (see Phyllis Rosendale, "The Indonesian Terms of Trade, 1950-1973," Bulletin of Indonesian Economic Studies, November 1975, p. 80; and, for more recent years, "Survey of Recent Developments," Bulletin of Indonesian Economic Studies, November 1978).

11 Australia and the New International Economic Order

Heinz W. Arndt

INTRODUCTION

No attempt is made in this chapter to cover all the NIEO issues areas. A selection has been made to highlight those aspects with respect to which Australia's experience, position, or approach differs from that of other OECD countries. The three main sections of this chapter deal with NIEO Philosophy and Principles; Commodity Problems; and Problems of Market Access for Third World Manufactures. Shorter sections are provided on Development Assistance and Transfer of Technology.

NIEO PHILOSOPHY AND PRINCIPLES

Australia is a developed country, a member of OECD, and ranks among the first ten in terms of per capita income. Australian official and public opinion on the New International Economic Order, therefore, has much in common with that of other OECD countries, although it differs significantly in attitude from most other OECD countries for three important reasons related to its history, economic structure, and geographic position. There is much sympathy with the problems of the Third World, concern about poverty, and a desire to help. But there is also skepticism about the extent to which the problems of the Third World can be attributed to deficiencies of the international economic system, as contrasted with matters that lie within the province of domestic policy of national governments, and about the extent to which the specific NIEO policy proposals put forward by Third World countries are well designed to remedy such deficiencies of the international economic system.

The discovery, settlement, and development of Australia were part of the process of European expansion in the eighteenth and nineteenth centuries, with catastrophic effects for the sparse population of Stone-

Age aborigines. Australians are very conscious of the fact that a large continent, which contains much land (while largely uninhabitable) and other natural resources, is in the possession of only 14 million people. Thoughtful Australians, therefore, are sensitive to the argument that the world's resources are inequitably distributed among the world's population.

It would be unrealistic to claim that the average Australian suffers sleepless nights about the manner in which the antipodean continent became British in 1788, any more that the average Russian does about Siberia or the average Mexican or Argentinean about the historical origins of his country. He thinks of the enterprise, skills, and industry of new settlers and their descendants who in two centuries, often in the face of extreme hardships and difficulties, built a nation by applying science and technology to the development of a virtually empty continent. Toward the aboriginal people — some 50,000 full-blooded aborigines continue to live on tribal lands in the tropical north and another 50,000 or so detribalized people of mixed blood live on the fringes of Australian towns — Australians, especially young Australians, feel a collective guilt for past wrongs and are prepared to support generous government policies, whether to help integrate them into white society or to insulate them from it. But toward the countries of the Third World, Australians, much like the citizens of other developed countries, tend at best to acknowledge a general moral obligation upon the rich to help the poor. And even this sentiment, which finds expression in public support and even pressure for generous aid and liberal trade policies, has to contend with demands for public expenditure and protection policies from vulnerable groups and powerful sectional interests within the country.

Australia's exports still consist predominantly of primary products — minerals and agricultural commodities. Australia, therefore, shares with most countries of the Third World a direct interest in commodity problems in international trade, particularly concern about instability of commodity prices and agricultural protectionism of the industrial countries. Australia's economic position is also not unlike that of some of the more industrialized countries of the Third World in that her own substantial manufacturing sector has been fostered for almost a century by a deliberate policy of import substitution through tariffs and other forms of protection. Her high level of real wages, reflecting basically an ample natural resource endowment, a well-educated and skilled work force, and a high rate of capital formation, has recently got out of line through excessive wage inflation and now presents a difficult problem of structural adjustment to the change in comparative advantage that has come about through industrial development in lower-wage Third World countries.

Official spokesmen have sometimes claimed for Australia a position "midway" between the developed and the less developed countries. In the most obvious sense of the distinction, that between rich and poor countries, such a claim would be absurd. In that sense, Australia unquestionably is part of the First World. But because of its economic structure, as a country largely dependent on exports of agricultural and other primary products, on import of capital and technology, and on heavily protected home-market oriented manufacturing industries, Australia finds herself on a variety of international economic issues sharing the point of view of the Third rather than the First World. All the issues selected below for special discussion illustrate this ambivalence in Australia's position in varying degrees.

Australia's geographic position, on the fringe of Asia, separated (with New Zealand) from the OECD countries of the northern hemisphere, links her interests and fortunes with those of important parts of the Third World. Australia has political and security reasons for maintaining close and friendly relations with her Asian neighbors and for taking these into account in her foreign economic policies.

A sense of insecurity deriving from their geographic position as countries of European settlement on the far side of Asia has been part of the national psyche of Australia and New Zealand from their earliest days. During the nineteenth century, they enjoyed the protection of the British navy, for much of the twentieth that of the ANZUS alliance with the United States. Now that neither of these can be counted upon, Australians are conscious of the need to stand on their own feet and to foster close relations with their Asian neighbors, especially the ASEAN countries with whom they share regional security interests. These political concerns influence Australian attitudes toward the Third World, giving them a strong regional bias in favor of Southeast (and to a less extent South and East) Asia at the price of relative neglect of Africa and Latin America.

For all these reasons, the Australian government takes the North-South dialogue about the issues of a New International Economic Order very seriously. An enquiry into its implications for Australia by the Standing Committee on Foreign Affairs and Defence of the Australian Senate has been under way for some time; and, early in 1978, the government appointed a high-level committee to advise it on all aspects of Australia's relations with the Third World.

COMMODITY PROBLEMS

Four-fifths of Australia's merchandise exports consist of primary products, including several of those specified in the Integrated Programme for Commodities (iron ore, copper, bauxite, sugar, and meat). Australia, therefore, shares many of the interests and concerns of Third World primary producing and exporting countries. It has over the years participated in a number of international commodity agreements, both as a producer (wheat, sugar, meat, tin) and as a consumer (coffee), and it has, in international discussions since UNCTAD IV, given general support to the IPC and to specific proposals, such as those for a Common Fund, for buffer stocks, and for primary producer associations. With respect to all three, however, this support has been subject to certain reservations.

Generally, Australia favors a producer/consumer approach, rather than a developed/developing country approach, to commodity problems, since the latter might result in concentration on commodities of interest to Third World countries to the exclusion of commodities (such as wool, wheat, dairy products, fruit) of concern to Australia, and might lead to discrimination in favor of Third World countries against Australia in relation to the former group of commodities.

Like primary producers everywhere, Australian farmers readily persuade themselves that prices always move against them, and Australian government spokesmen have at times made statements reminiscent of the Prebisch thesis about a declining secular trend in the terms of trade for primary products.   But the emphasis in the Australian approach to world commodity problems is not on action to raise prices – it is generally recognized that there are few if any primary products other than oil that lend themselves to cartel action of the OPEC kind – but on price stabilization. Even here, long experience with domestic price stabilization schemes has made Australian informed opinion very conscious of the pitfalls.

For most commodities, complete elimination of price fluctuations by buffer stock operations is prohibitively expensive. If the objective is merely to eliminate fluctuations of, say, plus and minus 15 percent, few commodities require action. Even buffer stock schemes ostensibly aimed at price stabilization tend, under pressure from producer interests, toward optimism about the long-term trend and thus to become insolvent. In any case, stabilization of prices does not necessarily promote the more important objective, which is stability in the earnings of producers; where the cause of instability is fluctuations in supply, such as good and bad harvests, to stabilize prices may well be to destabilize earnings.

Despite such reservations, the Australian government, after initially expressing a skeptical view about the IPC and Common Fund proposals at UNCTAD IV, came out in favor of the Common Fund at the CIEC Ministerial Meeting in Paris in May 1977 and then canvassed support for the proposal among fellow OECD member countries. As the Minister for Foreign Affairs explained to Parliament in May 1978,

In the interest of resolving outstanding differences, the Government has re-examined the Australian position. . . . In February the Prime Minister indicated that we were prepared to go a long way to meet the views of developing countries by modifying our position on points which had proved a stumbling block in earlier negotiations. In so doing we have moved ahead of the great majority of developed countries. . . . The Government now accepts that the fund should have direct Government subscriptions as well as deposits from participating commodity organisations, and borrowings. We accept also that the fund could have a role in measures other than the financing of buffer stocks. . . .

A later statement from another official source added the cautious rider that "this does not represent a blank cheque commitment to 'other measures.' Clearly, much work needs to be done to define what these 'other measures' might be and in which circumstances they might be funded."

Australian official statements, while in principle favoring buffer stock schemes, have taken a jaundiced view of compensatory financing schemes for the stabilization of export earnings of developing countries. STABEX-type arrangements have been dismissed as inappropriate since Australia is not a major importer of primary products, and compensatory arrangements have been declared to be unsatisfactory substitutes for buffer stocks on the curious ground that they "are only treating the consequences, not the causes, of market instability." Australian academic economists tend to take the opposite view. While having considerable doubts about the usefulness of international buffer stock schemes, for the various reasons given above, they favor compensatory financing schemes. Such schemes, they argue, focus on stability of earnings rather than prices, and this is what matters to the country's balance of payments and the incomes of producers. If the recently expanded IMF facility could be further liberalized, it would be particularly helpful to the poorer developing countries which do not have the same access to the private capital market as the larger and more advanced ones. It is true that compensatory financing involves some repayable debts; but, provided the schemes are carefully designed to compensate for fluctuations around a sustainable trend, they should be substantially self-liquidating.

Australia's interest as a major exporter of agricultural products also influences Australia's official position on multilateral trade negotiations. Australia has, from the earliest days of GATT, neglected no opportunity to castigate the inequity of the industrial countries in promoting liberalization of imports of industrial products while refusing to moderate their own policies of agricultural protection. In the course of the 1978 Multinational Trade Negotiations, Australia offered a 40 percent formula cut in its industrial tariff structure in return for substantial liberalization of trade in agricultural products. In demanding a more even-handed approach to the liberalization of world trade, as between industrial and agricultural products, Australian official spokesmen believe themselves to be promoting Third World interest as well as Australia's own.

The official position on producer associations is that, while preferring a joint producer-consumer approach to international commodity problems, Australia believes that producer associations can play a role in the exchange of information, but rejects cartel action of the OPEC type as unlikely to benefit producers of most commodities. This view is generally shared by informed public opinion.

MARKET ACCESS FOR THIRD WORLD MANUFACTURES

Next to New Zealand, Australia has the highest average rates of tariff protection for domestic manufacturing industries among OECD countries. Protectionism is deeply rooted in Australian public opinion and politics. Progress toward more liberal policies during the 1960s and early 1970s suffered a setback with the world recession which began in 1974-75. The explanation for this situation lies in Australia's economic and social history.

Industrialization as a deliberate policy began in Australia in the aftermath of the gold rush of the 1850s. When the eastern Australian gold fields were worked out, thousands who had been lured to Australia by gold drifted to the cities looking for work. Governments promoted manufacturing industry to create employment and, to counter the unparalleled concentration of population in a few large cities, pursued a policy of decentralization by encouraging the location of textile, footwear, and similar industries in small towns. In the two decades after World War II, a wide range of new manufacturing industries developed, from steel to heavy engineering, oil and metal refining, chemical, motor vehicle, electronics, and other technology-intensive industries. A large proportion of over two million immigrants attracted to Australia by a policy of assisted migration found employment in these industries, while others moved into the even more rapidly expanding service sector. But the older labor-intensive sector, though shrinking slowly, has continued to employ a significant part of the work force, a considerable proportion consisting of relatively immobile female labor.

During the 1960s, it came to be increasingly recognized that, even in its own economic interests, Australia needed to move away from the policy of high protection and concentrate on a narrower range of resource-based and skill-intensive industries in which she could hope to have a comparative advantage, and gradually leave the domestic market for labor-intensive manufactures to imports from lower-wage countries of the Third World. Some steps toward liberalization were taken. A modest LDC Preference Scheme, granting low-rate or duty-free entry to most Third World manufactures (but subject to quota limits), was adopted in 1966 and later extended. A few tariff rates were cut under the Kennedy Round agreements and more substantially in the course of tariff reviews from 1970 on. More far-reaching were the steps taken by the Labor government which took office in December 1972 to correct the imbalance in Australia's external accounts that had developed with the massive mineral exports and capital inflows of the preceding years. The Australian dollar was appreciated in steps by 30 percent against the US dollar and all tariffs were cut across the board by 25 percent. But the timing of this overdue adjustment proved unfortunate. By the time the changes took effect in expanding imports, boom had given way to recession. Australian manufacturing industries, caught between a domestic wage explosion and intensified import competition, ran into serious difficulties. As unemployment rose to the highest rates since the Great Depression of the 1930s, manufacturers and trade unions demanded emergency protection, a demand to which

first the Labor government and then the Coalition government that succeeded it in November 1975 responded by imposing quantitative import restrictions and, in some cases, higher tariffs.

These restrictive measures affected most severely those countries which had benefited most from the abnormally rapid expansion of the Australian market for their manufactures during the years of Australia's inflationary boom and trade liberalization, especially Malaysia and the Philippines which, during those same years, had embarked on a new phase of export-oriented industrial development, following the earlier examples of Taiwan, Hong Kong, Korea, and Singapore. Supported by their ASEAN partners, they have been severely critical of Australia's protectionist policies. The Australian government has frequently acknowledged that "one of the major problems facing developing nations is that of getting secure access to markets of the developed world" and, in particular, that "the emergence of many middle income developing countries in the region, whose growth strategies have been built around export-oriented labour-intensive manufacturing industries . . . has increased pressure for markets in Australia and other countries and will undoubtedly generate pressures for adjustment in Australian industry." But it has also stressed that "given the short-term difficulties Australia has experienced over the past few years, there is little prospect of imports from ASEAN continuing to grow at the rapid rate of the last five years at the further expense of Australian industry. There will be further opportunities for ASEAN's exports to Australia to increase when the economic and employment situation in Australia improves."

In defense of its position, the Australian government quotes statistics showing that Australian imports from developing countries have increased (at current prices) at an average annual rate of 16 percent; that, more particularly, imports from ASEAN countries grew at an annual rate of 30 percent between 1970-71 and 1976-77, and that more than half of these now consist of manufactures; and that, with respect to textiles, clothing, and footwear, Australia's imports on a per capita basis are higher than those of any other developed countries.   Those critical of the present protectionist stance, including the Industries Assistance Commission, point out that the rate of growth in Australian imports of manufactured goods from developing countries in the period 1962 to 1973 was no higher than that of most other developed economies, and that, although it accelerated markedly in 1972-73, it was well below the comparable rate for Japan. The share in total Australian imports of manufactures from the developing countries rose from 2.0 percent in 1968 to 4.9 percent in 1973.   The comparable figures in the latter year were 17.2 percent for Japan, 11.5 percent for the United States, 5.1 percent for the United Kingdom, and 2.0 percent for the EEC.

In Australia, as in other developed and indeed in Third World countries, the strength of protectionism derives in part from intellectual failure: the public and politicians see the favorable effects on employment in protected industries but the adverse effects which import barriers can have on other industries are not generally appreciated. The Industries Assistance Commission, in its last Annual Report, summed up the likely net effects on employment in Australia as follows:

> Industries which have recently been most heavily assisted have tended to be more labour-intensive than the average for manufacturing industry. This might suggest that the employment gains in those which benefited would exceed the employment losses in those which are disadvantaged, resulting in a net increase in employment. However, among the industries likely to be disadvantaged are those which are more suited to Australian conditions and which could be expected to contribute more to the economy's growth. Thus, where recession is prolonged, the generation of real wealth will be increasingly prejudiced and with it the economy's ability to generate employment in fields such as construction and its capacity to alleviate the welfare consequences of unemployment.

But intellectual failure merely reinforces the pressures of conflicting group interests. The benefits of protection are concentrated, the costs are diffused. Employers and trade unions in vulnerable high-cost industries, and whole communities in regions dependent on such industries, are able to subject governments to political pressures for protection which are not usually matched by all those who are in various indirect ways adversely affected. The Australian government is seeking ways of moderating these pressures through measures of adjustment assistance and has appointed a high-level committee to recommend appropriate policies. But it is generally recognized, even by critics of the government's protectionist policies, that the prospects for liberalization depend overwhelmingly on improvement in the employment situation in Australia which, in turn, is linked with the rate of recovery from the world recession throughout the First World.

With respect to specific NIEO proposals, the Australian government, while claiming credit for its own modest LDC Preference Scheme, takes the view that Third World countries have more to gain by pressing for nondiscriminatory MTN concessions by OECD countries, and especially cuts in tariffs and nontariff barriers on manufactures of special interest to them, than from GSP schemes. Australia is also concerned that preferences for Third World manufactures will discriminate against her own actual and potential exports of manufactures. Australia, however, welcomes moves toward regional cooperation, including trade liberalization, among ASEAN countries because it regards ASEAN as a factor for economic development and political stability in the Asian-Pacific region. The Australian government is anxious to promote closer economic relations with the ASEAN countries and can be expected to give this objective high priority over the next decade.

DEVELOPMENT ASSISTANCE

Australian governments, with the support of public opinion, acknowledge Australia's moral obligation as a rich country to assist the poor countries of the Third World. Many idealists, especially among the young, are ashamed of the meagerness of Australia's contribution. But the obstacles to translating good intentions into a substantially larger budget allocation to development assistance are no less formidable in Australia than in other developed countries. The claims of the Third World have to compete with those of sectional interest groups at home for larger public expenditure on health and education and urban renewal, for assistance to old age pensioners, unemployed, aborigines, and other disadvantaged groups, and for relief from the burdens of high taxation. Unlike governments of totalitarian countries which can proclaim the single-mindedly altruistic motives of their foreign aid policies, Australian governments, like those of all democratic countries, have to justify foreign aid to their citizens and inevitably do so as best as they can in terms of the country's enlightened self-interest, thus giving ammunition to Third World critics of the First World's selfishness.

In terms of global figures, Australia's record among Development Assistance Committee donors has been and remains relatively good. Australia ranks eighth (out of 17) in terms of official development assistance as percent of GNP, with 0.47 percent in 1976-77, and has declared its intention of working toward the 0.7 percent target as rapidly as economic and budgetary constraints permit. A very large part of total Australian development assistance goes to Papua-New Guinea toward which Australia believes itself to have a continuing special responsibility. Of the rest, 70 percent goes to least developed countries and multilateral institutions.

Australian development assistance policy has come under attack in recent years from domestic critics as being too narrowly concentrated on neighboring countries in the Asian-Pacific region and too much directed at modern sector growth, instead of social objectives such as employment and basic needs. Defenders of the current policy reply to the first criticism that, quite apart from considerations of foreign policy, Australia has a comparative advantage in terms of local knowledge and contacts in the Asian-Pacific region and, as a small donor, should not spread its aid effort too thinly; and, to the second, that the areas of development policy which deserve the highest priority in a Third World country's national development effort are not necessarily those best suited for financial or technical assistance by foreign governments. It is also pointed out that the major part of Australian development assistance that goes to Papua-New Guinea consists of untied cash grants which that government is free to use for whatever purposes it chooses.

In one respect, Australia's record as aid donor is unique. From the beginning, almost all of Australia's development assistance to Third World countries has taken the form of grants, not loans. Australia, therefore, supports Third World pressure for a further shift from loans toward grants. On the other hand, while not directly concerned as a creditor, Australia does not favor across-the-board debt relief which would not distribute relief according to need and would endanger future Third World access to the international capital market.

TRANSFER OF TECHNOLOGY

As a country heavily dependent on the import of technology, largely through direct investment by transnational corporations, Australia favors any moves that will facilitate the freest possible international flow of technology and has supported the concept of a code of conduct that will reconcile the interests of suppliers and recipients. But, while there are sections of Australian public opinion that deplore the trend of the postwar period toward increasing foreign ownership and control of Australian industries, the substantially bipartisan official guidelines on foreign investment are specifically designed to enable Australia to continue to attract foreign capital and technology for development. For this reason, also, Australia has reservations about any code which would discriminate in favor of Third World countries at its own expense.

In a country whose economic development over 200 years has depended, and continues in considerable measure to depend, on import and adaptation of technology developed overseas, and on immigration and training of people with the skills necessary to make effective use of such technology, one has difficulty in comprehending approaches to the problem of transfer of technology which seem to imply that foreign technology can be had for nothing and that it need merely be made available to be effectively applied. Whether a small country can secure the technology it needs more economically and efficiently by importing it from abroad through direct investment or joint ventures, or through purchase by licensing and other agreements, or by developing its own R&D capability, are questions much debated in Australia. The answers are not obvious and will clearly vary with the type of technology and many other factors.

Australia's own experience does suggest that reliance on import of manufacturing technology through direct investment has the effect of inhibiting development of an independent R&D capacity by local manufacturing firms and that this, while not a major ground for concern during the import-substitution phase of industrialization, may become a serious handicap to an export-oriented industrial strategy. To be ahead of competitors in new technology of some kind is one of the most important ways of breaking into export markets for the more capital and technology-intensive manufactures. This is probably also one reason why Australia's role as a supplier of technology to Third World countries is largely limited to the provision of technical assistance in areas where research and development are mainly a public sector responsibility, such as agricultural and livestock industries, public health, mineral exploration, and aerial navigation.

But this is beginning to change, as Australian manufacturers find advantage in locating some of their operations in lower-wage countries of Southeast Asia. As and when Australia undertakes the structural adjustment of her manufacturing industries, which in the longer run is agreed to be inevitable, Australian manufacturing industries will, both as a necessary condition and in consequence, acquire a capacity to innovate in certain specialized areas which will, in turn, make possible transfer of some of this new technology to Third World countries through Australian direct investment abroad.

Index

About the Editors and Contributors

JORGE A. LOZOYA is the UNITAR/CEESTEM project co-director and research coordinator at CEESTEM. He studied international relations at El Colegio de Mexico and Chinese modern history at Stanford University. He was secretary-general of the 30th World Congress of Social Sciences in Asia and North Africa.

A.K. BHATTACHARYA, Research Associate, UNITAR, and Assistant Professor of International Business, Pace University, New York.

EUGENIO ANGUIANO, Harvard University.

HEINZ W. ARNDT, The Australian National University.

NIRMAL K. CHANDRA, Indian Institute of Management.

LIM CHONG-YAH, University of Singapore.

PAUL T.K. LIN, McGill University.

VICHITRONG NA POMBHEJARA, Institute of Southeast Asian Studies.

MASAHIRO SAKAMOTO, National Institute for Research Advancement, Tokyo.

M.T.R. SARMA, National Council of Applied Economic Research, New Delhi.

ROMESH THAPAR, Seminar, New Delhi.

JONG YOUL YOO, Hyung Hee University, Seoul.